Changing France

Advance Reviews

'This lively, lucid, and meticulously researched book will be a rich resource for those wishing to know more of the burgeoning material culture of Second Empire France. It breaks new ground both in its exploration of how that culture, even at its most apparently trivial, reflected larger social and political anxieties; and in its compelling account of how the literature of the period responded to and engaged with it.'

—*Professor Heather Glen, University of Cambridge*

'Anne Green has applied a deep knowledge of social history to the gamut of texts produced during the Second Empire, from the works of major novelists to railway manuals and fashion magazines. The result is a brilliant and engaging tour de force of literary and cultural analysis. This book should be required reading throughout the humanities and social sciences.'

—*Professor Patricia Mainardi, City University of New York*

'A brilliant account of how literature responded to a materially changing world in Second Empire France. For laptops, spaceships, and climate change, read cameras, trains, and urban redevelopment. Meticulously researched, shrewdly argued, and beautifully written, this book offers important new perspectives on the relationship between culture and our lived environment.'

—*Professor Roger Pearson, University of Oxford*

'Anne Green's innovative and observant study engages illuminatingly with the responses of writers to certain fundamental changes affecting life in Second Empire France. *Changing France* will be read with profit and enjoyment by specialists and the general Francophile reader alike, while reinforcing Green's reputation as a leading authority on Flaubert.'

—*Dr Michael Tilby, University of Cambridge*

'This beautifully crafted study is essential reading for anyone interested in the cultural history of Second Empire France. With immense erudition, exemplary clarity and an eye for the telling detail, Anne Green shows us how texts of every variety reflect the social, political and industrial upheavals of the era.'

—*Professor Timothy Unwin, University of Bristol*

Changing France

Literature and Material Culture in the Second Empire

Anne Green

ANTHEM PRESS
LONDON · NEW YORK · DELHI

Anthem Press
An imprint of Wimbledon Publishing Company
www.anthempress.com

This edition first published in UK and USA 2013
by ANTHEM PRESS
75–76 Blackfriars Road, London SE1 8HA, UK
or PO Box 9779, London SW19 7ZG, UK
and
244 Madison Ave. #116, New York, NY 10016, USA

First published in hardback by Anthem Press in 2011

Copyright © Anne Green 2013

The author asserts the moral right to be identified as the author of this work.

Cover image 'Madame Paul-Sigisbert Moitessier, née Marie-Clotilde-Inès de Foucauld, Seated' by Jean Auguste Dominique Ingres, oil on canvas, 1856. Image reproduced courtesy of the Bridgeman Art Library, UK.

All rights reserved. Without limiting the rights under copyright reserved above, no part of this publication may be reproduced, stored or introduced into a retrieval system, or transmitted, in any form or by any means (electronic, mechanical, photocopying, recording or otherwise), without the prior written permission of both the copyright owner and the above publisher of this book.

British Library Cataloguing-in-Publication Data
A catalogue record for this book is available from the British Library.

Library of Congress Cataloging-in-Publication Data
The Library of Congress has cataloged the hardcover edition as follows:
Green, Anne, 1947–
Changing France : literature and material culture in the Second Empire / Anne Green.
p. cm.
Includes bibliographical references and index.
ISBN-13: 978-0-85728-777-9 (hardback : alk. paper)
ISBN-10: 0-85728-777-X (hardback : alk. paper)
1. French literature–19th century–History and criticism. 2. Literature and society–France. 3. France–Intellectual life. I. Title.
PQ292.G74 2011
840.9'008–dc22
2011014785

ISBN-13: 978 1 78308 070 0 (Pbk)
ISBN-10: 1 78308 070 1 (Pbk)

This title is also available as an ebook.

CONTENTS

Acknowledgements   vii

Chapter One
Introduction   1

Chapter Two
Exhibitions   5

Chapter Three
Transport   35

Chapter Four
Food   65

Chapter Five
Photography   91

Chapter Six
Costume   117

Chapter Seven
Ruins   147

Chapter Eight
Conclusion   169

Appendix: Second Empire Timeline   173

Bibliography   187

Index   195

ACKNOWLEDGEMENTS

I am very grateful to the AHRC and to King's College London for funding research leave without which this book would not have been completed. I should also like to thank all those friends and colleagues who have helped with information, advice or encouragement, particularly Simon Gaunt, Heather Glen, Nick Harrison, Deborah Jaffe, Robert Lethbridge, Jo Malt, Michael Tilby and Timothy Unwin.

An earlier version of part of chapter 2 appeared in 'France Exposed: *Madame Bovary* and the Exposition Universelle', *The Modern Language Review*, vol. 99, no. 4 (October 2004), 915–23.

Chapter One

INTRODUCTION

This is a book about writing and change – about changes affecting everyday life in Second Empire France, about the extraordinarily diverse and creative responses of writers to those changes, and about ways in which writing itself evolved during this period. It raises questions about how the material world impinges upon literature, and how writers, in turn, use that world as a way of negotiating change.

France had been rocked by momentous changes for more than half a century before the Second Empire came into being in December 1852. After the impact of the French Revolution of 1789, the country had gone through a series of revolutions, lurching from Republic to Empire to Monarchy and back to Republic again with the revolution of 1848, when the monarchy was finally abolished. But the failure of that short-lived Second Republic was seen by many as a particular betrayal. On 2 December 1851 Parisians woke to find that Louis Napoleon Bonaparte, President of the Second Republic, had dissolved the Legislative Assembly and proclaimed martial law. Over the next few days several hundred protestors and a number of innocent bystanders were killed by troops, and many thousands were subsequently deported to North Africa or exiled elsewhere. Although a plebiscite indicated that a majority of Frenchmen approved the move, for many the violence of Louis Napoleon's coup d'état and his overthrow of the 1848 constitution he had sworn to uphold was to be a long-lasting and bitter source of resentment. The following year, the Second Empire was officially proclaimed on the anniversary of the coup d'état, the imperial eagle was restored to the French flag, and Louis Napoleon took the title of Napoleon III, Emperor of the French. But the shock of his coup d'état and the repressive manner in which the Empire was established were not readily forgotten.

For many writers, the coup d'état and its aftermath marked a watershed. Those who had been drawn into the political debate during the events surrounding the 1848 revolution turned away from political engagement in disgust, and their reluctance to involve themselves in political commentary was reinforced by the new regime's strict censorship laws and close control of the press. As Charles Baudelaire famously put it, 'the 2nd of December *physically depoliticised* me'.[1] Maxime Du Camp, at that time editor of the *Revue de Paris*, noted in his memoirs that many minor writers who had made their living by writing for newspapers and journals were ruined when the administration suppressed these outlets, and he recalled that Gérard de Nerval had abandoned a plan to write about Hassan-ibn-Sabbah, the legendary eleventh-century founder of the Assassin sect, for fear that people would see allusions to the Emperor in it.[2]

Such reactions explain a recurrent image in Second Empire literature – that of a room with windows or shutters closed to shut out a raging tempest, while the writer sits inside, creating a world of his own in his imagination and apparently oblivious to the turmoil outside. This is the central image of both Théophile Gautier's 'Préface', where the poet composes his poems '[p]aying no attention to the hurricane/ That lashed against my closed windows',[3] and of Baudelaire's 'Paysage', where the poet refuses to be distracted by '[t]he Riot raging in vain at my window', instead shutting out the outside world in order to conjure up images of his own.[4]

But while writers may have used such images to dramatise their unwillingness to engage directly with current affairs, they were not oblivious to the wider changes taking place around them. After the turbulence of the first half-century, the country was changing on all fronts – not only politically, but socially, economically and physically.[5] An energetic foreign policy meant that French armies once again ranged widely, dominating Algeria, fighting against Russia in the Crimea, and against Austria in support of Italian unification – a war whose peace terms gave Nice and Savoy to France. Further afield, there were ambitious French military campaigns in West Africa, Indochina, Syria, New Caledonia and, disastrously, Mexico. This was also the period of the

---

1 'Le 2 décembre m'a *physiquement dépolitiqué*.' Charles Baudelaire, *Correspondance*, ed. Claude Pichois, 2 vols. (Paris: Gallimard-Pléiade, 1973) I, 188.
2 Maxime Du Camp, *Souvenirs littéraires* (1882–83; Paris: Aubier, 1994), 380–381.
3 'Sans prendre garde à l'ouragan/ Qui fouettait mes vitres fermées'. Théophile Gautier, *Émaux et camées* (1852 and 1856; Lille and Geneva: Giard and Droz, 1947), 3.
4 'L'Émeute, tempêtant vainement à ma vitre.' Charles Baudelaire, *Œuvres complètes*, ed. Marcel A. Ruff (Paris: Seuil, 1968), 95. Cf. Eugène Fromentin, *Dominique* (1862; Paris: Flammarion, 1987), 80–84, which features a curious enclosed room whose walls and windows are covered with the protagonist's impassioned, youthful writings. It contains political works dating from the build-up to the 1848 revolution and represents Dominique's past, but he makes it clear that he no longer writes: 'Oh no, that's all over and done with!' ['Oh! Pour cela, non, c'est fini!']
5 See Appendix for an indication of some of these changes.

greatest developments of the steam age: the country's infant rail industry grew into a massive programme of railway construction that carved its way across France, opening up links with neighbouring countries and giving access to trade with North Africa and the Near East. Manufacturing industries were transformed by new industrial processes; cities expanded rapidly as workers moved in from the countryside; and as fortunes were made and lost, social hierarchies loosened and changed. Recently developed technologies such as photography offered new ways of seeing the world, and ambitions and expectations shifted as the Second Empire forged a new identity for itself.

Modern readers' perceptions of this period tend to be coloured by Émile Zola's Rougon-Macquart series of novels which vividly trace the fortunes of one extended family during the Second Empire. Zola, however, was writing after the event, looking back over that extraordinary eighteen-year period in full knowledge of the Empire's sudden and ignominious end in September 1870 when Napoleon III surrendered at Sedan after a series of humiliating defeats in the war against Prussia. The writers discussed in this book, however, were writing during the Second Empire itself, unsure of how events would unfold, yet acutely sensitive to the changes going on around them. The picture of Second Empire France that emerges from their work does so obliquely, for perhaps without their realising it, their hugely diverse responses to the here-and-now of existence reveal much about that time.

As writers embraced 'modernity' and incorporated new technologies, inventions and fashions into their work, French literature itself underwent a fundamental change. Writers frequently complained that art was becoming industrialised and commodified, yet they found ways of appropriating the industrial and transforming it into art as they incorporated commodities into their writing and breathed new life into literary forms. In the chapters that follow, it will become clear that the new literary focus on the material world was not the simple 'realist' reflection of external reality that critics often assume. Rather, Second Empire writers recognised that depicting apparently innocent little details of modern life could be a subtle and versatile means of thinking about deeper issues in the wider world. Embedded in the trivial and unregarded details which bring their work to life are ideas and associations that add a richness of meaning often lost to a modern reader.

One of the ways in which this book tries to identify these associations is by examining some of the myriad non-literary texts, now largely forgotten, that explored the modern world – contemporary practical guides, commentaries and manuals which purported to help readers negotiate aspects of new cultural phenomena such as train travel, photography or fashion. Many of their concerns seem strikingly modern – there are worries about image, diet, stress, lack of time, and the frustrations of public transport – but as these texts turn the outside world into language and interpret it for readers, they often reveal more than expected. Although the guides and manuals claim simply to offer practical advice to readers, in doing so they betray contemporary political tensions and social anxieties. Beneath their descriptions and recommendations lie barely expressible attitudes to the nature of change and to the new social order. In some cases reactions that could not be expressed openly for fear of censorship bubble to the surface; in others, attitudes and ideas that are still half-formed seem to emerge unconsciously from the practical text. Read in conjunction with these guides and manuals, literary works reveal unexpected new resonances and meanings: sometimes what critics have taken to be an original feature will turn out to be a contemporary commonplace, or, conversely, an apparently unremarkable detail will be revealed as having special import.

The aim of this book is neither to discuss aspects of the material world in order to decide whether literary descriptions of them were factually accurate, nor to plunder literary texts in order to elucidate some aspect of the material world or to bolster a social or historical analysis. Rather, it attempts to bring literary and non-literary texts together with key areas of material culture, to show how writing itself changed as writers recognised the extraordinarily rich possibilities of expression opened up to them by the changing material world. It does not try to be comprehensive. Other areas such as medicine were undergoing changes quite as momentous as those examined here. The many original sources referred to are only a sample of the vast body of guides, manuals and commentaries published during the period, and the literary texts discussed are a small selection of the examples that might have been chosen. If certain authors appear to dominate – and Flaubert's presence is particularly obvious – it is because they seem exceptionally sensitive to the tremors of the time, and more aware of the complexities of changing circumstance. But if, like all great artists, Flaubert has his finger on the pulse of the age in a way that lesser writers did not, their simpler, more wooden responses can often be just as revealing. By reading these works in context, by weaving between different types of text and attempting to tease out layers of meaning whose significance is no longer evident to a modern reader, the chapters that follow show how literature itself changed during the Second Empire as it responded to a changing France.

Chapter Two

EXHIBITIONS

Nowhere were the changes taking place in mid nineteenth-century France displayed in more concentrated form than at the two international exhibitions held in Paris in 1855 and 1867. The exhibition of 1855, announced by Napoleon III barely four months after the proclamation of the Second Empire, was seen as an opportunity for France to stamp its new identity on the world. It was to be an occasion for France to assert its superiority over other nations and to show off the achievements of the new Empire to the hordes of visitors who were confidently expected to travel from far and wide to see it and to marvel. The exhibition's aims were explicit: as Prince Napoléon, the Emperor's cousin, declared in a speech to the first meeting of the Imperial Commission, its purpose was 'to illustrate nineteenth-century France and Europe'.[1] But what did it mean, 'to illustrate [. . .] France'? How was France to be presented?

From the outset, the 1855 exhibition, like its successor, was closely identified with the imperial family and the new régime. An Imperial Commission under the supervision of Prince Napoléon planned the exhibition. The Emperor set the scheme in motion and officiated at the opening ceremony, his profile was stamped on the exhibition medals, his sculpted bust presided over the main entrance, and he and the Empress made numerous public visits. Moreover, the innovatory idea of incorporating fine arts into what was originally conceived of as an exhibition of agriculture and industry was publicly attributed to the Empress, who was appointed patron of the art section.[2] From the outset, then, the exhibition was to be a showcase for the aims of the new Empire and an

---

1 '[I]llustrer la France et l'Europe du dix-neuvième siècle'. Prince Napoleon's speech to the first meeting of the Imperial Commission, 29.12.1853. *Exposition des produits de l'industrie de toutes les nations. Catalogue officiel publié par ordre de la Commission impériale* (Paris: E. Panis, 1855), v.
2 As the imperial decree explained, 'May it be particularly the role of France, whose industry owes so much to the fine arts, to grant them the place they deserve at the forthcoming universal exhibition.' ['Qu'il appartient spécialement à la France, dont l'industrie doit tant aux beaux-arts, de leur assigner, dans la prochaine exposition universelle, la place qu'ils méritent.'] Decree of 22.6.1853. *Exposition des produits de l'industrie de toutes les nations*, iii.

expression of a new national and imperial identity – an image of Second Empire France for display to the nation and the world.

We can trace the gradual emergence of this image by examining some of the common features of the many texts written directly for or about the two exhibitions – official reports, speeches, articles, catalogues and guide-books – and it is worth looking at them at some length, since the values and attitudes they convey form a basis for exploring the literature of the period. Most of the literature with which the present book is concerned adopts a position in relation to this emerging identity. Consciously or not, writers reinforced or challenged the values implicit in the exhibitions, for these were emblematic of a certain way of responding to a changing France.

Glossing over the dubious legitimacy of the new regime, texts surrounding the exhibitions were suffused with images of continuity and organic growth – images that implied that the exhibitions had evolved as a natural and inevitable manifestation of the essential nature of Frenchness. Even the design for the exhibition palace was portrayed as if it had emerged spontaneously from the French soil,[3] and the exhibitions themselves, seen as 'the truest and most complete expression of the forces and trends of the new world',[4] were presented as the culmination of a natural and inexorable process that had brought France to its present, enviable state. Inscribed within a natural, God-given order that moves inevitably towards perfection, the exhibitions were shown to exemplify that process. In the words of Prince Napoleon at the opening ceremony, the exhibition of 1855 marked 'a new step towards perfection, that law laid down by the Creator, which is the first requirement of mankind and the necessary condition for social organisation'.[5] By wrapping the exhibitions in this discourse of inevitability and naturalness, and by presenting them as having been conceived in accordance with divine will, these writings work to legitimise the new Empire.

In the language of the exhibition texts, newness becomes an exemplary attribute. Associated with genius, creativity and wonder, newness marks a fundamental and essential break with the past. Despite these texts' emphasis on continuity, despite France's long tradition of industrial exhibitions, and despite London's hugely successful Great Exhibition of 1851, the *Exposition* of 1855 is presented as novel, unique, exceptional and without precedent. It is the first French *exposition universelle*, the first ever to bring together industry and fine arts

---

3 See for example *Les Douze expositions de l'industrie en France de 1798 à 1855* (Paris: Martinon, 1855), 41.

4 '[L]'expression la plus vraie et la plus complète des forces et des tendances du monde nouveau.' *Les Douze expositions…*, 5.

5 '[U]n nouveau pas vers le perfectionnement, cette loi qui vient du Créateur, ce premier besoin de l'humanité et cette indispensable condition de l'organisation sociale'. Ibid., 45.

('a combination so well-suited to our genius for innovation', says the official catalogue),⁶ the first ever to indicate the price of the exhibits ('a bold innovation that was not introduced in London'),⁷ and the items on display, of course, represent all that is most modern. The new Palace of Industry, constructed mainly of iron, is repeatedly described as unlike anything built before, while its exhibits exemplify 'the nature of this solemn celebration which is truly unique in our history.'⁸ Yet its successor, the 1867 exhibition, is also presented as unique and without precedent. The new exhibition palace is again said to be unlike anything built before. One writer even describes the 1867 exhibition site, the Champ de Mars, as a 'Parisian desert', a once-arid plain that the exhibition has transformed into a hive of activity in a lush, green setting – conveniently overlooking the fact that the 'desert' was a former swamp.⁹

But if one strand of discourse emphasises a rupture with the past and the sudden emergence of the original and new, another strand stresses continuity. The exhibitions *do* have a history: they have their origins in the French Revolution, whose values of liberty and equality they are said to exemplify. As one commentator wrote in 1855,

> Their origins go back to the time when industry, for centuries bowed, oppressed and stifled by corporate control, had been newly emancipated by the laws of 1791. [...] But as soon as industry, labour and human thought had burst free of their age-old chains and been galvanised by liberty, then and only then did the idea of exhibitions come into being, for they aimed to favour and develop all the powerful instincts of the new society created by the immortal revolution of 1789.¹⁰

---

6 '[A]lliance qui va si bien à notre génie initiateur'. *Exposition des produits de l'industrie de toutes les nations*, v.

7 '[I]nnovation hardie qui n'avait pas été faite à Londres'. *Les Douze expositions…*, 45.

8 '[L]e caractère de cette solennité vraiment unique dans nos annales.' 'Le Palais de l'Industrie' in Alexandre Dumas, Théophile Gautier et al, *Paris et les Parisiens au XIXe siècle. Mœurs, arts et monuments* (Paris: Morizot, 1856), 316.

9 *Paris-Guide, par les principaux écrivains et artistes de la France* (Paris: Librairie internationale, 1867), II, 2006; Pierre Larousse, *Grand dictionnaire universel du XIXe siècle*, (Paris: Administration du grand dictionnaire, 1865–1890), 1211.

10 'Leur origine remonte à l'époque où l'industrie, courbée, opprimée, étouffée depuis des siècles sous le régime des corporations, venait d'être émancipée et rendue à la liberté par les lois de 1791. [...] Mais aussitôt que l'industrie, que le travail, que la pensée humaine eut pu briser ses chaînes séculaires et se ranimer au contact électrique de la liberté, alors, mais alors seulement, l'idée des Expositions dut se faire jour et prendre naissance, car elles tendaient à favoriser et à développer tous les instincts puissants de la société nouvelle, telle que l'immortelle révolution de 89 l'avait faite.' *Les Douze expositions…*, 5–6.

The rupture with the past has effectively been displaced from the coup d'état that brought the Second Empire into being. Instead, the historical break has been moved back to the Revolution, allowing the Second Empire to appropriate the values of liberty, equality and fraternity as its own.

Yet these texts perform another historical displacement, and propose a second point of origin. The exhibitions may stem from the Revolution, but they also carry echoes of imperial Rome. In 1855 ancient Rome was repeatedly invoked as a point of comparison with France, and the 1867 exhibition palace was frequently likened to the Coliseum (though to one dissenting commentator it looked more like a giant gasometer). Thus we can see urgency in the construction of the new identity as it absorbed paradoxes, instabilities and contradictions, and presented them as seamlessly consistent. Exhibition rhetoric glossed over the inconsistencies: deemed to be new and without history or precedent (and therefore a phenomenon of creative genius), France was at the same time located within a historical process that originated both in ancient Rome and at the French Revolution.

The discourse surrounding the exhibitions also hints at their sacred nature. More than a simple association of Church and State,[11] the exhibitions and all they represent are themselves represented as the expression of a God-given order. Indeed the solemn and religious connotations of the word '*exposition*' are very much to the fore in these texts, where the exhibition itself is often referred to as a *solennité*[12] as the distinctions between the commercial and the sacred become blurred. The exhibition palaces are described as places of veneration – as temples or cathedrals with monumental stained-glass windows and great transepts and naves where the exhibits are solemnly displayed. The machine gallery is 'the temple of work', and the exhibition a 'Mecca', a place of pilgrimage for all the peoples of the earth.[13] At the heart of this secular cathedral is the unseen presence of the Emperor himself, represented by the raised imperial throne which dominated the central 'nave' of the exhibition, its rich draperies embroidered with the golden bees of the Napoleonic dynasty.[14] (The 1867 exhibition took the ecclesiastical association further

---

11 Patricia Mainardi points out that 'the primary purpose of Second Empire patronage was to conciliate the Church, which had supported the coup d'état, and to glorify the regime'. *Art and Politics of the Second Empire. The Universal Expositions of 1855 and 1867* (New Haven and London: Yale University Press, 1987), 38.

12 '[S]olemn celebration'. E.g. Edmond Renaudin, *Paris-Exposition ou guide à Paris en 1867* (Paris: Ch. Delagrave & Cie., 1867), 329; see also the 'Expositions' entry in Larousse, *Grand dictionnaire universel*.

13 '[L]e temple du travail'; Kaempfer, 'L'Exposition universelle', *Paris-Guide*, II, 2007.

14 'Le Palais de l'industrie' in Dumas, Gautier et al, *Paris et les Parisiens au XIXe siècle*, 316.

and displayed one section in 'a church which was none other than a special *exhibition* of religious artefacts'.[15] Thus by attributing spiritual associations to the exhibitions and by suggesting that they were the truest and most complete expression of the forces and tendencies of the modern world – in other words, of the Second Empire – these texts imply that the 'naturalness', 'inevitability' and creative genius of the exhibitions were enshrined in the new regime itself, and that both had divine sanction.

Furthermore, the exhibition discourse conveys a picture of France as the embodiment of harmony, peacemaker supreme. One of the stated aims of the imperial decree that announced the 1855 exhibition was to commemorate the nation's forty war-free years since Waterloo, an aim underlined by Napoleon III at the opening ceremony when he declared: 'It is with great pleasure that I declare open the Temple of Peace, which invites all nations to live in harmony'.[16] Expressions of peace and harmony abound in these texts: the exhibitions are temples of peace, and France itself is the peacemaker who extends the hand of friendship to all nations and guarantees future accord. Honest competition is represented as replacing international rivalry: France and England 'will shake hands as powerful nations who have faith in a peaceful future',[17] and commentators delight in pointing out that old enemies such as Austria and Switzerland have forgotten their former hostilities and are now exhibiting alongside one another.[18] In May 1867 Flaubert commented to George Sand that people had stopped talking about war and no longer discussed anything of substance, because 'the exhibition alone occupies everyone's minds.'[19] Readers were assured that France, with its 'call for peace', had brought disparate cultures and beliefs together in harmony, on neutral territory.

But this part of the French image was hard to sustain. By the time the so-called Temple of Peace opened in 1855, there was no longer a forty-year peace to commemorate. The Crimean war had begun the previous spring, and the exhibition texts' rhetoric of peace is suffused with the terminology of war. Exhorting the jury selecting works of art to remember that France's high artistic reputation must be maintained, Prince Napoleon announced: 'We must come to this peaceful battle only with well-chosen arms, so that in this struggle

---

15 '[U]ne église, qui n'était autre chose qu'une *exposition* particulière d'objets du culte.' *Grand dictionnaire universel*, 'Expositions' entry.
16 'J'ouvre avec bonheur le temple de la Paix, qui convie tous les peuples à la concorde.' Cit. in *Les Douze expositions*, 46.
17 '[E]changeront la poignée de main des nations fortes qui ont foi dans un pacifique avenir.' Kaempfer, 'L'Exposition universelle', *Paris-Guide*, II, 2011.
18 *Paris-Guide*, II, 2021.
19 'L'Exposition seule occupe tous les esprits.' Gustave Flaubert, *Correspondance*, ed. Jean Bruneau and Yvan Leclerc (Paris: Gallimard-Pléiade, 1973–2007), III, 642 (17.5.67).

our artists may prove themselves worthy of those other children of France who are fighting our country's enemies with such valour.'[20] Within the Temple of Peace, France was to fight a bloodless battle to defend her honour. This idea of an oxymoronic 'bataille pacifique' infiltrated the discourse surrounding both exhibitions, and the coliseum-like shape of the 1867 exhibition palace allowed writers to conjure up an image of nations locked together in peaceful gladiatorial combat.[21] Nevertheless it was made clear that the victor in these non-battles would always be France.

Yet a very real threat of war with Prussia hung over the opening of the 1867 exhibition. Prussia exhibited cannons of all shapes and sizes, dominated by the largest cannon ever made, a gigantic 50,000kg Krupp steel cannon capable of firing 550kg shells, which was trained dramatically on the palace.[22] Military equipment filled the exhibition park. France displayed sabres, bayonets, guns, cannon, howitzers, mortars, shells and bullets, and the Austrians, recently crushed by Prussia at Sadowa, were said to be trying to defeat the Prussians on the Champ de Mars.[23] The British exhibit was no different. Kaempfer states that '[t]he English are very warlike in their park: one building is a military hospital, another houses an exhibition of munitions, yet another has a government display of cannon which are large enough and powerful enough to give Prussia's monster-cannon pause for thought.'[24] But he still ends his account by reasserting the vision of France as a source of universal peace and harmony. Despite the slaughter enacted metaphorically on the exhibition sites (and enacted in reality in Crimea and Mexico), hostility and rivalry were blandly represented in the guidebooks and commentaries as part of a

---

20 'Il ne nous faut arriver à cette bataille pacifique qu'avec des armes bien choisies, afin que nos artistes se montrent dans cette lutte dignes de ces autres enfants de la France qui combattent si vaillemment les ennemis de notre patrie.' *Exposition des produits de l'industrie de toutes les nations. Catalogue officiel publié par ordre de la Commission impériale* (Paris: E. Panis, 1855), 111.

21 '[P]eaceful battle'. The palace is 'a circus where all nations in the world fight in a peaceful fray'. ['un cirque où luttent dans une mêlée pacifique tous les peuples de l'univers'.] Kaempfer, *Paris-Guide*, II, 2007. See also Edmond Renaudin, *Paris-exposition ou guide à Paris en 1867*, 329–330.

22 Kaempfer says the cannon seems to be saying '"If I wanted to, I could smash, overthrow and obliterate all of that." Fortunately it condescends not to want to.' ['"Si je voulais, je briserais, je renverserais, j'anéantirais tout cela." Par bonheur, il daigne ne pas vouloir.'] *Paris-Guide*, II, 2022.

23 Kaempfer, *Paris-Guide*, II, 2021.

24 'Les Anglais sont très belliqueux dans leur parc: cette construction est une caserne-hôpital, cette autre loge une exposition de munitions de guerre, cette autre des canons exposés par le Gouvernement et qui sont de taille et de calibre à donner à réfléchir au canon-monstre de la Prusse.' Kaempfer, *Paris-Guide*, II, 2027.

co-operative commercial exchange. While France was increasingly drawn into military conflict abroad, the rhetoric of the exhibition texts promoted a nation at peace, and confident of its supremacy.

These texts represent imperial France as a country at peace not only with its neighbours but with itself, having left the violent upheaval of its past revolutions safely behind. The values of liberty, equality and fraternity remain and define the nation, and the exhibitions themselves are presented as expressions of these ideals: they are perceived as exemplifying 'equality in work'[25] and striving to improve the lot of the working classes. Prizes were offered to outstanding workers. Claiming to satisfy 'the sense of equality, so dear to our country, in all that is satisfactory, honorable and truly legitimate',[26] the exhibitions' avowed aim was to consecrate all forms of labour. A favourite attraction was the French display of manual labour where visitors could watch human workers as they went about the business of manufacturing items such as hats, shoes, artificial flowers, lorgnettes or meerschaum pipes. The machines in the spectacular 1867 machine gallery – 'the workshop of the whole world'[27] – were themselves described as a legion of majestic workers, disciplined and tractable. Represented as obedient servants, these machines were shown to carry out their prodigious tasks rhythmically, methodically, and, of course, unquestioningly. No hint of tension between manual and industrial modes of production ruffles the harmonious and egalitarian image that these texts project.

A central tenet that emerges from the exhibitions is the notion that France represents the quintessence of civilisation. The exhibition is a 'vast and various competition to which France has invited the civilised world'; the machine gallery is evidence of France's own 'material civilisation',[28] and further proof comes from what was generally agreed to be the outstanding elegance, taste and refinement of France's artistic contributions:

> Where France is unrivalled, where she reigns supreme, is in everything that appeals to the imagination and delights it – in other words in objects of fantasy, taste and luxury. France truly comes into her own in the Saint-Louis and Baccarat hall, in the Sèvres and Gobelins room, and in the display of Parisian gold plate.

---

25 '[L]'égalité devant le travail'.
26 '[L]e sentiment de l'égalité, si cher à notre pays, dans ce qu'il a d'acceptable, d'honorable et de vraiment légitime.' *Les Douze expositions*, 3.
27 '[L]'atelier du monde entier'.
28 '[V]aste et multiple concours où la France a convoqué le monde civilisé'; 'civilisation matérielle'. *Les Douze expositions*, 57.

A foreigner dropped into the midst of such luxuries would immediately recognise where he was and exclaim, 'I am in France.'[29]

Converging on France, on Paris, on the exhibition sites, contributors and visitors were drawn from far and wide by the promise of seeing the world of the future. What they found, of course, was not only the mass of *curiosités* – the dizzying display of art and industry – but each other. They too were on display; they were part of the exhibition. They were even included in the guidebooks, which pointed out that the *exposition universelle* was also a cosmopolitan exhibition of inhabitants from all corners of the earth. Visitors were told they would find a stroll along the crowded exhibition promenade just as interesting as a tour of the galleries.[30] 'All nationalities rub shoulders there, all languages can be heard, and all the costumes are different from one another.'[31] Here we see another essential element of France's new image taking shape: France not only attracts and welcomes other nations but absorbs and appropriates them. Contemporary accounts stress that the exhibition site is not only an embodiment of Second Empire France, it is the world in miniature.[32] 'Europe, Asia, Africa, America, Oceania with their racial types, their animals, plants, minerals, natural resources, industry, science and fine arts are all contained within those forty hectares.'[33] Buildings of all shapes, styles and periods rise above the trees; domes, steeples, blast-furnace chimneys, towers, lighthouses, cupolas and minarets stand out against the skyline; and the wasteland the Champ de Mars once was has become 'the most visited place in the world; or rather, the whole world itself'.[34] The new France projected by these texts stretches far beyond the country's physical boundaries to colonise the

---

29 '[Là] où elle est sans rivale, où elle est maîtresse et maîtresse incontestée, c'est dans ce qui parle à l'imagination et la ravit, c'est enfin dans les choses de la fantaisie, du goût et du luxe. La France est vraiment elle-même et uniquement elle, dans la salle de Saint-Louis et de Baccarat, dans celle de Sèvres et des Gobelins, dans celle de l'orfèvrerie parisienne.'; 'Je suis en France.' Kaempfer, *Paris-Guide*, II, 2009.
30 M. de Parville, *Itinéraires dans Paris, prédédé de Promenades à l'exposition* (Paris: Garnier, 1867), 17.
31 'Toutes les nationalités s'y coudoient, toutes les langues s'y font entendre, tous les costumes y contrastent.' Larousse, *Grand dictionnaire universel*, 'Expositions' entry.
32 Larousse, *Grand dictionnaire universel*, 'Expositions' entry.
33 'L'Europe, l'Asie, l'Afrique, l'Amérique, l'Océanie avec leurs types humains, leurs animaux, leurs plantes, leurs minéraux, leurs produits naturels, leur industrie, leurs sciences, leurs beaux-arts tiennent dans ces quarante hectares.' Kaempfer, *Paris-Guide*, II, 2006.
34 '[L]e lieu le plus fréquenté du monde; mieux que cela, le monde entier lui-même.' Kaempfer, *Paris-Guide*, II, 2006. See also Edmond and Jules de Goncourt's description in their *Journal* (Paris: Robert Laffont, 1989) II, 86–87 (27.5.1867).

globe,³⁵ in a process which *The Communist Manifesto* had neatly described in 1848: 'The bourgeoisie[...]draws all [...]nations into civilisation. [...] It compels all nations, on pain of extinction, to adopt the bourgeois mode of production; it compels them to introduce what it calls civilisation into their midst, i.e. to become bourgeois themselves. In one word, it creates a world after its own image.'³⁶

The examples of that image as conveyed by the exhibition texts are remarkably consistent. The view – the profoundly bourgeois view, as Marx and Engels suggest – of France as civilised and artistic, spreading peace and harmony, superior but egalitarian, rooted in tradition yet forging ahead into a future of perfectibility, and benevolently dominating the world, emerges loud and clear from these writings. This, then, was the ideological background to the literature of the Second Empire, and as we shall see, these are the values which that literature examines, challenges, upholds, subverts or creatively transforms.

Above the main entrance to the 1855 exhibition was an enormous sculpture depicting the figure of France standing with outstretched arms laden with palms and wreaths, and with two allegorical figures sitting at her feet. One, busy with hammer and anvil, represented Industry; the other, with her head resting on her hand as she gazed pensively into space, was the melancholy figure of Art. As one commentator put it, 'it is nineteenth-century Art searching for the right path but not finding it yet.'³⁷ In a curious way, however, the exhibitions were to focus the attention of artists – and of writers in particular – on a way forward.

Although Ernest Renan complained that the 1855 exhibition had passed without giving rise to any memorable poetry, and 'without speaking to the imagination', his pessimism was misplaced.³⁸ Renan believed the exhibition

---

35 This was a phenomenon which Flaubert had deplored when he travelled to the East and saw how the old Orient was vanishing as French influence spread. He complained that the Orient had been contaminated by Paul de Kock, Béranger and the newspapers; he bemoaned the fact that the gardens of Top-Kapi were starting to look like Versailles, and that Turkish cafés had installed billiard tables; and he predicted that in a few years' time Egyptian beauties would all be wearing hats and corsets and reading novels. Flaubert, *Voyage en Orient*, *OC* II, 622 and 645.
36 Karl Marx and Friedrich Engels, *The Communist Manifesto*, tr. S Moore (London: Penguin, 1967), 84.
37 '[C]'est l'Art au dix-neuvième siecle qui cherche sa voie et qui ne l'a pas encore trouvée.' Anon., 'Le Palais de l'Industrie', in Dumas, Gautier et al, *Paris et les Parisiens au XIXe siecle*, 312.
38 '[S]ans rien dire à l'imagination'. Ernest Renan, 'La poésie et l'Exposition', in *Essais de morale et de critique* (Paris: Lévy, 1859), 353–374. Flaubert recommended this essay to Princess Mathilde when she found the 1867 exhibition boring – 'a sentiment I entirely share' ('sentiment que je partage entièrement'), he added. Flaubert, *Corr.* III, 584 (late Dec. 1866 – early Jan. 1867).

demonstrated that technological progress had coincided with a great moral and intellectual decline to produce a world of base pleasures, devoid of moral beauty and intellectual thought. That very idea, however, was to provide the central theme of much of the literature of the Second Empire. If exhibitions were the obsession of the age ('the delirium of the nineteenth-century', as Flaubert later called them),[39] they also afforded writers a prism through which to observe the world in all its modernity, and an aesthetic that shaped the way writers expressed what they saw.[40]

What they saw, however, was often at odds with the rhetoric of the exhibitions. Far from viewing Paris as the centre of the universe, drawing people of all nations to its heart, many writers felt estranged from their city and alienated by what was on show. As Flaubert commented to George Sand after visiting the 1867 exhibition, 'One feels very far from Paris there, in a vast, new, ugly world which may be the world of the future.'[41] The Goncourt brothers were also struck by that exhibition's curiously disorientating effect; instead of capturing the present in all its modernity, the display made them feel as if they had been projected into the future and were looking back into the past at a Paris transformed into an oriental city.[42] Resistant to the exhibitions' image as a phenomenon that drew in and absorbed all comers, several writers reacted by distancing themselves imaginatively in time, in an attempt to adopt a detached perspective. In *Paris nouveau et Paris futur*, for example, Victor Fournel pictured the Paris of a hundred years into the future, and envisioned a city that had finally achieved its aim of turning itself into pure exhibition, to the detriment of its own inhabitants:

> The great goal pursued for so long had finally been achieved: that of turning Paris into an object of luxury and curiosity rather than of function; an *exhibition city*, placed under glass; the world's hotel, admired and envied by foreigners, but impossible for the people who lived there.[43]

---

39 '[L]e délire du dix-neuvième siècle.' Flaubert, *Dictionnaire des idées reçues*, 'Exposition' entry. *OC* II, 308.
40 For more on the influence of the exhibition aesthetic on nineteenth-century France see Philippe Hamon, *Expositions: Littérature et architecture au XIXe siècle* (Paris: Corti, 1989).
41 ' On se sent là très loin de Paris, dans un monde nouveau et laid, un monde énorme qui est peut-être celui de l'avenir.' Flaubert, *Corr.* III, 635 (George Sand, 6.5.1867).
42 Goncourt, *Journal*, II, 86, 90.
43 'On avait enfin atteint le grand but poursuivi depuis si longtemps: celui de faire de Paris un objet de luxe et de curiosité plutot que d'usage, une *ville d'exposition*, placée sous verre, hôtellerie du monde, objet d'admiration et d'envie pour les étrangers, impossible à ses inhabitants.' Victor Fournel, *Paris nouveau et Paris futur* (Paris: Jacques Lecoffre, 1865), 241.

For Hippolyte Taine, however, that vision of a Paris of the future already existed in reality: the city had become 'a kind of permanent exhibition, open to the whole of Europe', and its dehumanised inhabitants had been reduced to the level of mercantile goods circulating within it: 'A salon is a permanent exhibition', he wrote; 'you are a commodity, and a commodity can only be sold by being put on display.'[44]

Such comments mark a sense that the city's emphasis on exhibition and display was at the expense of its own inhabitants' welfare, and an awareness of a disparity between outward spectacle and an underlying reality of neglect is prevalent in much of the literature of the period. The Goncourts' *Germinie Lacerteux*, for example, ends with a moving description of paupers' graves in the Montparnasse cemetery, followed by a bitter outburst directed at an unfeeling Paris. Couched in terms that simultaneously echo and mock the discourse that pervades exhibition texts, the passage exposes the hidden human cost of the capital's spectacle:

> O Paris! You are the heart of the world; you are the great human city, the great city of charity and fraternity! You are gentle in spirit, compassionate in manner, and generous in spectacle! The poor are as much your citizens as the rich. Your churches speak of Christ; your laws speak of equality; your newspapers speak of progress; all your governments speak of the common people. And yet look at where you throw those who die in your service, or kill themselves producing your luxuries, or perish from your harmful industries – those who have sweated away their lives toiling for you and creating your comforts, pleasures and splendour! Look at where you cast those who generated your loud, lively bustle, and who devoted their entire lives to your continuance as a capital city, thronging your streets and peopling your grandeur![45]

---

44 '[U]ne sorte d'exposition permanente, ouverte à toute l'Europe'; 'Un salon est une exposition permanente; vous êtes une denrée, et on ne place pas une denrée qu'en l'exposant.' Hippolyte Taine, *Notes sur Paris. Vie et opinions de Monsieur Frédéric Thomas Graindorge* (Paris: Hachette, 1867), 283.

45 'O Paris! tu es le cœur du monde, tu es la grande ville humaine, la grande ville charitable et fraternelle! Tu as des douceurs d'esprit, de vieilles miséricordes de mœurs, des spectacles qui font l'aumône! Le pauvre est ton citoyen comme le riche. Tes églises parlent de Jésus-Christ; tes lois parlent d'égalité; tes journaux parlent de progrès; tous tes gouvernements parlent du peuple; et voilà où tu jettes ceux qui meurent à te servir, ceux qui se tuent à créer ton luxe, ceux qui périssent du mal de tes industries, ceux qui ont sué leur vie à travailler pour toi, à te donner ton bien-être, tes plaisirs, tes splendeurs, ceux qui ont fait ton animation, ton bruit, ceux qui ont mis la chaîne de leurs existences dans ta durée de capitale, ceux qui ont été la foule de tes rues et le peuple de ta grandeur!' Edmond and Jules de Goncourt, *Germinie Lacerteux* (Paris: Union Générale d'Editions, 1979), 247–48.

The exhibition discourse's emphasis on the role of Paris in bringing people of all nationalities and walks of life together in a spirit of equality and harmony glossed over such social problems. Items displayed in the exhibition cases and listed in the catalogues were detached from their own environment. New and depersonalised, they were presented without history or troubling context. Creative writers, however, frequently staged exhibition scenes of a very different kind in their work. Favouring salerooms, museums, shops, salons – any space where objects were amassed and put on show – writers borrowed from the exhibition ethos as they dramatised an alternative vision of France.

In Second Empire literature, the auction room in particular lent itself to an ironic rewriting of the exhibition. In the salerooms of fiction, the objects on display are re-engaged with humanity; they are given a history, and often a poignancy that is noticeably absent from the official accounts. Fictional items on display are not merely emblems of commercialism, consumption and class; they carry memories and traces of past experience. At the sale of Madame Arnoux's possessions in Flaubert's *L'Éducation sentimentale*, for example, human beings and objects alike are segregated into distinct and corresponding categories. The shoddiest goods and people are on show together in the courtyard. 'You could see [...] washstands without basins, armchair frames, old baskets, shards of porcelain, empty bottles, mattresses', and alongside are their equally battered human counterparts: 'men in overalls or dirty overcoats, quite grey with dust, and with vile features.'[46] Inside, one room is full of gentlemen with catalogues who examine the paintings on display, while another exhibits a collection of Chinese weaponry. There is superficial order in the room containing the Arnoux's possessions, with objects arranged according to size, curtains and carpets displayed on the walls, and auctioneer, assistants, dealers and general public all occupying their own separate spaces. But that order soon collapses as categories dissolve and dreams fade. In direct contrast to the forward-looking optimism of exhibition texts, images of despair and death invade the description. As Madame Arnoux's petticoats and chemises and fichus are tossed through the air before being sold off, Frédéric feels he is witnessing her corpse being picked at by crows, while his own heart breaks as each of her possessions is put under the hammer. Whereas the exhibitions displayed static, dehumanised items and wrapped them in a rhetoric of egalitarianism

---

46 'On voyait[...]des lavabos sans cuvettes, des bois de fauteuils, de vieux paniers, des tessons de porcelaine, des bouteilles vides, des matelas; et des hommes en blouse ou en sale redingote, tous gris de poussière, la figure ignoble.' Flaubert, *L'Éducation sentimentale*, OC II, 157.

and harmony, here we see a display of commodities in circulation, reflecting the painful trajectories of their owners.

Like the exhibitions themselves, the fictional auction house or saleroom is often presented as a social melting-pot where rich and poor may rub shoulders,[47] but whereas exhibition discourse glossed over issues of social difference, these scenes dramatise individuals' anxious progression up or down the social ladder, a movement that is marked by sales and purchases as the commodification of private lives is exposed. Ernest Feydeau's 1868 novel, *La Comtesse de Châlis ou les mœurs du jour*, draws attention to the instability of social hierarchies by describing the pre-auction show of the possessions of Florence, a celebrated courtesan. When the dissolute Comtesse de Châlis arranges for a private viewing of the display, she unexpectedly encounters Florence amidst her possessions, an encounter that forces the Countess to acknowledge that 'in a word, there is almost no difference between her and … and us'.[48] In *L'Éducation sentimentale*, too, the sale-room episode breaks down social categories and brings together courtesan (Rosanette) and *grande dame* (Madame Dambreuse) to examine and appraise one another as if they, too were objects on show. Moreover each is drawn to the saleroom by the prospect of seeing the enactment of Madame Arnoux's social ruin, as the intimate remnants of her life are displayed and dispersed.

As Champfleury points out in *L'Hôtel des commissaires-priseurs*, in the auction-house 'all classes are merged'.[49] Social hierarchies dissolve, as do the categories into which objects on show are initially sorted. Changing hands, circulating, tracking the rise and fall of individuals, the displayed items reveal a social dynamic that exhibition discourse worked to hide. The fictional saleroom thus undermines all that the exhibitions stood for. Its emphasis is on the dispersal of the objects on display rather than on their accumulation; on private failure rather than public triumph; on the banal rather than the extraordinary; on repetition and monotony rather than on creative diversity; on rupture and

---

47 In Champfleury's words, 'rich enthusiasts and poor enthusiasts, influential art-dealers and small merchants, bankers and princes, foreigners and natives, artists and the middle-classes, brokers and girls of easy virtue, the greedy and the curious' all come together, 'united by the freemasonry of the curio'. ['les amateurs riches et les amateurs pauvres, les gros bonnets de la curiosité et les petits marchands, les banquiers et les princes, les étrangers et les indigènes, les artistes et les bourgeois, les coulissiers et les lorettes, les avides et les curieux'… 'reliés par la franc-maçonnerie du bric-à-brac'.] Champfleury, *L'Hôtel des commissaires-priseurs* (Paris: Dentu, 1867), vii–viii.

48 'Enfin il n'y a presque pas de différence entre elle et…et nous autres.' Ernest Feydeau, *La Comtesse de Châlis ou les moeurs du jour* (Paris: M. Lévy, 1868), 262.

49 '[T]ous les rangs sont confondus.' Champfleury, *L'Hôtel des commissaires-priseurs*, vii–viii.

disintegration rather than progress. This is no doubt why Flaubert chose to place his emblematic saleroom scene at a point in the novel where all the main emotional and political strands of his narrative come together before disintegrating, and to set it on 1st December 1851, the eve of Louis-Napoleon's coup d'état that heralded the Second Empire.

As writers of this period draw on the exhibition ethos for inspiration, in their work all kinds of locations become exhibition spaces. In *L'Éducation sentimentale*, M. Dambreuse's house, bursting with showy possessions, explicitly evokes the exhibitions and their quasi-religious reverence for consumerist display:

> the sideboard resembled the high altar of a cathedral or an exhibition of gold plate, so many dishes, covers, cutlery and spoons made of silver or silver-gilt were there, alongside items of cut crystal which radiated [...] shafts of iridescent light. The other three salons were crammed with art objects [...]

– and so the catalogue continues.[50] Indeed, in *L'Éducation sentimentale* Flaubert shows how the contemporary mentality turns virtually everything – even natural surroundings – into a commodity to be put on display. Frédéric and Rosanette respond to natural phenomena such as spiders' webs, puddles and butterflies 'as if they were curios', and their coachman presents the forest of Fontainebleau as a series of tourist sites, pointing out famous trees, listing their names, and slowing down 'so that they could be admired'.[51]

Elsewhere, the much-vaunted architectural features of the exhibition buildings find themselves transposed into literature. The multiple aisles and side-chambers of the 1855 Palace of Industry, its famous roof with over 400 windows of toughened glass that allowed daylight to flood the exhibits, and the concentric layout of the 1867 exhibition hall all leave their traces on the literature of the period. Examples include the vast hall with radiating corridors leading to other commodity-filled galleries that is Hamilcar's store-house in

---

50 '[L]e buffet ressemblait à un maître-autel de cathédrale ou à une exposition d'orfèvrerie, – tant il y avait de plats, de cloches, de couverts et de cuillers en argent et en vermeil, au milieu des cristaux à facettes qui entrecroisaient [...] des lueurs irisées. Les trois autres salons regorgeaient d'objets d'art.' Flaubert, *L'Éducation sentimentale*, *OC* II, 65.

51 '[C]omme une curiosité'; 'pour les faire admirer'. *L'Éducation sentimentale*, *OC* II, 127, 125. Shortly after, a man shows them three snakes displayed in a box (II, 127).

Flaubert's *Salammbô*; the luminous ceiling that sheds a soft, clear light over the display cabinets and shelves of Captain Nemo's submarine collection in Verne's *Vingt mille lieues sous les mers*; the Pharaoh's palace in Gautier's *Le Roman de la momie*, pointedly situated next to the military parade ground and full of luxurious artefacts including many images of the Pharaoh himself with his raised throne at its centre; and even the mortuary in Zola's *Thérèse Raquin*, where a 'varied and disparate public' walk up and down viewing corpses neatly laid out on display behind glass.[52] All are examples of writers borrowing from the exhibition aesthetic and transforming it into their own, darker and more troubling reflection of Second Empire France.

One of the most striking examples of the transposed exhibition space comes in Hugo's *Les Travailleurs de la mer*, where Gilliatt finds himself in an extraordinary sea-cave with galleries and side-chambers running off it. Flooded with a strange light from the sea, the cave is described in terms that are markedly reminiscent of the famous glass roof of the exhibition palace: 'Its rectilinear radiance, divided into long, straight strips, [...] looked like interposed sheets of glass.'[53] In an extension of the exhibition palace analogy, a vast range of sea-life is displayed in 'small side-caves, the aisles of the central cavern', which are illuminated by light from 'this window beneath the sea'. The natural objects Gilliatt sees there are described in terms of an exhibition of exquisite artefacts. The display includes 'the rarest gems from the ocean's jewellery-box', rock which is 'engraved with the most delicate, natural incisions', or which 'represented a vague bas-relief' worthy of Michelangelo, or is 'damascened like a Saracen shield or nielloed like a Florentine bowl. It had panels that seemed to be made of Corinthian bronze, and arabesques reminiscent of a mosque door.' Under Hugo's pen, this curiously transposed exhibition scene is transformed into something both seductive and disturbing whose metaphorical resonance gradually becomes clear. 'There is nothing more troubling and more enigmatic than the splendours in this cave,' he writes. The cavern exercises a strange fascination – 'What dominated was a sense of enchantment' – yet this is no Salon of Fine-Arts or Palace of Industry: it is a sinister 'Palace of Death'. In a further subversive echo of exhibition discourse, it has something of the sacred ('tabernacle', 'sanctuary', 'altar'), yet is presided over by a monster – a hideous, giant octopus with greedy tentacles, described as a hypocrite and a traitor that holds tight to whatever it can seize. At the

---

52 '[P]ublic mêlé et disparate'. Emile Zola, *Thérèse Raquin* (Paris: Garnier Flammarion, 1970) 132.

53 'Ses rayonnements rectilignes, découpés en longues bandes droites, [...] imitaient des interpositions de lames de verre.' Victor Hugo, *Les Travailleurs de la mer* (Paris: Gallimard, 1980), 347.

heart of Hugo's marine exhibition palace we recognise the embodiment of all he detested about Napoleon III.[54]

The *expositions universelles* were accompanied by a proliferation of catalogues. Listing, enumerating and classifying, these catalogues rarely attempt to explain or interpret their contents for the reader, but instead organise items into categories and impose an order on the objects on display. Although Janell Watson has referred to catalogues as 'a form of writing born of the profane sphere of material culture, not the sanctified sphere of "literary" writing',[55] it was nevertheless a form that mainstream literature readily assimilated during this period, and passages containing lists and inventories are one of the most characteristic features of Second Empire creative writing. The works of authors such as Victor Hugo, Jules Verne and the Goncourt brothers abound in passages of enumeration; reviewing *Salammbô*, Sainte-Beuve commented that Flaubert had listed the contents of Hamilcar's treasure-house 'with all the detail and precision of an inventory' and compared him 'to an auctioneer having fun'.[56] These literary 'catalogues', however, are very different from the real thing. Whereas the exhibition catalogues impose order on a profusion of items, the literary form of inventory generally subverts order, questions categories, and undermines confidence in classification. If, as Pierre Bourdieu has suggested, classification is a form of domination, the myriad examples of literary 'cataloguing' work to resist such domination and all it stands for.

In *Vingt mille lieues sous les mers*, for example, Verne describes the vast exhibition room that lies at the heart of Captain Nemo's submarine. In the terse style of a contemporary catalogue, the text lists without comment the paintings that hang, uniformly framed, on its walls:

> The various schools of the old masters were represented by a Raphael Madonna, a Leonardo da Vinci Virgin, a Correggio nymph, a woman by Titian, an Adoration by Veronese, an Assumption by Murillo, a portrait by Holbein, a monk by Velasquez, a martyr by Ribera, a fair by Rubens,

---

54 '[P]etites caves latérales, bas-côtes de la caverne centrale'; 'cette fenêtre sous la mer'; 'les plus rares bijoux de l'écrin de l'océan'; 'travaillé des plus délicates ciselures naturelles'; 'figurait un vague bas-relief'; 'damasquinée comme un bouclier sarrasin ou niellée comme une vasque florentine. Elle avait des panneaux qui paraissaient de bronze de Corinthe, puis des arabesques comme une porte de mosquée.'; 'Rien de plus troublant et de plus énigmatique que ce faste dans cette cave.'; 'Ce qui dominait, c'était l'enchantement'; 'Palais de la Mort'. Hugo, *Les Travailleurs de la mer*, 345–352, 438, 444.
55 Janell Watson, *Literature and Material Culture from Balzac to Proust. The Collection and Consumption of Curiosities* (Cambridge: Cambridge University Press, 1999), 109.
56 '[A]vec la minutie et l'exactitude d'un inventaire'; '[U]n commissaire-priseur qui s'amuse'. Charles Augustin Sainte-Beuve, '*Salammbô* par Monsieur Gustave Flaubert', *Le Constitutionnel*, 15 December 1862.

two Flemish landscapes by Teniers, three little genre paintings by Gérard Dow, Metsu, and Paul Potter, two pictures by Géricault and Prudhon, and some seascapes by Backhuysen and Vernet. Among the works by modern painters were canvases bearing the signatures of Delacroix, Ingres, Decamps, Troyon, Meissonier, Daubigny, etc; and some admirable marble and bronze statues, after the finest antique models, stood on pedestals in the corners of this magnificent museum.[57]

Music is represented by 'scores by Weber, Rossini, Mozart, Beethoven, Haydn, Meyerbeer, Herold, Wagner, Auber, Gounod, and a number of others'. The main exhibition, 'in elegant, copper-framed glass cases, [...] classed and labelled', displays 'the most precious productions of the sea that had ever been presented to the eyes of a naturalist',[58] and these, too, are listed at great length. Yet Verne turns the exhibition ethos on its head. Even more spectacular than the exhaustive list of exhibits in Captain Nemo's museum is the display that lies beyond the confines of the submarine. The luminous ceiling that shines on Nemo's exhibits suddenly goes dark, and the visitors turn to view the world outside, illuminated by the submarine's electric light. What they see is so immeasurably greater than the supposedly unsurpassed collection of specimens in the museum, that it defies any attempt to name and list and classify: 'What a spectacle! What pen could describe it?' says the narrator;[59] 'I shall not mention all the varieties that passed before our dazzled eyes, all the collection of the seas of Japan and China.'[60] Unlike official catalogues, literary

---

57 'Les diverses écoles des maîtres anciens étaient représentées par une madone de Raphaël, une vierge de Léonard de Vinci, une nymphe du Corrége, une femme du Titien, une adoration de Véronèse, une assomption de Murillo, un portrait d'Holbein, un moine de Vélasquez, un martyr de Ribeira, une kermesse de Rubens, deux paysages flamands de Teniers, trois petits tableaux de genre de Gérard Dow, de Metsu, de Paul Potter, deux toiles de Géricault et de Prud'hon, quelques marines de Backuysen et de Vernet. Parmi les œuvres de la peinture moderne apparaissaient des tableaux signés Delacroix, Ingres, Decamp, Troyon, Meissonnier, Daubigny etc., et quelques admirables réductions de statues de marbre ou de bronze, d'après les plus beaux modèles de l'antiquité, se dressaient sur leurs piédestaux dans les angles de ce magnifique musée.' Jules Verne, *Vingt mille lieues sous les mers* (Paris: Hetzel et cie, n.d.), 78–79.
58 '[D]es partitions de Weber, de Rossini, de Mozart, de Beethoven, d'Haydn, de Meyerbeer, d'Herold, de Wagner, d'Auber, de Gounod, et nombre d'autres'; 'sous d'élégantes vitrines fixées par des armatures de cuivre, étaient classés et étiquetés les plus précieux produits de la mer qui eussent jamais été livrés aux regards d'un naturaliste.' Verne, *Vingt mille lieues sous les mers*, 78–79.
59 'Quel spectacle! Quelle plume le pourrait décrire!' Verne, *Vingt mille lieues sous les mers*, 103.
60 'Je ne citerai pas toutes les variétés qui passèrent ainsi devant nos yeux éblouis, toute cette collection des mers du Japon et de la Chine.' Verne, *Vingt mille lieues sous les mers*, 109.

lists such as Captain Nemo's museum inventory draw attention to their lack of exhaustiveness, and, as here, celebrate the notion that life exceeds classification and resists any attempt to quantify and control.

Despite Sainte-Beuve's comment about *Salammbô*, Flaubert's account of Hamilcar's storehouse is far from being a straightforward inventory. It, too, dramatises the irrepressible, uncontrollable nature of its contents. Exotic gums overflow their containers; gold dust spills thorough the gaping seams of sacks; subtle fumes escape from the amassed perfumes, leathers, spices and ostrich feathers and hang over the collection. Just as the contents elude containment, so they resist identification. There are lists of precious commodities with exotic names, but one sample turns out to be a fake and thus throws the rest of the inventory into question. The catalogue form fails again when faced with objects that defy classification or evaluation – 'mysterious things which had no name, and were of incalculable value.' As the inventory of Hamilcar's wealth continues, it becomes less a list of what has been amassed than a catalogue of what has been lost or destroyed – it becomes an inventory of absence that seems to mock the exhibitions' message of peace and prosperity: 'Three thousand trees were felled in Maschala, and in Ubada the granaries were destroyed and the cisterns filled in! In Tedès, they carried off fifteen hundred *gomors* of flour; in Marassana, they killed the shepherds, consumed the flocks, and burned down your house [...] The slaves fled to the mountains; and of the donkeys, hinnies, mules, Taormino cattle and oryngis horses, not one remains! All were taken!'[61]

Other literary texts undermine the exhibition ethos even more overtly. An 1855 drama entitled *Dzing! Boum! Boum!* features an 'Exposition de la Bêtise' – an 'Exhibition of Stupidity' where a jumbled mass of ridiculous objects is presented in a great exhibition hall. So unimpressive is the exhibition that the visitors smash the display in a particularly vivid dramatisation of a counter-current of fragmentation, discontinuity and disintegration that frequently emerges from literary texts of the period, as if in defiance of the establishment discourse of harmony and integration. In a parody of the exhibition texts' celebration of internationalism, these visitors are resolutely provincial and parochial: 'people from Normandy, Gascony and

---

61 '[D]es choses mystérieuses, qui n'avaient pas de nom, et d'une incalculable valeur'; 'Trois mille pieds d'arbres sont coupés à Maschala, et à Ubada les greniers défoncés, les citernes comblées! A Tedès, ils ont emporté quinze cents gomors de farine; à Marassana, tué les pasteurs, mangé les troupeaux, brûlé ta maison, [...] Les esclaves [...] se sont enfuis vers les montagnes; et les ânes, les bardeaux, les mulets, les boeufs de Taormine, et les chevaux orynges, plus un seul! tous emmenés!' Flaubert, *Salammbô*, *OC* I, 735, 736, 738.

the Auvergne, natives of Marseilles from the Cannebière, people from Berry, and women from Brittany and Burgundy who come to attend the opening of the exhibition [...] to admire [...] articles from the world in general, and from their own *département* in particular.'[62]

The aspect of exhibition rhetoric that celebrated France's all-encompassing welcome to other nations is subverted more subtly elsewhere. In *Manette Salomon*, for example, the Goncourt brothers describe the artist Coriolis's studio in terms that both evoke and undermine the concepts of universality and display prevalent in exhibition discourse. The studio is presented (as the exhibitions themselves had been) as a dazzling microcosm, a display of people and artefacts from all corners of the globe, past and present:

> It was as if people from all nations and all centuries were crowded together within these four walls radiant with light. History and space seemed to have been brought together there. The whole universe was rubbing shoulders. It was as if the figures in a Museum had stepped out of their frames and were jostling one another at the Carnival. Fabrics, fashions, drawings, lines, memories, countries, all mingled together in a dizzying confusion of colours. There were examples from every civilisation, pieces from all over the world.[63]

Drawing both on the crush of international visitors to the *expositions universelles* and on the artefacts on display there, over the space of several pages the authors list a profusion of people and costumes. There are specimens from every corner of the world. The heterogeneous objects crammed into the studio are as 'universal' as its visitors, and the repeated references to display cabinets and shelving strengthen the sense that we are in an exhibition space as much as in an artist's studio. But in contrast to the exhibition palaces, this exhibition space

---

62 'Des Normands, des Gascons, des Auvergnats, des Marseillais de la Cannebière, des Berrichons, des Bretonnes, des Bourguignottes qui viennent assister à l'ouverture de l'Exposition...pour y admirer...les produits de l'univers en général, et en particulier ceux de leur département.' A. Guénée, C. Potier and E. Mathieu, *Dzing! Boum! Boum! Revue de l'exposition* (Paris: Mifliez, 1855), 2.

63 'Entre les quatre murs rayonnant de lumière, on eût cru voir se presser un peu de toutes les nations et de tous les siècles. L'histoire et l'espace semblaient ramassés là. L'univers se coudoyait. C'était comme une évocation, où le peuple d'un Musée, descendu de ses cadres, se cognait au Carnaval. Les étoffes, les modes, les dessins, les lignes, les souvenirs, les pays, tout se mêlait dans le tohubohu étourdissant des couleurs. Il y avait des échantillons de toutes les civilisations, des morceaux de toute la terre [...].' Edmond and Jules de Goncourt, *Manette Salomon* (Paris: Union Générale d'Editions, 1979), 226.

is chaotic, disordered and unexplained: 'The display and jumble of baroque luxury, the accumulation of strange, exotic, disparate objects, souvenirs, and pieces of art-work, the quantity and diversity of things from every period, every style, and in every colour, the confusion of things picked up by an artist, traveller or collector combined to produce a chaotic orgy of clutter.'[64] Unlike the destructive chaos depicted in many literary 'exhibitions', however, this is a creative disorder. The Goncourts' text is subtly subversive, for the reader is led to understand that the chaos of objects is what enables Coriolis's artistic creation. In pointed contrast to the much-vaunted organisation and methodology of the *expositions*, this disordered display will produce real art.

Clearly, not everyone was open to the exhibitions' message of confident optimism. However controlled and ordered the display of objects, its reception remained problematic. The catalogues, with their interminable lists of artefacts and commodities, were impersonal and impartial; interpretation was left to the spectator who might come away overwhelmed and confused, like Flaubert, who wrote of his visit to the 1867 exhibition: 'It's overpowering. There are some splendid and very interesting things. But man was not designed to swallow infinity. You would have to know all the Sciences and all the Arts to take an interest in everything you see at the Champ-de-Mars.'[65] Something of this resistance to the exhibitions' ideology, this failure to engage with accumulated display, finds its way into the literature of the period as characters repeatedly fail to respond to amassed objects, and in particular to industrially-produced items.

In Flaubert's *Éducation sentimentale*, Jacques Arnoux, as proprietor of *L'Art industriel* and dealer in mass-produced goods, epitomises a brash confidence in modern manufactured articles. He is constantly exhibiting, whether from the display in the offices of *L'Art industriel*, his 'museum', his factory, or his shop selling religious artefacts. (In naming this character, did Flaubert perhaps have in mind *Le Travail universel, revue complète des œuvres de l'art et de l'industrie exposées à Paris en 1855*, by one J. J. Arnoux?)[66] Arnoux embodies some of the aspects that Flaubert most abhorred about the association between art and

---

64 'L'étalage et le fouillis d'un luxe baroque, un entassement d'objets bizarres, exotiques, hétéroclites, des souvenirs, des morceaux d'art, l'amas et le contraste de choses de tous les temps, de tous les styles, de toutes les couleurs, le pêle-mêle de ce que ramasse un artiste, un voyageur, un collectionneur, y mettaient le désordre et le sabbat du bric-à-brac.' Goncourt, *Manette Salomon*, 136.

65 'Cela est écrasant. Il y a des choses splendides et extra-curieuses. Mais l'homme n'est pas fait pour avaler l'infini. Il faudrait savoir toutes les Sciences et tous les Arts pour s'intéresser à tout ce qu'on voit dans le Champ-de-Mars.' Flaubert, *Corr.* III, 635 (George Sand, 6.5.1867).

66 2 vols. (Paris: Bureaux de la patrie, 1856).

industry celebrated by the universal exhibitions. Showing off the incongruous objects crammed into his shop, he insists to Frédéric that 'you can put art everywhere'. But Frédéric, like Flaubert at the exhibition, fails to respond as he should: 'Arnoux's displays bored Frédéric, who was cold and hungry.'[67] The lack of a 'proper' response is characteristic of Flaubert's presentation of exhibition sequences. Whether it be the guide trying to show Emma and Léon round Rouen cathedral in *Madame Bovary*, or Rosanette's lack of enthusiasm for the sights of the Chateau de Fontainebleau, or Frédéric's reluctant tour of Arnoux's porcelain factory later in *L'Éducation sentimentale*, exhibition-like displays are portrayed in his novels as interfering irrelevances that stand in the way of the characters' real desires.

This is indeed how the reader often experiences the catalogues of objects that are such a feature of the literature of the period: these lists seem to get in the way of the plot, and we are uncertain how to interpret them. Like many of the exhibition catalogues, the Second Empire literary text provides little guidance for the reader. In this respect, the Goncourt's description of Coriolis's cluttered studio in *Manette Salomon* offers a striking contrast with Balzac's 1831 description of an equally cluttered antique shop in *La Peau de Chagrin*.[68] Whereas Balzac frames and organises his description and offers a narrator, Raphael, through whose eyes the mass of objects on display is interpreted and understood, the Goncourts provide no such help; the reader of *Manette Salomon*, like the visitor to the exhibitions, is overwhelmed by the heterogeneous objects and must make of them what he or she will. Faced with such a description, or with Verne's pages-long lists of sea-creatures or prehistoric animals, we are tempted to respond as Flaubert did to the exhibition: '*cela est écrasant...*'

Yet display, excess and commodification were grist to the mills of writers who sought to capture 'modern life'. In their desire to represent modernity, Second Empire writers seem to have discerned an analogy between the characteristics of exhibition practice and their own literary enterprises:[69] the writer's task of collecting a mass of source material, organising it, privileging the visual, bringing together characters from a variety of types, behaviours and classes to people their novels, and displaying a wealth of detail to the reader with the

---

67 '[O]n peut mettre de l'art partout'; 'Les démonstrations d'Arnoux ennuyaient Frédéric, qui avait froid et faim.' Flaubert, *L'Éducation sentimentale*, *OC* II, 47.
68 For an extended discussion of these novels, see Janell Watson, *Literature and Material Culture*, 119–128.
69 In 1867 Flaubert wrote to Amélie Bosquet that, 'jealous of industrialists, gentlemen of letters have set about "creating a work for the Exhibition". Sentences are being lined up alongside enema syringes. Hurrah for progress!' ['MM. les gens de lettres, jaloux des industriels, se sont mis "à faire un ouvrage pour l'Exposition". Les phrases s'alignent à côté des clysopompes. Vive le progrès!'] Flaubert, *Corr.* III, 608 (17.2.1867).

minimum of explanation or interpretation, was a process akin to that of the *expositions universelles*. Novels became a form of exhibition. Unlike French fiction from the earlier part of the century, which had tended to reflect inwardly, they put the outward world on display. Uneasy about a future of industrialisation and commodification, however, and suspicious of the manipulative nature of official rhetoric, writers were particularly conscious of linguistic erosion, and many feared that language, too, was in danger of becoming debased and commodified. When Madame Arnoux takes Frédéric on a tour of the porcelain factory in *L'Éducation sentimentale*, for example, Flaubert makes it clear that language itself has been caught up in the industrial display. Among the specimens exhibited are words and letters churned out by Arnoux's machinery: 'pots embellished with arabic writing [...] letters for shop-signs, wine labels'. Madame Arnoux's own language seems to have become debased in turn: '"Those are the *patouillards*," she said. The word sounded grotesque to him, almost indecent, coming from her lips', and as Sénécal takes over as guide, the text degenerates into a long list of technical terminology, harsh-sounding and incomprehensible. 'Frédéric understood none of it.'[70]

In this novel the text frequently takes on the attributes of the exhibition catalogue as it moves from narrative to simple lists. There is a list of cafes ('café Gascard, café Grimbert, café Halbout, estaminet Bordelais, Havanais, Havrais, Bœuf-à-la-mode, brasserie Allemande, Mère Morel') whose international names echo the internationalism of the exhibitions and are almost – but significantly not quite – in alphabetical order.[71] A list of Rosanette's lovers is meaningless to the reader and even to the protagonists, since it fails to distinguish between two brothers: 'She has slept with Jumillac, with Flacourt, with little Allard, with Bertinaux, with Saint-Valéry, the pockmarked one. No! The other one! It doesn't matter, they're brothers.'[72] Even different types of language are classified and catalogued: 'All sorts of remarks followed: puns, anecdotes, boasts, wagers, lies taken to be true, implausible assertions, a tumult of words that soon dispersed into private conversations.'[73] Yet there is something subversive about these lists: not quite alphabetical, not quite specific,

---

70 '[D]es pots rehaussés d'écritures arabes [...] des lettres d'enseigne, des étiquettes à vin'; '"Ce sont les patouillards," dit-elle. Il trouva le mot grotesque, et comme inconvenant dans sa bouche'; 'Frédéric n'y comprenait rien.' Flaubert, *L'Éducation sentimentale*, *OC* II, 79–80.

71 Flaubert, *L'Éducation sentimentale*, *OC* II, 46.

72 'Elle a couché avec Jumillac, avec Flacourt, avec le petit Allard, avec Bertinaux, avec Saint-Valéry, le grêlé. Non! L'autre! Ils sont deux frères, n'importe!' Flaubert, *L'Éducation sentimentale*, *OC* II, 67.

73 'Toute sorte de propos s'ensuivirent: calembours, anecdotes, vantardises, gageures, mensonges tenus pour vrais, assertions improbables, un tumulte de paroles qui bientôt s'éparpilla en conversations particulières.' Flaubert, *L'Éducation sentimentale*, *OC* II, 53.

language here struggles to resist the classificatory threat, and a formless 'tumult of words' overwhelms the imposed order before reconstituting itself into new meanings, new conversations. With these examples Flaubert seems to show language caught up in a quasi-industrial process of ordering and control, yet working to break free from systematisation. Running counter to the exhibition ethos, language's resistance to well-organised regulation here implies, like the disorder of Coriolis's studio, a more creative alternative.

Of all Second Empire writers, it is perhaps Flaubert whose literary response to the changing world promoted by the exhibitions is most intricately woven through his work. Although he once included the universal exhibitions in a long list of things that annoyed him,[74] his subtle exploitation of the exhibition mentality in *Madame Bovary* turns out to be so comprehensive that it merits a more detailed examination. In September 1851, only a few days after starting to write *Madame Bovary*, Flaubert had travelled to London with his mother to visit the Great Exhibition. Rather to his surprise he was impressed by what he saw, took copious notes,[75] and pronounced the exhibition 'very fine, though admired by everyone'.[76] As he continued to work on *Madame Bovary*, exhibition fever took hold in France,[77] and it left an indelible mark on this novel (completed in 1856) which charts the gradual industrialisation of France and ends in the Second Empire with Homais triumphant.

Nowhere in the text are echoes of the exhibition more evident than in Flaubert's description of the eagerly-awaited agricultural fair. Set under the July Monarchy, these *comices agricoles* of course predate the first *exposition universelle*. Yet from the start of the chapter it is clear not only that Flaubert was acutely conscious of the rhetoric surrounding the build-up to the exhibition and the image of France it promoted, but that his absurd provincial agricultural fair is a deliberate ironic reworking of both. Yonville becomes the exhibition space, bedecked with tricolours like the Palais de l'Industrie. In 1855 the palace's main entrance was marked by four tall flagpoles, each flying a long banner.[78] In a diminished echo of this, Yonville's fair is announced by four makeshift

---

74 *Sottisier* no. 8, ms g 226¹, fol. 277. Cit. in Anne Herschberg-Pierrot (ed.), Gustave Flaubert. *Le Dictionnaire des idées reçues et Le Catalogue des idées chic* (Paris: Livre de Poche, 1997), 181.
75 See Jean Seznec, *Flaubert à l'exposition de 1851* (Oxford: Clarendon Press, 1951).
76 '[U]ne fort belle chose, quoique admirée de tout le monde.' Flaubert, *Corr.* II, 34 (E. Chevalier, 17.1.1852).
77 By the end of 1853 Flaubert was already aware that he would have to hurry to reserve lodgings in Paris if he wanted to be there during the exhibition period. See Flaubert, *Corr.* II, 490 (L. Colet, 28.12.1853).
78 See for example A. Deroy's picture of the Palais de l'Industrie, 1855, reproduced in Mainardi, *Art and Politics of the Second Empire*, 41.

posts erected outside the Mairie, each of which bears a little banner of greenish cloth adorned with inscriptions in gold lettering. Literally spelling out the agricultural fair's subliminal link with the *Exposition universelle*, these golden letters read 'To Commerce', 'To Agriculture', ' To Industry' and 'To the Fine Arts'. Despite the fact that industry and the fine arts are conspicuously absent from Flaubert's agricultural fair, (and Homais accuses the mayor of being 'completely lacking in what is known as artistic genius') they are repeatedly evoked – by Lieuvain, whose speech praises the monarch's role in cultivating trade, industry, agriculture and the arts, and again by Homais, who proposes a toast 'to industry and the fine arts, those two sisters!'[79] The *idea* of industry and the fine arts is thus constantly present at the Comices, but it is an empty presence that merely serves to draw the reader's attention to their absence.

A curious little episode earlier in the novel had prepared the reader for such an undermining of the exhibition ethos, when Homais takes Charles, Emma, Leon and his children on an outing to show them a new linen mill under construction.[80] This strange, empty building carries subversive overtones of the design of the modernistic Palace of Industry with its celebrated glass roof. Like the exhibition palace, Flaubert's mill is a long, rectangular structure adorned with tricolours, with a large number of windows and a roof through which the sky is clearly visible. But instead of standing in an exhibition park surrounded by a proud display of machinery, the mill is situated in a bleak open space dotted with a few rusting gear-wheels. Its value as a focus of interest is nil, for 'nothing [...] was less curious than this curiosity'. Homais' strange fascination with this desolate structure starts to make sense if we recognise it as an oblique reference to the innovative exhibition building, a reference reinforced when he calculates the thickness of its walls and the strength of its floors (echoing the kind of calculations made by commentators on the Palais de l'Industrie),[81] and expatiates

---

79 'Au Commerce', 'À l'Agriculture', 'À l'Industrie', 'Aux Beaux-Arts.' Flaubert, *Madame Bovary*, *OC* I, 619; 'compètement dénué de ce qui s'appelle le génie des arts' (I, 622); 'à l'industrie et aux beaux-arts, ces deux soeurs!' (I, 626).
80 Flaubert, *Madame Bovary*, *OC* I, 608.
81 E.g. 'The external measurements of the Palace of Industry are 254 metres 40 centimetres in length, by 110 metres 49 centimetres wide, giving a surface area of 28,055.76 square metres, and if we add to that the six pavilions that adjoin the palace, we arrive at an overall total of 31,939.28 square metres of buildings covering the ground in one piece, or alternatively, 3 hectares 19 ares and 39 centiares.' [Le Palais de l'Industrie mesure *hors oeuvres des murs*, c'est-à-dire extérieurement, une longueur de 254 mètres 40 centimètres, sur une largeur de 110 mètres 49 centimètres. Ce qui nous donne une surface de 28,055 mètres 76 centimètres carrés, et si l'on y joint les six pavillons qui flanquent le palais, on arrive à un total général de 31,939 mètres 28 centimètres carrés de bâtiments, d'un seul tenant, couvrant le sol, ou, si l'on veut, 3 hectares 19 ares 39 centiares.'] Dumas, Gautier et al, *Paris et les Parisiens au XIXe siècle*, 313–14.

on 'the future importance of this establishment.'[82] Flaubert's phantom 'Palace of Industry' thus offers a sardonic comment on the bleakness of an industrial future that will eventually claim Emma and Charles' daughter, Berthe.[83]

If the visit to the empty linen factory can be read as an indirect commentary on the industrial ethos of the *exposition universelle*, Emma and Léon's visit to Rouen Cathedral provides a subversive counterpoint to the exhibition's fine-arts display. Whereas exhibition texts had emphasised the sacred quality of the *exposition universelle* with its cathedral-like exhibition palaces, here that notion is turned on its head. The artistic and spiritual glories of Rouen's great cathedral are reduced to statistics such as the weight of the great bell, the height of the spire, or the size of a benefactor's legacy, and secularised – the church itself resembles 'a gigantic boudoir'. Full of paintings and sculptures which the guide wants to display '*in the right order*', and which Emma inspects through her lorgnette like a gallery visitor, the cathedral is presented as an exhibition space where *curiosités* are displayed in nave and transept: 'Would Sir care to see the curiosities of the church?' asks the verger; 'Would Madam care to see the curiosities of the church?'[84] Recommended itineraries and titles of paintings are listed in the perfunctory tones of a catalogue entry: 'Exit [...] by the north door [...] to see the *Resurrection*, the *Last Judgment*, *Paradise*, *King David* and the *Damned* in the fires of Hell.' And like the exhibition itself, the cathedral generates excessive numbers of explanatory publications: the guide is seen carrying twenty or so bound volumes '*that dealt with the cathedral*.'[85] Under Flaubert's ironic pen the guided tour of this 'Palais des Beaux-Arts' rings as hollow as the visit to the empty linen mill.

If Flaubert turns Rouen Cathedral into a debased and secularised art exhibition, he presents the agricultural fair as a *solennité* with all the quasi-sacred overtones that permeate the discourse surrounding the universal exhibition. During the official speech-making, M. Derozerays emphasises the close relationship between agriculture and religion and their joint contribution to civilisation, while M. Lieuvain associates the flourishing of commerce and fine arts with a strengthened religion which 'smiles on all our hearts.'[86] Yonville's exhibition space itself is suffused with the smell of incense and

---

82 'Rien[...]n'était moins curieux que cette curiosité'; 'l'importance future de cet établissement.' Flaubert, *Madame Bovary*, *OC* I, 608.
83 Orphaned, Berthe ends up working in a cotton mill.
84 '[U]n boudoir gigantesque'; '*dans l'ordre*'; 'M. désire voir les curiosités de l'église?'; 'Madame désire voir les curiosités de l'église?' Flaubert, *Madame Bovary*, *OC* I, 655–56.
85 'Sortez[...]par le portail du nord[...]pour voir la *Résurrection*, le *Jugement dernier*, le *Paradis*, *le Roi David* et les *Réprouvés* dans les flammes d'enfer'; '*qui traitaient de la cathédrale*.' Flaubert, *Madame Bovary*, *OC* I, 656–57.
86 '[S]ourit à tous les cœurs.' Flaubert, *Madame Bovary*, *OC* I, 622.

candlewax emanating from the church chairs hired out by Lestiboudois in his own personal amalgam of commerce and religion, so that villagers sitting on them watch the proceedings 'with a certain veneration'.[87]

Whereas contemporary commentators revelled in the image of crowds converging on the *exposition universelle* from all over the world, Flaubert presents a diminished image of crowds streaming towards the agricultural fair from the surrounding Norman countryside – 'like the waves of a tempestuous sea', says Homais.[88] They arrive on foot or on carthorse, in ironic counterpoint to M. Lieuvain's fulsome tribute to the new railway system which, in another echo of exhibition rhetoric, he calls 'the new means of communication, like so many new arteries in the body politic'.[89] But whereas exhibition texts stressed how diverse in appearance and nationality the crowds who flocked to the *exposition universelle* were, Flaubert uses that commonplace image only to turn it on its head to emphasise the crowd's dumb uniformity. At his *Comices*, 'all those people looked alike [...] All the waistcoats were made of velvet, with shawl collars; all the watches had an oval cornelian seal on a long ribbon; [...] all the mouths in the crowd were wide open.'[90]

The speeches these crowds drink in resound with the same rhetoric that surrounded the universal exhibition. Taking up the familiar image of the peaceful battle, M. Lieuvain explains that the *comices* are 'a peaceful arena' from which the victor will emerge to extend a fraternal hand to the vanquished.[91] With frequent references to progress and civilisation and to the guiding hand of the beloved monarch who knows how to 'ensure respect for peace as for war, industry, trade, agriculture and the fine arts', he reinforces the association between exhibition and State, reiterating the idea that 'our fine nation' is a place where art and industry flourish and where religion smiles on all.[92] Subtly undermining this discourse of French harmony, however, is the bitter rivalry

---

87 '[A]vec une certaine vénération.' Flaubert, *Madame Bovary*, *OC* I, 621.
88 'Comme les flots d'une mer en furie.' Flaubert, *Madame Bovary*, *OC* I, 626.
89 '[L]es voies nouvelles de communication, comme autant d'artères nouvelles dans le corps de l'État.' Flaubert, *Madame Bovary*, *OC* I, 622.
90 'Tous ces gens-là se ressemblaient [...] Tous les gilets étaient de velours, à châle; toutes les montres portaient au bout d'un long ruban quelque cachet ovale en cornaline' [...] 'toutes les bouches de la multitude se tenaient ouvertes.' Flaubert, *Madame Bovary*, *OC* I, 622–23.
91 '[D]es arènes pacifiques.' Flaubert, *Madame Bovary*, *OC* I, 624. In an early draft, the fair is described as 'peace struggles' ('luttes de la paix') See online transcription at www.flaubert.univ-rouen.fr, L'Atelier Bovary, Brouillons vol. 3, fol. 68v.
92 '[F]aire respecter la paix comme la guerre, l'industrie, le commerce, l'agriculture et les beaux-arts'; 'notre belle patrie.' Flaubert, *Madame Bovary*, *OC* I, 622.

between the tellingly-named innkeeper, Madame Lefrançois, and the *Café de France* with its equally pointed title. Moreover, the fact that this speech is made by Lieuvain instead of the expected *préfet* adds a further subversive note, for during the Second Empire it was not uncommon for a Prefect to absent himself from such ceremonies and send a last-minute substitute in a tacit mark of hostility to the regime.[93]

Like most commentators on the 1855 exposition, Flaubert's Lieuvain paints a picture of social harmony, where everyone works for the betterment of all and the support of the State. He praises the docile workers whose labour is at last being rewarded by this benevolent new regime: 'And you, venerable servants! Humble domestics, whose painful toil no government has ever taken into account until now, step forward to receive a reward for your silent virtues'.[94] The silent, virtuous, but uncomprehending figure of Catherine Leroux, described as 'this half-century of servitude'[95] shows the hollowness of that rhetoric, her fifty-four years of service rendering the 'reward' derisory. While Lieuvain's speech stresses the familiar notion that the present regime is different from and better than any previous one, M. Derozerays takes up the other strand of origin spun by the exhibition texts and evokes the Roman Empire in an allusion to Diocletian planting cabbages. The familiar reference points of the new French identity promoted by the universal exhibition are all here in diminished or ludicrous form.

Meanwhile, as these speeches are seducing the crowd, Rodolphe's words are seducing Emma. The two sets of discourse intertwine so that Rodolphe's repeated references to a world of dream and illusion serve to undermine the fantasies spun by Lieuvain and Derozerays. 'People throw themselves like that into all kinds of fantasies and foolishness', says Rodolphe to Emma as Lieuvain holds forth in the background about 'the current state of our fine nation'.[96] Rodolphe appears to distance himself both literally and metaphorically from the patriotic rhetoric of Lievain and Derozerays: full of mockery for the fair, he steers Emma away from the speeches and asks, 'Doesn't that social conspiracy disgust you?'[97] Yet as Rodolphe uses his own seductive power on Emma,

---

93 See Matthew Truesdell, *Spectacular Politics. Louis-Napoleon Bonaparte and the Fête Impériale, 1849-1870* (New York, Oxford: Oxford University Press, 1997), 174.
94 'Et vous, vénérables serviteurs! humbles domestiques, dont aucun gouvernement jusqu'à ce jour n'avait pris en considération les pénibles labeurs, venez recevoir la récompense de vos vertus silencieuses'. Flaubert, *Madame Bovary*, *OC* I, 624.
95 '[C]e demi-siècle de servitude' *Madame Bovary*, *OC*, I, 625.
96 '[L]'on se jette ainsi dans toutes sortes de fantaisies, de folies'; 'la situation actuelle de notre belle patrie.' Flaubert, *Madame Bovary*, *OC* I, 622.
97 'Est-ce que cette conjuration du monde ne vous révolte pas?' Flaubert, *Madame Bovary*, *OC* I, 624.

Flaubert shows us that he too is part of that politicised world of alluring but empty display. Significantly, this seduction mainly takes place in the Council Room of the Mairie, presided over by a bust of the monarch.

The constant presence at the agricultural fair of the image of the monarch, presiding in sculpted form or invoked in speeches, echoes the omnipresent image of the Emperor that dominated the *exposition universelle* from its inception. But the fair is also dominated by another ubiquitous figure – Homais. Member of the consultative committee, member of the jury, author of a treatise on cider, proposer of a toast to art and industry, contributor of his own 'exhibition text' to the *Fanal de Rouen*, Homais is a physical embodiment of the *exposition universelle* as he tries to dazzle Madame Lefrançois by displaying his knowledge of agronomy, botany, building construction, chemistry, geology, meteorology, mineralogy, pomology, nutrition and principles of hygiene. In a deeply symbolic moment, Flaubert portrays this grotesque character as he listens with rapt attention to Lieuvain's speech, with his legs straddling the tiny figure of his son – whose name is Napoleon. Is it purely coincidental that Flaubert sketched out his *Comices agricoles* chapter on the same day that he wrote an effusive letter in praise of Victor Hugo's vituperative *Napoléon le petit?*[98]

Madame Bovary vividly dramatises the hollowness of the exhibition's rhetoric, and as the agricultural fair comes to an end Flaubert deals a final blow to the image it sought to project:

> The meeting was over; the crowd dispersed; and now that the speeches had been read out, everyone resumed their former rank and everything went back to normal; the masters ill-treated the servants, and the servants beat the animals, those lethargic victors returning to their cowsheds with green wreaths around their horns.[99]

With the speeches over, the fantasy conjured up by the rhetoric collapses as violence and discord and social inequality reassert themselves. Masters abuse servants, servants beat animals. Particularly telling is the reference to the 'green wreath', for the laurel wreath was an important feature of

---

98 See Flaubert, *Corr.* II, 382–83 (Victor Hugo, 15.7.1853) and II, 386 (Louise Colet, 15.7.1853).

99 'La séance était finie; la foule se dispersa; et, maintenant que les discours étaient lus, chacun reprenait son rang et tout rentrait dans la coutume; les maîtres rudoyaient les domestiques, et ceux-ci frappaient les animaux, triomphateurs indolents qui s'en retournaient à l'étable, une couronne verte entre les cornes.' Flaubert, *Madame Bovary*, *OC* I, 625.

the iconography of power surrounding Napoleon III, and French uses the same word for 'wreath' as for 'crown'. In an early plan of the novel the derogatory association was more direct: there, the animals are described as 'unconcerned monarchs eating their leafy crowns.'[100] Thus what emerges victorious from Flaubert's *exposition* is very different from those values the universal exhibitions sought to project. Instead of the harmony, progress, art and industry of a dominant civilisation, the *comices agricoles* convey the exact opposite. In their place, we see the triumph of indolence, greed, and bovine stupidity – and those, for Flaubert, were dominant characteristics of Second Empire France.

---

100 '[M]onarques insoucieux qui mangeaient leur couronne de feuillage.' *Madame Bovary, Plans et scénarios*, ed. Yvan Leclerc (Paris: Zulma, 1995), 45. The same folio (fol. 26r) contains an even more subversive reference to a 'crowned pig' ['cochon couronné'].

Chapter Three
TRANSPORT

Many of the farthest-reaching changes that took place during the Second Empire derived, directly or indirectly, from France's new railway network, and indeed the universal exhibitions could not have taken place on such a scale if it had not been for steam transport. The first French passenger line had opened under the July Monarchy, but the real expansion occurred between 1852 and 1870 in a great surge of growth that added 15,000 kilometres to the system. A line from Paris to the German border was completed in 1853 and another linked the capital with the Mediterranean during the Crimean War; by 1860 the network had reached Italy and Spain; and by the end of the Second Empire the modern pattern of the French railway was already in place. Its impact was immense. Production of iron and steel soared, and speculators made and lost fortunes as the railways transformed trade and commerce. City centres were rebuilt to accommodate stations and equipment yards, and the French landscape changed dramatically as new lines and tunnels and cuttings sliced through it.

But the railway's effects were not merely physical or financial, for the expansion of the rail network brought with it a broadening of social and mental horizons. Goods and passengers could now move from one end of the country to the other with unprecedented ease as the railways brought people and produce from different parts of the country – or indeed from different countries – together as never before. The middle classes began travelling regularly for pleasure, particularly to the seaside, and these and more extensive journeys abroad to fashionable destinations, such as the 'mer de glace' in the Swiss Alps, opened up new horizons and stimulated new appetites. As Dr Emile Decaisne, the author of an 1864 medical guidebook for travellers, declared: 'Locomotion may be classed as one of the most intense and persistent passions of the 19th century [...] it is as if humanity can no longer bear to stay in one place: travel is a necessity.'[1]

---

1 'La locomotion peut être classée parmi les passions les plus intenses et les plus vivaces du XIXe siècle [...] on dirait que l'humanité ne peut plus rester en place: voyager est une nécessité.' Emile Decaisne, *Guide médical et hygiénique du voyageur* (Paris: Albessard, 1864), iii, vii,. See also Flaubert's ironic 'Chemin de fer' entry in his *Dictionnaire des idées*

Steam travel changed people's lives in subtler ways too, as it entered the public imagination and helped to shape popular consciousness. Offering a wealth of images of modernity and a rich and endlessly manipulable cultural metaphor, the strong imaginative appeal of the railway supplied writers with a fresh source of inspiration. It also fostered speculation about the future, for if horse-drawn vehicles were being superseded by steam transport, was it not possible that in its turn, it too would be eclipsed by some new method? Jules Verne imagined a futuristic rocket-train that would one day speed from the Earth to the moon with none of the bumps or jolts or fear of derailments that marred rail travel.[2] The distant prospect of air or submarine or space travel intrigued many and added yet another layer to the rich seam of metaphor that the new transport offered. The railway was not only a new phenomenon but a new subject, waiting to be transformed by the writer's imagination, while writing, in turn, would be transformed by the arrival of the railway.

Many writers at this period seized on the idea of rail travel as a means of articulating their thoughts about a changing France, and confidently pronounced that the railway heralded the greatest political, economic and social revolution the world had ever known.[3] Benjamin Gastineau argued that it would break all the old moulds, allow the free exchange of enlightened ideas, and bring about a new social order.[4] More flamboyantly, Maxime Du Camp proclaimed that the sparks that flew from the steam engine would illuminate the hereafter.[5] The very words 'chemin de fer' ['railway'] conveyed optimism and a belief in progress, as the rhapsodic 'Railway' entry in the *Grand dictionnaire universel* shows: '*Chemin de fer*! What magical words, and bathed in such an aura when we see them as synonymous with civilisation, progress and fraternity!'[6]

---

    reçues which shows the extent to which railway travel became a middle-class obsession: 'Be rhapsodic about the invention and say "I, Sir, who am sitting here talking to you, was at X this morning, I went there by the X train, I did what I needed to do there, and I was back home by X o'clock!' ['S'extasier sur l'invention et dire: "Moi, monsieur, qui vous parle, j'étais ce matin à X; je suis parti par le train de X; là-bas, j'ai fait mes affaires, etc., et à X heures, j'étais revenu!"] Flaubert, *OC* II, 305.

2 Jules Verne, *De la terre à la lune* [1865] (Paris: Librairie générale française, 2001), 163.

3 Adolphe Joanne, the author and director of the 'Guides Joanne' (a hugely successful series of railway guidebooks), cit. in *Grand dictionnaire universel*, 'Chemins de fer' entry.

4 Benjamin Gastineau, *Les Romans du voyage. La Vie en chemin de fer* (Paris: Dentu, 1861), 110–11.

5 'From me there will shoot forth the spark / That will illuminate the hereafter.' ['De moi jaillira l'étincelle / Qui doit éclairer l'avenir.'] Maxime Du Camp, 'La Locomotive', *Les Chants modernes*, nouvelle ed. (Paris: A. Bourdilliat et Cie, 1860), 203.

6 '*Chemins de fer*! Quels mots magiques, et de quelle auréole ils sont environnés quand ils nous apparaissent comme synonymes de civilisation, de progrès et de fraternité!' *Grand dictionnaire universel*, 'Chemins de fer' entry, 1148.

In that entry and elsewhere, the physical, geographical link created by the railway line was seen as representing a moral and spiritual link that would bring nations together in fraternal harmony: viewed from this perspective, the railway would act as a force for peace by obliging hostile countries to abandon their old quarrels in the interests of economic prosperity. For Gastineau, the railways had not only created a new moral order but had transformed the very nature of mankind:

> Mark my words, a new moral universe dates from the inception of the railways; man's nature has changed; he has become the Proteus of the universe, betrothed to movement – a liberated, winged, radiant being! Steam will create a new humanity and trace a new map of the globe by crossing human races and mingling the interests and blood of all peoples. – Hail, beautiful races of the future, fathered by the railway![7]

Such effusive reactions lent themselves to poetic expression. One anonymous poet (who signs himself simply as 'un chauffeur' ['an engine-driver']), produced a collection of railway poems which also hail the railway as the harbinger of a new moral order. His 'Chant du chauffeur' compares the locomotive to a soaring eagle (which of course was the imperial emblem of Napoleon III), and exhorts it to spread harmony, freedom and enlightenment beyond the boundaries of France:

> Fly off, untamed eagle,
> Crossing borders to bear
> Light and liberty
> To nations who have become brothers.[8]

And in a poem entitled 'La Locomotive', Maxime Du Camp attributes a clear-cut set of values to the railway engine, so that it becomes emblematic of his vision of how the people of France ought to be: strong, yet obedient; respectful and God-fearing; industrious and productive; working together for a fraternal

---

7 'Qu'on le sache bien, un nouveau monde moral date de la création des chemins de fer; l'homme a changé de nature; il est devenu le protée de l'univers, le fiancé du mouvement, l'être émancipé, ailé et rayonnant! La vapeur créera une nouvelle humanité, fera une nouvelle carte du globe, en croisant les races humaines, confondant les intérêts et le sang de tous les peuples. – Salut à vous, belles races de l'avenir enfantées par le chemin de fer!' Gastineau, *Les Romans du voyage*, 112.

8 'Va-t-en, franchissant les frontières / Porter, aigle au vol indompté, / Chez les peuples devenus frères / La lumière et la liberté!' 'Le Chant du Chauffeur', *Poésie des chemins de fer, par un chauffeur* (Paris & Lyon, 1855), 78.

future where poverty and misery will be unknown. In this incarnation, the steam-engine has been transformed into a powerful spiritual force that brings mankind into closer contact with God:

> Every work is a prayer to Thee, O Lord!
> The tool is a fine breviary;
> It is the best means of drawing closer to Thee;
> And steam is incense
> Dear to Thy heart.[9]

Transformed by language, the railway engine of these relentlessly positive texts is always more than a mere piece of industrial machinery. It is repeatedly described as bathed in a magical aura and possessing mysterious, supernatural qualities. Writers compare it to a dragon flying at great speed and breathing flame from its nostrils,[10] or to the magic talisman of oriental fairytales which carries out the magician's wishes by transporting him halfway round the world in a twinkling. To write about trains in these terms was not merely an expression of confidence and optimism about the future, but also a means of incorporating the railway into a familiar and delightful world of pre-existing myths. It was a way of glossing over the railway's disruptive capacity and threatening newness, for what could possibly be disruptive about something that brought man closer to God, and had the magical attributes of familiar fairytales? And if the railway was described as being as essential as a beating heart that brought lifeblood to the limbs (as it frequently was), what could be threatening about an invention that was reassuringly presented as such an integral part of nature? Several writers use a conceit that weaves the railway into a timeless bucolic landscape as a means of eliding the disturbance it brought. In the preface to his collection of railway poems, for example, the engine-driver poet shamelessly describes railway tracks as 'an invisible line across the vast fields of creation' and argues that an engine belching smoke would be quite at home in one of Virgil's landscapes, where shepherds would find the shriek of the train's whistle no more disturbing than the cawing of crows.[11] Gastineau, too, implicitly roots the railway in the mythical past by evoking the fantastical view from a train speeding through a landscape peopled

---

9 'Toute œuvre te prie, ô Seigneur! / L'outil est un bon bréviaire; / C'est le meilleur auxiliaire / Pour t'approcher; et la vapeur / Est l'encens qui plaît à ton cœur!' Du Camp, 'La Locomotive', *Les Chants modernes*, 202; cf. also 'La Vapeur', 172–176.
10 *Poésie des chemins de fer*, 78.
11 '[L]igne imperceptible à travers les vastes champs de la création.' *Poésie des chemins de fer*, 2.

by Titans, sphinxes and Egyptian gods.[12] With its origins thus reassuringly embedded in nature and in myth, the railway is incorporated by writers such as these into a timeless world of peace and harmony. For them it embodies the dawn of a new age of enlightenment.

Yet Second Empire texts proposing such optimistic visions of rail travel were very much in the minority. Far from projecting an aura of civilisation, progress and fraternity, for many commentators the railway symbolised fundamental and disturbing ways in which their world was changing. Texts praising a swift new French transport system as a metaphor for a nation steaming confidently towards a better future were vastly outnumbered by works that appropriated the railway for altogether different purposes. To the modern reader, the many references to steam-travel in novels, plays and poems of this period may seem innocent enough – simply a 'realistic' reflection of a modern phenomenon. They begin to yield up less innocent messages, however, when read in the context of a little-explored but prolific sub-genre of the period, the railway manual.

The publication of large numbers of books of advice for rail travellers was one of the more intriguing literary consequences of the Second Empire obsession with *la locomotion*. They have titles such as *Indispensable guide-manuel du voyageur en chemin de fer*; *Le Voyageur, les chemins de fer et l'hôtel*; *Les Dames en voyage*; or, *Les Chemins de fer au point de vue sanitaire*. At first sight these little manuals seem perfectly straightforward – a useful source of practical tips and information for inexperienced passengers. They explain how to negotiate the complex and unfamiliar formalities of rail travel, and offer medical or legal advice to passengers in case things go wrong. But if we read more closely, we soon notice strange contradictions that alert us to the presence of an insistent subtext. Exploiting the railway's metaphorical resonance, these manuals offer an indirect commentary on a nation which, like the inexperienced traveller, is embarking on a journey into the unknown.

Perhaps their most striking feature is the level of anxiety that surrounds the advice they offer. Whereas Benjamin Gastineau describes the railway station as a microcosm of society where people of different ages and backgrounds mingle happily before setting out on their journey to admire 'all the brilliant facets of the gem of creation',[13] most of these manuals paint a different picture. Book after book warns of the dangers lying in wait for unsuspecting travellers,

---

12 Gastineau, *Les Romans du voyage*, 53–54.
13 '[T]outes les brillantes facettes du joyeau de la création'. Gastineau, *Les Romans du voyage*, 18, 20–22.

who are advised to ensure they are well rested and in excellent health before daring to embark on any journey by train.[14] The first hazard is the railway station itself. Variously described as a labyrinth, a maze, a prison, a swirling maelstrom, a hell where the traveller suffers the torments of the damned, the station in these texts is a deeply threatening place which subverts all the supposed benefits of train travel. Instead of promising swift transportation to a chosen destination, railway stations are described in terms that suggest the very opposite of forward movement: the station is a place of confusion in whose swirling vortex the traveller is trapped. Rushing to buy tickets, register luggage, complete all the necessary formalities and find the right train, passengers are caught in a terrifying chaos from which, they are warned, they are unlikely to emerge unscathed.[15]

More mundane difficulties at the railway station underscore the idea that the individual is at the mercy of an incomprehensible and possibly incompetent authority. (The entire French railway system was under government control, although the rail companies were privately owned.) Writers talk of insolent station employees, of the risk of missing the train, of getting on one going in the wrong direction, or of relying on an inaccurate timetable which includes 'connections that do not connect.'[16] The passenger in these manuals seems lost in a nightmarish and constantly shifting world where nothing is certain and where obstacles appear at every turn. The authors offer advice on every problem passengers might encounter even before setting foot on the train: what to do if the ticket office fails to open in time, or if the clerk issues them with the wrong ticket, or if they lose their ticket before boarding, or buy two tickets by mistake. What if they lose their luggage registration ticket, or indeed the luggage itself?[17] What if they miss the train because station employees have failed to announce its departure? These warnings no doubt had an immediate practical point, but they also shade into larger questions of political authority, social order, personal advancement, social divisions and class structure. Readers are left in no doubt about the struggle they face if they are not to be left behind when the train of life sets off, for only the elite will have an easy ride. So to the alert reader of these guidebooks, the Second Empire station is

---

14 Decaisne, *Guide médical*, 18.
15 Eugene Delattre, *Tribulations des voyageurs et des expéditeurs en chemin de fer. Conseils pratiques* 2nd ed. (Paris: Taride, 1858), 11 and 17; and Decaisne, *Guide médical*, 20–21.
16 '[D]es correpondances qui ne correspondent pas.' Théophile Astrié (Avocat), *Indispensable guide-manuel du voyageur en chemin de fer, indiquant les dispositions légales et réglementaires, les moyens et les formes propres à faire valoir les droits et aboutir les réclamations du voyageur* (Paris: Le Bailly, 1869), 17ff.; and Delattre, *Tribulations des voyageurs*, Chapter XII.
17 Delattre, *Tribulations des voyageurs*, 22ff., 43–46. See also p. 169.

far from the utopian gateway envisioned by Gastineau; instead it becomes a place from which to contemplate the dangers and inequities of an uncertain future over which they may have little control. Gustave Claudin, writing in 1862, describes Paris, at the hub of the railway system, as a 'universal station' where one witnesses the strange spectacle of a new civilisation imposing itself brutally on the old way of life.[18]

The segregation of trains into three separate 'classes' gave physical form to existing class divisions, and writers of these guidebooks exploit the question of where the passenger should sit with an insistence that again betrays the workings of a social metaphor. Readers are repeatedly warned of the difficulties of finding a seat and are urged to position themselves in a proper social context, for, as Eugène Delattre noted pointedly, first class passengers travel in comfort, 'forgetful of dangers and cares, and of all the social wretchedness huddled in third class'.[19] Passengers are advised not only to keep away from overripe cheeses and baskets of fish, but also to avoid socially undesirable companions – very fat people (who will sweat and refuse to open a window), smokers, drunkards, workmen in filthy clothes, or women carrying lap-dogs or parrots or both.[20] There is much discussion of where to find the safest or most comfortable seats,[21] and of the unscrupulous or violent means by which some people try to claim these; readers are warned that the best places will be won only by force.[22] Advice about the process of choosing a seat is thus suffused with concerns about maintaining or improving one's social status, and recent memories of violent social disruption lie beneath the superficially innocent recommendations.

The underlying threat of violence runs through many of these texts. One writer makes the chilling claim that when one opens the carriage door, instead of seeing someone sitting there one often finds only a corpse.[23] Women are warned to be wary of fellow passengers in case they turn out to be rapists

---

18 Gustave Claudin, *Paris* (Paris: Dentu, 1862), ii.
19 '[O]ublieux des dangers, des soucis, et de toutes les misères sociales qui grelottent en troisièmes'. Delattre, *Tribulations des voyageurs*, 107. Cf. Honoré Daumier's series of drawings of 'The Third Class Carriage', which date from the 1860s.
20 Delattre, *Tribulations des voyageurs*, 114; and Eugène Chapus, *Voyageur, prenez garde à vous!* (Paris: Decaux et Dreyfous, 1855), 27–29. See also Astrié, *Indispensable guide-manuel*, 21, 24. *Poésie des chemins de fer, par un Chauffeur*, 20, refers to a passenger carrying a parrot, a dog and a lobster.
21 Astrié, *Indispensable guide-manuel*, 24, advises passengers to choose the middle of the train (safer in case of accident) and to face away from the engine (fewer draughts). Delattre, *Tribulations des voyageurs*, 41, advises corner seats.
22 Delattre, *Tribulations des voyageurs*, 41.
23 Larousse, *Grand dictionnaire universel du XIXe siècle*, 1158.

who use chloroform to overpower their victims, and men are advised to arm themselves with a swordstick or a good revolver in case they find themselves travelling with bandits, madmen or murderers.[24] Empty trains, however, have their own dangers. In a book bracingly entitled *Voyageur, prenez garde à vous!* (1855) [*Traveller, Beware!*], Eugène Chapus warns travellers never to enter a compartment with only one other passenger for fear of being attacked or robbed if they fall asleep. The railway carriage thus becomes emblematic of a world where the threat of violence and sexual and social disruption is always present.

Set against this were frequent expressions of regret for the more leisurely world of coach-travel, and for the less brutal and less stressful way of life it was felt to represent.[25] As one anonymous writer put it: 'Nowadays we no longer travel, we arrive',[26] whereas the enclosed privacy of the unhurried stagecoach had long enjoyed a reputation for encouraging amorous intrigues. Chapus notes that 'feelings moved fast in carriages: it was a *well-known* fact in the days of the stage-coach',[27] and Emma and Léon's famous carriage ride in *Madame Bovary* should be read not as a daringly adventurous seduction but as a deliberately ironic cliché. But the agreeable flirtations that went on in horse-drawn vehicles were seen as having given way, under the Second Empire, to the sexual brutality of the railway: 'Formerly, people made amorous conquests; nowadays they commit rape.'[28] The now vanishing *diligence* was frequently remembered as a relaxed and sociable way to travel, which allowed passengers to form new friendships and indulge in laughter and song, while its leisurely pace gave them time to sketch the slowly passing scenery.[29] To mourn its disappearance and lament its replacement by the railway was much more than mere nostalgia for a vanishing mode of transport – it was an expression of distaste for contemporary society, a way of marking the writer's sense of alienation from the world of the Second Empire. The leisurely pace of the horse-drawn coach was seen as emblematic of a relaxed and congenial way of

---

24 Chapus, *Voyageur, prenez garde à vous!*, 51–55. See also Decaisne, *Guide médical*, 26
25 'Be nostalgic for the days of the stagecoach' ['Regretter le temps des diligences'] is one of the platitudes listed in Flaubert's *Dictionnaire des idées recues. OC* II, 307.
26 'On ne voyage plus, aujourd'hui, l'on arrive.' Quoted in Larousse, *Grand dictionnaire universel*, 'Chemins de fer' entry, 1162.
27 '[L]e sentiment allait vite en voiture: c'était une vérité *courante* à l'époque des diligences.' Chapus, *Voyageur, prenez garde à vous!*, 52.
28 'Autrefois on faisait des conquêtes; aujourd'hui on perpètre des viols.' Larousse, *Grand dictionnaire universel*, 'Chemins de fer' entry, 1162.
29 See for example Decaisne, *Guide médical*, 14–15, 39; *Poésie des chemins de fer*, 3.

life which seemed to have gone for good, leaving in its place a society that was sad, cold and fragmented. As Emile Decaisne put it:

> The railways have revolutionised not only mechanics, industry and movement, but also morals and manners; one may even assume that they have a powerful influence on the temperament of the generation that has grown up with them [...] Gaiety is dying, gaiety is dead; people used to sing in coaches, but no one even feels like humming in a railway carriage; joyful songs have been replaced by the engine's whistle.[30]

Here the steam train comes to represent all that is antagonistic to art and creativity. In the age of the railway there is no more music, no more drawing, and whereas travel by coach is remembered as 'poetic', travel by rail is seen as utterly 'prosaic'.[31]

In an extension of this perspective, the joyless atmosphere of the Second Empire station waiting room becomes a metaphor for the bleakness of modern life. As Delattre explains: 'Nowadays people are bored there. Nothing nice to look at. Bare walls, wooden struts and dismal faces. Our times are dark and cold.'[32] Readers of railway manuals are regularly warned against being infected by a mood of gloom when travelling by train: 'avoid sad people like the plague', advises Decaisne.[33] This bleak vision of travel was not confined to the railway, however, for in the early years of the Second Empire a similarly desolate view of social change was projected onto the Paris omnibus. Described as representing 'the democratisation of the vehicle' since it brought members of different ranks of society into close proximity, the

---

30 'Les chemins de fer ont révolutionné non-seulement la mécanique, l'industrie, la locomotion, mais encore les mœurs et les habitudes; il est même à présumer qu'ils exerceront une très grande influence sur le tempérament de la jeune génération qui est venue avec eux [...] La gaieté se meurt, la gaieté est morte; on chantait dans les diligences, mais on n'a pas même la velléité de fredonner dans les wagons; les sifflements de la locomotive ont remplacé les joyeux refrains.' Decaisne, *Guide médical*, 39.

31 E. g. 'Railway travel is as prosaic as can be. You cover the ground in a straight line, which [...] is fundamentally repugnant to the poetry of travel.' ['Le voyage en chemin de fer est on ne peut plus prosaïque. On franchit l'espace en ligne droite, ce qui [...] répugne essentiellement à la poésie du voyage.'] Larousse, *Grand dictionnaire universel*, 'Chemins de fer' entry, 1162.

32 'Aujourd'hui, on s'y ennuie. Rien qui flatte la vue. Des murailles nues, des barres de bois et des visages mornes. Notre siècle est sombre et froid.' Delattre, *Tribulations des voyageurs*, 79.

33 '[F]uyez comme pestiférées les personnes qui sont tristes.' Decaisne, *Guide médical*, 60–62, and 7.

omnibus revealed the growing economic, social and psychological distances that separated them. Nothing was more conducive to melancholy than taking frequent omnibus rides, wrote the authors of *Paris-en-omnibus*,[34] for the passengers, like those on trains, were morose, silent and inward-looking, and deliberately shut themselves off from their companions. 'The omnibus makes people unsociable and misanthropic... You sit down next to one another without saying anything; women lower their veils, men pull their hats down over their eyes.'[35] The 'democratic' omnibus, the crowded railway-carriage and the bleak waiting-room are thus all associated with a society that has lost its social cohesiveness and *joie de vivre*, and is being propelled into an uncertain and threatening future.

Moreover, that future is one over which the traveller has no control. As Théophile Astrié points out in the introduction to his *Indispensable guide-manual du voyageur en chemin de fer*:

> Every passenger may sometimes be made anxious or even be injured by the railway companies or their employees [...]. The railway companies are powerful; they have at their disposal the power of capital combined with intelligence. The traveller, on the other hand, is on his own, and his complaint is all the more timid because he does not know whether he has the right to express it, or whether it will have any effect.[36]

In other words, the passenger, like the common citizen, is at the mercy of the authorities and unable to make his protest heard.

As the social metaphor develops, so does the level of anxiety that these texts express. Readers are warned that even with a good seat and honest and hygienic neighbours, they can never feel safe. Rail travel has other potential hazards in store, including (in alphabetical order) apoplexy, blindness, deafness, depression, epilepsy, haemorrhage, miscarriage, palpitations, paralysis of the lower limbs, pathological nervous excitement,

---

34 Edmond Texier, *Le Tableau de Paris*, 1853, cit. in Richard D. E. Burton, *The Flâneur and his City: Patterns of Daily Life in Paris, 1815–1851* (Durham: University of Durham, 1994), 42; Anon., *Les Petits Paris: Paris en omnibus* (Paris: Alphonse Taride, 1854), 11.

35 'L'omnibus rend farouche et misanthrope... On s'assoit à côté les uns des autres sans rien dire; les femmes abaissent leur voile, les hommes ramènent leur chapeau sur leurs yeux.' *Paris-en-omnibus*, 54–55.

36 'Tout voyageur peut quelquefois être inquiété, lésé même par les Compagnies de chemins de fer ou leurs employés [...] Les Compagnies de chemins de fer sont puissantes; elles disposent des forces du capital unies à celles de l'intelligence. Le voyageur, au contraire, est isolé et sa plainte est d'autant plus timide qu'il ne sait pas s'il est en droit de la formuler, ou si elle aboutira.' Astrié, *Indispensable guide-manuel*, v.

pneumonia, rheumatism, stiff neck and toothache.[37] Every aspect of rail travel comes to be a source of anxiety. Travellers who try to distract themselves by reading risk missing their station,[38] damaging their eyesight, or going blind.[39] Those unwise enough to eat on a train are likely to suffer disastrous after-effects, but those who alight to eat at a station are liable to food poisoning.[40] Passengers who leave the train to use the station lavatory risk getting back on the wrong train or being left behind, but if they stay on the train they risk contracting 'incurable and even fatal illnesses caused by retaining the urine for too long'.[41]

But even these worries pale before the threat posed by accidents. The ultimate fear articulated in these manuals is that, far from speeding onward bearing light and liberty, as Gastineau and Du Camp had argued, the rail journey of the Second Empire would end in catastrophe. Not only are hapless readers warned they risk being run over if they stray on to the line,[42] or being dragged to their death if their clothing gets caught in the train's wheels, but they are reminded that throughout their journey they will be at the mercy of landslides, bursting dams, broken bridges, floods, lightning strikes and earthquakes.[43]

The manuals' most pointed warnings, however, are directed not at Acts of God, but at hazards created by an uncaring or incompetent authority whose inability to safeguard its customers' welfare echoes, it is implied, that of an uncaring or incompetent political regime. Official accident statistics are quoted with relish,[44] and disastrous potential scenarios are described to readers in graphic detail. Delattre includes a lengthy section on accidents in his appropriately titled *Tribulations des voyageurs et des expediteurs en chemin de fer: Conseils pratiques* [*Tribulations of Railway Passengers and Dispatchers: Practical Advice*].

---

37 Decaisne, *Guide médical*, 87ff. and 45–46. See also E. L. Bertherand, *Les Chemins de fer au point de vue sanitaire* (Paris: Arbois, 1862), 21 and 23.
38 Delattre, *Tribulations des voyageurs*, 155.
39 Delattre, *Tribulations des voyageurs*, 85–86.
40 Delattre, *Tribulations des voyageurs*, 85–86.
41 '[D]es maladies incurables, et même mortelles, occasionnées pour avoir retenu trop longtemps son urine.' Decaisne, *Guide médical*, 28; see also 93.
42 Dr Bertherand recommended that locomotives be fitted with a kind of metal cowcatcher that would scoop up anyone who walked or fell in front of the train. Bertherand, *Les Chemins de fer au point de vue sanitaire*, 24–35.
43 M. ***, Avocat, *Le Voyageur, les chemins de fer et l'hotel: Les Dames en voyage* (Paris: Dezobry, S. Magdeleine & Cie, 1860), 79; Astrié, *Indispensable guide-manuel*, 35–36.
44 E. g. Delattre says there were 513 railway accidents between 1835 and 1855, causing 2,374 fatalities, but points out that rail travel in France carried much the same risk as travelling by coach. He compares French transport with the very much safer German railways (*Tribulations des voyageurs*, 140).

Somewhat surprisingly, this section was added at the suggestion of Flaubert.[45] As Flaubert had foreseen, Delattre was able to milk the idea of accidents to the full and weave into it a satirical web of class commentary. Was it safer to travel first class, since carriages nearer the engine were more likely to be derailed or destroyed by fire or explosion? Would the soft upholstery in first class not protect passengers, giving them more time to escape while those in second and third class met their fate? Or were first-class carriages more likely to be crushed because they had fewer internal partitions to support the roof? And when carriages were crushed together in an accident, might it not be better to be in third class where the hard wooden benches would cut off passengers' legs cleanly at the knee 'in a neat manner that avoids the bother of amputation', whereas first class upholstery would crush legs horribly, making amputation more difficult? The conclusion is that 'accidents are so various that it is impossible to choose a seat that is safe from them'.[46] In an amusing if ghoulish way, Delattre is making a serious point: railway accidents were indeed a real hazard over which passengers had no control. But behind his mockery of callous bourgeois indifference to social inferiors and warnings of the threat of accidental death lay a thinly veiled attack on France's apparent willingness to sacrifice human life in other contexts. As he says, 'In France[...]it takes piles of corpses and pools of blood to calm our excitement and remind us that the first duty of any society is to preserve human life.'[47] A contemporary reader would immediately recognise that such a comment applied equally well to the blood shed in France's ongoing military exploits as to railway fatalities. As other writers pointed out, the railways had changed the conditions of war, with devastating consequences: 'wholesale slaughter takes place over greater stretches of battle-lines; thus the clearest effect of applying the railway to warfare has been increased carnage.'[48]

---

45 See Anne Green, 'La contribution inattendue de Flaubert à un manuel de chemin de fer', *Bulletin des Amis de Flaubert et de Maupassant,* no. 8 (2000), 13–21.

46 '[D]'une façon nette qui évite la peine d'une amputation'; 'les accidents sont si variés qu'il est impossible de choisir une place qui en soit à l'abri'. Delattre, *Tribulations des voyageurs,* 146–151.

47 'En France [...] il nous faut des monceaux de cadavres et des mares de sang pour calmer notre effervescence et pour nous rappeler que le premier devoir d'une société est de se montrer avare de la vie humaine.' Delattre, *Tribulations des voyageurs,* 14.

48 '[L]'hécatombe se consomme sur de plus grandes étendues de lignes de bataille; ainsi le résultat le plus clair de l'application des chemins de fer à la guerre, c'est l'accroissement du carnage.' Larousse, *Grand dictionnaire universel,* 'Chemins de fer' entry, 1148. See also Bertherand, *Les Chemins de fer au point de vue sanitaire,* 28. Astrié, *Indispensable guide-manuel,* 23–24, warns passengers to beware of large, obstructive packages on trains, particularly when they contain 'loaded or unsheathed weapons' ['des armes chargées ou démunies de fourreau'].

So although these manuals purport to serve the straightforward practical purpose of explaining how to use the railway system, and claim to reassure the inexperienced traveller, they nevertheless amass an alarming catalogue of the dangers of travel and implicitly evoke parallels with the social order. While stating that travel is necessary, pleasurable and beneficial to health, they vividly portray its potentially damaging or, indeed, fatal consequences. Their claims to offer guidance and reassurance sit uneasily with the profuse accounts of what may go wrong, and the reader is left with the strongest possible sense of danger and confusion.

One might argue that the manuals were merely drawing attention to genuine risks – it was certainly the case that the new forms of transport could be confusing, stressful, and sometimes highly dangerous. (Flaubert himself was nearly run over by a locomotive in 1859. 'It would have been a loss to literature, I know', he wrote to a friend.)[49] But in fact trains were no more dangerous than travel by stagecoach had been. In 1860 alone, carriage traffic in Paris caused nearly as many deaths as had occurred on the entire French railway system in the previous ten years.[50] Nevertheless, the new technology became an apt metaphor through which to project generalised unspoken fears. The authors of these books were conscious that changing modes of transport heralded wide-ranging social changes that could not be checked. In Decaisne's words: 'A revolution has taken place in our manners and customs, and nothing can stop it.'[51]

Couched in the veiled terms characteristic of much Second Empire writing, politically charged points emerge from these seemingly innocent guidebooks. The railways are pictured as highroads of civilisation leading to an imposing but terrifying future, or as rivers of iron, bearing an anxious humanity away to unknown shores.[52] The vulnerable individual is at the mercy of the authorities – political as well as industrial – who cannot necessarily be trusted to give direction and avert disaster.[53] As Flaubert immediately noticed when he read Delattre's *Tribulations*, this was not simply a book about trains. Thanking Delattre for sending him a copy (which he read twice), Flaubert wrote: 'throughout, one can sense the protest of the individual against the

---

49 'C'eût été une perte pour la littérature, je le sais.' Flaubert, *Corr.* III, 40 (to Ernest Feydeau, 21.9.1859).
50 Delattre, *Tribulations des voyageurs*, p. 139; Bertherand, *Les Chemins de fer au point de vue sanitaire*, 25.
51 'Il s'est […] opéré dans nos mœurs et dans nos habitudes une révolution que rien ne saurait arrêter dans son développement.' Decaisne, *Guide médical*, vii.
52 Delattre, *Tribulations des voyageurs*, 3, 82.
53 Astrié, *Indispensable guide-manuel*, pp. v–vi.

monopoly, against power [...]. [T]his book puts forward a host of ideas. In a few years' time it will be very interesting to consult it as history. People will conclude that we were still living in a state of total barbarism.'[54] The proliferation of these manuals during the Second Empire, and their constant reiteration of the same anxious preoccupations, must be read as evidence of a widespread unease about a changing world, for no alert reader could fail to see an analogy between the repeatedly evoked perils lying in wait for the train as it hurtles along the line, and uncertainties about what the future might hold for France.

It is against such a background of anxiety and suspicion that we should read the literature of the Second Empire. As modern readers, conscious of the nineteenth-century realist writer's desire to *faire vrai* and describe the world in all its physical detail, it is all too easy for us to miss the freight of metaphorical meaning that literary references to steam transport may carry. Read in the light of the non-fictional texts, however, they turn out to have unexpected resonance.

Perhaps surprisingly, it was only after the fall of the Second Empire that the sinister subtext hinted at by the railway manuals was exploited to full dramatic effect. The famous final scene of Émile Zola's *La Bête humaine* (1890) depicts the ultimate horror – a driverless, runaway locomotive hurtling towards inevitable catastrophe, in an apocalyptic vision of what lay ahead for France. 'What did they matter, those victims the machine crushed in its path! Was it not going on into the future anyway, regardless of bloodshed? Driverless in the darkness, like a deaf and blind beast unleashed in the midst of death, it raced on, and on...'[55] Zola's description clearly draws on a popular imagery that had already become commonplace under the Second Empire. During the Second Empire itself, however, the railway's literary symbolism was generally more subtle. Flaubert had no more confidence than Zola in the benefits of the machine age or in the governing powers, but he makes the point more obliquely in *L'Éducation sentimentale* with Pellerin's painting of a locomotive purporting to represent the Republic, or Progress, or Civilisation being driven through virgin forest in the

---

54 '[O]n y sent partout la protestation de l'individu contre le monopole, contre le pouvoir [...] [C]e livre suggère une foule d'idées. Il sera dans quelques années bien curieux à consulter comme histoire. La conclusion en sera que nous étions encore en pleine barbarie.' Flaubert, *Corr.* III, 3 (to E. Delattre, 10.1.1859).
55 'Qu'importaient les victimes que la machine écrasait en chemin! N'allait-elle pas quand même à l'avenir, insoucieuse du sang répandu? Sans conducteur, au milieu des ténèbres, en bête aveugle et sourde qu'on aurait lachée parmi la mort, elle roulait, elle roulait...' Émile Zola, *La Bête humaine* (Paris: Fasquelle, 1979), 435.

safe hands of Jesus Christ.⁵⁶ The absurdity of this image (which has echoes of Du Camp's poem 'La Locomotive'), undermines any such misplaced trust.

In some literary works the anxieties of the travel manuals reappear, virtually untransformed, simply as an atmospheric backdrop to the action. For example *Les Chemins de fer*, a play by Eugène Labiche that had great success when first performed in 1867, manages to incorporate virtually all the worries raised in the guidebooks. In this play passengers encounter traffic jams on their way to the station, and must contend with a rush for the train, confusion over seats, lost tickets, lost luggage, and anxieties about catching cold from draughts and being trapped on a train with an upset stomach. It features passengers with hacking coughs and smelly babies and foul tobacco, and an incompetent railway employee who not only smears passengers' clothes with axle grease but also causes mayhem when he mistakenly uncouples two full coaches in mid journey. The play introduces worries about eating at a station buffet and missing the train, and conjures up images of incompetent authority by alluding both to wrongly-switched points that send a train to Dijon instead of Angoulême, and to a derailment. This onslaught of detail creates a powerful background of tension and disorder against which the main action is set, but in fact the main action is so inconsequential that the essence of the drama is the mood of anxious confusion itself, playing as it does on more general fears of 'going off the rails' or of ending up, through no fault of one's own, at the wrong destination in life.

This was not, of course, the first time that Labiche had exploited the railway's physical and metaphorical possibilities in one of his plays. He set the first act of *Le Voyage de M. Perrichon* (1860) in a bustling railway station, where Perrichon becomes increasingly flustered as he tries to organise tickets and porters and luggage for his first ever train journey. This famous opening is more than just a visually striking comic device to show up the central character's personal flaws, however. The stress and anxiety Perrichon feels when embarking on this journey to a foreign country by an unfamiliar form of transport serves to dramatise wider issues about adapting to change. Significantly, Perrichon has made his money from an obsolescent form of transportation – he is a former coachbuilder – while his daughter's suitors both owe their wealth, directly or indirectly, to steam transport,⁵⁷ and his preposterous farewell to 'France! the queen of nations!'⁵⁸ as he sets off on his train journey may be seen as a poignant farewell to a world that is changing beyond recognition.

---

56 Flaubert, *L'Éducation sentimentale*, *OC* II, 117.
57 Daniel runs a company operating steamships on the Seine, and as an 'amateur banker' Armand would implicitly benefit from railway investments.
58 'Adieu, France! Reine des nations!' Eugène Labiche, *Le Voyage de Monsieur Perrichon*, *Œuvres complètes* (Paris: Calmann Lévy, 1898), II, 20.

Mérimée's short story, *La Chambre bleue*, also exploits the usual worries of railway travel – being late, missing the train, sharing the compartment with an eccentric fellow passenger, alighting from the train without revealing one's legs. In this case these familiar apprehensions are used to dramatise a young couple's nervousness about spending an illicit night together. But a passing reference to Charles Jud, the notorious railway murderer,[59] taps into much deeper anxieties which intensify the mood into one of horror. The terrified couple spend a sleepless night in their hotel room, convinced not only that the dark stain from an overturned wine bottle is blood seeping from a murdered corpse, but that they are certain to be convicted of the crime and executed. Although *La Chambre bleue* is an insubstantial little tale, its comic suspense and its depiction of displaced sexual guilt rely entirely on the reader recognising and identifying with the terrors of railway travel, which were fast becoming a portmanteau metaphor for aspects of social unease.

In Théophile Gautier's 'Les Néréides', the brutality and dangers of steam travel are again exploited, only half-playfully, in a poem that is part mythological conceit and part pointed commentary on a new and overbearing State. With its flag identifying it with France, a noisy paddle steamer threatens injury to anything in its path as it bears down on a group of carefree seanymphs frolicking in the waves, who flee in terror:

> On the horizon – a piquant blend
> Of fable and reality –
> There appears a vessel which disturbs
> The terrified marine choir.
> Its flag is the tricolour;
> Its funnel belches steam;
> Its paddles thrash the resounding water
> And the nymphs dive in fear.
> [...]
> But the steamboat with its wheels,
> Like Vulcan beating Venus,
> Would strike their lovely cheeks
> And wound their naked limbs.[60]

---

59 For details of Jud's crime, see the *Grand dictionnaire universel*, 'Chemins de fer' entry.

60 'A l'horizon, – piquant mélange / De fable et de réalité, – / Paraît un vaisseau qui dérange / Le chœur marin épouvanté. // Son pavillon est tricolore; / Son tuyau vomit la vapeur; / Ses aubes fouettent l'eau sonore, / Et les nymphes plongent de peur. // [...] Mais le steam-boat avec ses roues, / Comme Vulcain battant Vénus, / Souffletterait leurs belles joues / Et meurtrirait leurs membres nus.' Théophile Gautier, 'Les Néréides', *Émaux et camées*, 87–88.

In much of the literature of the Second Empire, however, the predominant message conveyed by transport scenes is less one of terror than one of bewilderment and frustration. Instead of serving as a metaphor for rapid progress, transport is more often used to suggest a society that is blocked and unable to move forward; travel by train, steamship or horse-drawn carriage brings anxiety and disappointment. The nightmarish world of confusion, circularity, imprisonment and loss of identity that characterised railway manuals' descriptions of railway stations resurfaces in the fictional abortive journey that leads nowhere, for the paradox of Second Empire literary transport is that vehicles designed for rapid movement all too often find themselves stationary. As a character in the Goncourt brothers' *Manette Salomon* complains, 'I find the omnibus deadly dull...a machine that pretends to move forward but keeps stopping': it is often quicker to walk than to travel by 'a piece of engineering'.[61] In an age of urgency with everyone in a hurry to move forward, only a select few are able to advance rapidly, and the disappointment and frustration of slow progress by transport is seized on by Second Empire writers as a metaphor for a failure to progress in life, or indeed as a means of expressing the injustices of social rank.[62]

Whether travelling by omnibus, train, steamship or horse-drawn carriage, characters repeatedly find themselves mired in frustrating delays and obstructions, unable to advance. The traffic jam subverts the proud rhetoric that presented modern transport as the embodiment of speed and efficiency. Instead, recurrent references to impeded travel become emblematic of authors' jaundiced view of progress. Some of the most telling examples are to be found in Flaubert's *L'Éducation sentimentale*, where characters are constantly travelling, propelled by what the coachman in *Madame Bovary* refers to as a 'mania for locomotion',[63] but their journeys are repeatedly interrupted and frustrated. When Frédéric tries to return to Paris from Fontainebleau, for example,

[T]he Leloir messenger-coach had just left, the Lecomte berlins would not be running, the Bourbonnais stagecoach would not come until late at night and might be full; no one knew. After wasting a great deal of

---

61 'Je trouve ça mortel, l'omnibus...cette mécanique qui fait semblant d'aller et qui s'arrête toujours!' Goncourt, *Manette Salomon*, 177.
62 Théophile Gautier commented that the only difference between those who travel on foot in Paris and those who travel by carriage is the running board – 'it is the hyphen between the man who has nothing and the man who has all.' *Etudes philosophiques: Paris et les Parisiens au XIXe siècle* (Paris, 1856), 26, cit. in Walter Benjamin, *The Arcades Project*, trans. Howard Eiland and Kevin McLaughlin (London: Belknap Press, 1999), 93.
63 '[F]ureur de la locomotion' *Madame Bovary*, *OC* I, 657.

time on this information, it occurred to him to take a post-chaise. The postmaster refused to provide horses as Frédéric had no passport. Finally, he hired a barouche.[64]

Even then, his troubles are not over, for the coachman refuses to take him further than the station, where he discovers that the railway lines have been cut by revolutionaries. After transferring to a shabby cabriolet which then abandons him, he has to finish his journey on foot, getting arrested on the way. This is only one of this novel's many examples of frustrated travel which are accompanied (as the guidebooks have led us to expect) by a sense of urgency, anxiety and foreboding.[65] The overwhelming impression given by Flaubert's depiction of transport in *L'Éducation sentimentale* is one of confusion and disorder, without any sense of arrival – an effect inherent in the linguistic structure of these passages. An accumulation of carriage-terminology clogs the narrative and prevents the plot from advancing, just as the traffic-jam stops the forward flow of vehicles. The crush of carriages leaving the Champ de Mars – milords, berlines, landaus, calèches, briskas, wurts, tandems, tilburys, dog-carts, tapissières, demi-fortunes, victorias, coupés, fiacres and chaises – grinds to a halt in traffic that is as congested as the sentence containing the list of vehicles itself.[66] Yet Frédéric's smooth and rapid displacement by the train taking him from Paris to Nogent is hardly more successful since he immediately catches the next train back to his starting point.[67] Transport, in *L'Éducation*, is thus a means of articulating the novel's central theme of circularity and confusion which permeates both personal relationships and the politics of the time.

Woven into those descriptions of the carriages' erratic progress is also a representation of social hierarchy. Just as the railway manuals had hinted that the difficulties of finding a train seat, choosing a class, and deciding which passengers to associate with and which to avoid, had their counterpart in the individual's need to find and establish his or her own place in society, so Flaubert's text vividly conveys social tensions while purporting to offer

---

64 'La voiture des messageries Leloir venait de partir, les berlines Lecomte ne partiraient pas, la diligence du Bourbonnais ne passerait que tard dans la nuit, et serait peut-être pleine; on n'en savait rien. Quand il eut perdu beaucoup de temps à ces informations, l'idée lui vint de prendre la poste. Le maître de poste refusa de fournir des chevaux, Frédéric n'ayant point de passe-port. Enfin, il loua une calèche.' Flaubert, *L'Éducation sentimentale*, *OC* II, 129.
65 Cf. another such journey when Frédéric travels in search of Madame Arnoux first in Paris, then Creil, then Montataire. Flaubert, *L'Éducation sentimentale*, *OC* II, 77–78.
66 Flaubert, *L'Éducation sentimentale*, *OC* II, 83.
67 Flaubert, *L'Éducation sentimentale*, *OC* II, 159.

an innocent description of the facial expressions of the different vehicles' occupants. Jostling for position yet brought to a standstill, they are forced into an unwilling proximity, and the account of the looks of envy or haughty indifference or scorn or mute admiration that pass between the different classes of carriage echo the class divisions of the day:

> They stopped close together and inspected one another. From the crested coachwork, indifferent gazes ranged over the mob; eyes full of envy glittered deep inside the cabs; disparaging smiles responded to a haughty bearing; gaping mouths expressed imbecilic admiration; and here and there, some casual pedestrian wandering in the middle of the road leapt back to avoid a horseman who galloped between the carriages and managed to get clear of them.[68]

Undercurrents of envy and resentment which will soon erupt in violence are vividly represented in these carriages, as social difference is sharpened. Different classes are forced together yet kept pointedly segregated by their vehicles, while only the rare individual shows the aggressive bravado needed to forge ahead.

In contrast, the Goncourt brothers' description of a 'democratic' omnibus flattens out social difference to the point of dehumanising the passengers. They are observed passively, 'mechanically', as anonymous, sexless, shadowy silhouettes, while the stop-start movement of the vehicle is echoed by the text's jerky phrasing and interrupted typography as it enacts a failure to progress:

> I had been mechanically following the shadows cast on the shutters of the closed shops by the people in the omnibus which is forever starting off again...a series of silhouettes... Not one interesting person...all looking like people who travel by omnibus...women...sexless women, women carrying packages...[69]

---

68 '[O]n restait les uns près des autres, et l'on s'examinait. Du bord des panneaux armoriés, des regards indifférents tombaient sur la foule; des yeux pleins d'envie brillaient au fond des fiacres; des sourires de dénigrement répondaient aux ports de tête orgueilleux; des bouches grandes ouvertes exprimaient des admirations imbéciles; et, çà et là, quelque flâneur, au milieu de la voie, se rejetait en arrière d'un bond, pour éviter un cavalier qui galopait entre les voitures et parvenait à en sortir.' Flaubert, *L'Éducation sentimentale*, *OC* II, 84.
69 'J'en étais arrivé à suivre mécaniquement, sur les volets des boutiques fermées, l'ombre des gens de l'omnibus qui recommence éternellement...une série de silhouettes... Pas un bonhomme curieux...tous, des têtes de gens qui vont en omnibus...des femmes... des femmes sans sexe, des femmes à paquet...' Goncourt, *Manette Salomon*, 177–78.

This is a far cry from the conviviality of stagecoach scenes from earlier in the century. Instead, the crowded Second Empire omnibus here articulates that bleak vision of anomie to which the railway manuals also draw attention, and which was typified by the station waiting room.

The new speed brought by steam travel was an element ripe for exploitation by writers. While travel by coach, carriage, omnibus and steam train were all used at this period to evoke alienation, one might expect rail travel to be treated differently from horse-drawn transport where speed was concerned. After all, the railway allowed great distances to be covered more rapidly than ever before – so much so that Marseilles was talked of as a suburb of Paris[70] – and exclamations about how quickly one could move from place to place earned an entry in Flaubert's *Dictionnaire des idées reçues*.[71] Wolfgang Schivelbusch has argued that the uniform speed of the motion generated by the steam engine soon came to seem more natural than horse-drawn motion.[72] However, Second Empire writers rarely present it in this way. The shifting relationship between speed and time and space was not perceived in the same manner by all; still less was it taken for granted as 'natural'. Paradoxically, more time was spent in travelling than previously, and the promised ease and rapidity were often illusory. Delattre complained that although it took only ten minutes to travel by train from St. Denis to Paris, a passenger must allow an extra half hour to reclaim his luggage and spend another fifteen minutes waiting for a coach to his final destination in the capital.[73] While a few commentators do extol the speed of rail travel and see it as a manifestation of progress, for most literary authors it exemplified frustration, disorientation and delay.

As Nerval had graphically demonstrated in *Les Nuits d'octobre*, published only a few weeks before the Second Empire was formally declared, the new railway system disrupted a previous network of local coach services, and despite their reputation for speed and directness, trains could make travel slower and more complicated than before. As he explained:

> The railway system has disrupted all transport in the surrounding areas. The great expanse of country to the north of Paris has been deprived of any direct communication; in order to reach places one used to be able to get to in four hours, one has to travel by rail for ten leagues to

---

70 Decaisne, *Guide médical*, vii.
71 Flaubert, *Dictionnaire des idées recues*, *OC* II, 305.
72 Wolfgang Schivelbusch, *The Railway Journey: Trains and Travel in the 19th Century*, trans. Anselm Hollo (Oxford: Basil Blackwell, 1979), 18.
73 Delattre, *Tribulations des voyageurs*, 181–82.

the right or eighteen leagues to the left, and changing trains to get there adds another two or three hours to the journey.⁷⁴

Nerval takes pleasure in undermining trains' reputation for speed and directness – 'I love to thwart the railway', he writes.⁷⁵ Delighting in these slow, frustrating, indirect journeys, his creative genius turns them to literary effect. His labyrinthine progress is echoed in his equally meandering prose – indeed, he ends the *Nuits d'octobre* by explicitly acknowledging the relationship between his circuitous route and his prose style: the convoluted journey he has just narrated has cured him of the 'excesses of an over-strict realism'.⁷⁶

For Nerval, a discourse of confusion and uncertainly associated with transport develops into an aesthetic of disorientation. In *Les Nuits d'octobre* (which records in overwhelming and disorientating detail the many different possible routes and means of transport the narrator might take, and the many obstacles to reaching his destination), that sense of powerlessness and failure to progress reaches a peak when he is arrested in mid-journey for having no identity papers, and is chained, handcuffed and imprisoned. Here, as in Frédéric's flight from Fontainebleau in *L'Éducation sentimentale*, the impeded journey, recounted in a style that mimics its convolutions, is associated with impotence in the face of an alien authority. Far from celebrating speed, these literary journeys convey helplessness and obstruction.

A changing sense of time creeps into the literature of this period, often subverting the new punctuality and time-keeping that had been transplanted from railway operation into people's everyday lives.⁷⁷ Contemporary commentators regularly deplored the sense of urgency that pervaded modern life, with its new pressure to be 'on time'; yet stopped or mal-functioning

---

74 'Le système des chemins de fer a dérangé toutes les voitures des pays intermédiaires. Le pâté immense des contrées situées au nord de Paris se trouve privé de communications directes; il faut faire dix lieues à droite ou dix-huit lieues à gauche, en chemin de fer, pour y parvenir, au moyen des correspondances, qui mettent encore deux ou trois heures à vous transporter dans les pays où l'on arrivait autrefois en quatre heures.' Gérard de Nerval, *Les Nuits d'octobre*, *Œuvres complètes*, 3 vols., ed. J. Guillaume & C. Pichois (Paris: Gallimard Pléiade, 1993), III, 345.
75 'J'aime à contrarier les chemins de fer.' Nerval, *Promenades et souvenirs*, *OC* III, 686, 671.
76 '[D]es excès d'un réalisme trop absolu'. Nerval, *Les Nuits d'octobre*, *OC* III, 351.
77 Michael Freeman, *Railways and the Victorian Imagination* (New Haven and London: Yale University Press, 1999), 21. France did not, however, adopt a standard national time until 1891.

clocks appear with astonishing frequency in Second Empire novels,[78] arguably both a function of, and a reaction against, the new attitude to time and time-measurement that was a legacy of the railway's arrival. Baudelaire's observation that '[e]very moment we are crushed by the idea and the sensation of time' finds an echo in many texts of this period.[79] Repeatedly, time is presented as stagnant, or as somehow out of joint. In *Arria Marcella*, for example, Gautier plays with the temporal incongruity of taking the train to Pompeii. The central character 'in whom all sense of time was in confusion', and who fears his watch may have stopped, finds himself either transported back in time to a living Pompeii before the eruption of Vesuvius, or still in the present, with the ancient city strangely brought to life around him and drawing him in; the story ends with his dazed return to Naples by rail.[80] In this instance and many others like it, images of urgency and progress are undermined, to produce instead an anxious sense of disorientation, disruption, or stagnation.

The expected imagery of speed and progress thus turns out to be far more troubled than one might suppose. As Nerval had graphically demonstrated in *Les Nuits d'octobre*, trains could make travel slower and more difficult than before. Moreover, he associates them with social and economic inequity: he writes of once-thriving towns that have died after being bypassed by the railway. These abandoned towns 'sit sadly on the debris of their past fortunes, and turn in on themselves, casting a disenchanted eye

---

78 Perhaps the most famous example of the stopped timepiece is the ornate clock in Nerval's *Sylvie* which has not been wound for two hundred years and whose appearance conjures up a lost world of the past. It is 'one of those Renaissance tortoiseshell clocks, whose gilded dome topped by the figure of Time is supported by Medici-style cariatids which in turn rest on rearing horses. Historic Diana, leaning on her stag, is depicted in bas-relief beneath the clock face, where the enamel figures showing the hours are displayed against a nielloed background. Its movement – no doubt excellent – had not been wound up for two centuries. – It was not in order to tell the time that I bought this clock in Touraine.' ['une de ces pendules d'écaille de la Renaissance, dont le dôme doré surmonté de la figure du Temps est supporté par des cariatides du style Médicis, reposant à leur tour sur des chevaux à demi cabrés. La Diane historique, accoudée sur son cerf, est en bas-relief sous le cadran, où s'étalent sur un fond niellé les chiffres émaillés des heures. Le mouvement, excellent sans doute, n'avait pas été remonté depuis deux siècles. – Ce n'était pas pour savoir l'heure que j'avais acheté cette pendule en Touraine.'] Nerval, *Sylvie*, *OC* III, 544.
79 'A chaque minute nous sommes écrasés par l'idée et la sensation du temps.' Baudelaire, 'Hygiène Conduite Morale', *OC*, 640. Cf. 'L'Horloge' (94) and 'La Chambre double' (149–50) where he refers to Time's 'brutal dictatorship' ['brutale dictature']. See also Anne Green, 'Time and History in *Madame Bovary*', *French Studies*, XLIX, 3 (July 1995), 283–291.
80 '[E]n qui toutes les idées de temps se brouillaient'. Théophile Gautier, *Arria Marcella*, in *Romans et contes* (Paris: Charpentier, 1880), 273–74, 292.

over the wonders of a civilisation that condemns or forgets them.'[81] It is a bleak reflection on the values of civilisation, progress and fraternity that the railway was held to embody.

That bleak assessment is seen, too, at the end of *L'Éducation sentimentale*, when Frédéric and Deslauriers discuss the reason for their failed lives. Couching their lack of success in opposing terms that apply equally well to the linear directness of the railway and to the congested traffic circulating around Paris, they attribute their failure to 'the lack of a straight line' for the one, and to 'too great a directness' for the other.[82] Both explanations imply a desolate vision of a future that seems to be going nowhere. Although a commentator like Decaisne might claim that travelling was one of the most intense passions of the nineteenth century, such a comment would merely have confirmed Flaubert's own pessimistic view of his contemporaries. For him, the desire to travel signified a deluded belief that it was possible to escape from the limitations and tedium of the day. As he wrote to Louise Colet, 'Nothing proves the *limited nature* of human existence better than travel; the more you shake it, the hollower it sounds [...] our activity is nothing but constant repetition, however diverse it may seem.'[83]

Not all writers took such a defeatist view, however. Victor Hugo, passionately hostile to Napoleon III and his regime, produced a vivid example of stalled motion in *Les Travailleurs de la mer* when he described how the great steamship, La Durande, was run aground by its duplicitous captain, Clubin, and remained firmly wedged on the rocks. His steamship is heavily freighted with symbolic meaning, but the negative associations of its immobilisation are qualified by hope for the future. The vessel's tall funnel is a symbol of progress, writes Hugo; its compass points the way forward, and its steam-power allows it to follow the true path.[84] Wreathed with images of education, civilisation, peace and harmony, Hugo's steamship is an explicit metaphor for all that a civilised society should value: 'Navigation is education [...] Navigation is the opposite

---

81 '[S]'asseyent tristement sur les débris de leur fortune passée, et se concentrent en elles-mêmes, jetant un regard désenchanté sur les merveilles d'une civilisation qui les condamne ou les oublie.' Nerval, *Les Nuits d'octobre'*, *OC* III, 686.
82 '[L]e défaut de ligne droite'; 'excès de rectitude'. Flaubert, *L'Éducation sentimentale*, *OC* II, 162. The image of the straight line is much used at this period; the Goncourt brothers point out that it is a human invention, found nowhere in nature, and they associate it with Empire and tyranny. Goncourt, *Journal*, I, 922.
83 'Rien ne prouve mieux *le caractère borné* de notre vie humaine que *le déplacement*. Plus on la secoue, plus elle sonne creux [...] notre activité n'est qu'une répétition continuelle, quelque diversifiée qu'elle ait l'air.' Flaubert, *Corr.* II, 423–24 (Louise Colet, 2.12.1853).
84 Hugo, *Les Travailleurs de la mer*, 476.

of war. Navigation civilises barbarism, war barbarises civilisation.'[85] After a heroic struggle, the wrecked ship is salvaged at the end of the novel and steams triumphantly off into the distance. *Les Travailleurs de la mer* thus leads the reader to understand that the ship of state that has been stranded on the rocks by its treacherous captain will one day have a new master at the helm and forge ahead towards a glorious future. Hugo's confident prediction – expressed solely through his description of the fate of the steamship – is that France's progress will no longer be impeded once its present leader has gone.

But transport could articulate contemporary concerns in other ways. One was to focus on the shifting landscape seen from the window of a moving vehicle. In Gautier's *Arria Marcella*, for example, the Mediterranean scenery viewed from the window of the train to Pompeii is transformed into a smoke-blackened industrial landscape; the sunny, whitewashed villages 'have something plutonian and ferruginous about them, like Manchester and Birmingham; the dust there is black, and a fine layer of soot clings to everything; one can feel the great furnace of Vesuvius panting and smoking only feet away'.[86] Although purporting to describe the effects of the volcano, the description more vividly evokes the smoke and soot belching from the locomotive's furnace and their cheerless effect on the surroundings.

Seen fleetingly from a train window, the vanishing view offered writers a convenient analogy to a France that was rapidly changing. In such descriptions it is not the traveller who moves away from his or her surroundings, but rather the familiar surroundings that desert the traveller as they disappear into the distance. The observer is represented as sitting at the still centre, while the countryside or cityscape is in perpetual motion, hard to decipher, and constantly vanishing from sight. Those writers who are happy to cast off the past and welcome the new exploit this image to express their positive outlook. Benjamin Gastineau, for example, not only embraces change and accepts that time cannot be stopped, but openly acknowledges the metaphorical resonance of his description of rapidly vanishing surroundings. When his traveller glimpses scenes from the window of a speeding train that conjure up alluring visions of romance, he recognises the futility of his desire to be part of them, accepts change as an inherent part of man's brief life, and refuses to be despondent – indeed

---

85 'Navigation, c'est éducation [...] La navigation est le contraire de la guerre. La navigation civilise le sauvagisme, la guerre sauvagise la civilisation.' Hugo, *Les Travailleurs de la mer*, 554.
86 '[O]nt [...] quelque chose de plutonien et de ferrugineux comme Manchester et Birmingham; la poussière y est noire, une suie impalpable s'y accroche à tout; on sent que la grande forge du Vésuve halète et fume à deux pas de là.' *Arria Marcella*, in *Romans et contes*, 273.

by the end of this extended metaphor the traveller is identified with the engine itself as it forges ahead into the future:

> Oh! If only one could stop. But there is no station. We must continue on our way, bearing with us our regret for that vision of paradise. Seeing, regretting and continuing on one's way, that is what life is all about. Man is in this world for only a moment, and his passage is fleeting and frantic, as rapid as the steam-engine projecting the moving shadow of its carriages along the field's edge.'[87]

Maxime Du Camp was similarly aware of the tensions between nostalgia and progress. Travelling by train through Holland, he admired cottages glimpsed from his moving carriage, and uttered 'the exclamation familiar to travellers: I should like to live there!' The relentless speed of modern life makes him long for a simpler, more peaceful existence, and the little houses represent for him the antithesis of the noisy railway. In this variation on the Second Empire leitmotif of the cosy room whose windows are shuttered against the turbulent outside world, the cottages seen from the train offer the illusion of a refuge from the modern world, yet Du Camp recognises the futility of his daydream: 'What a strange and enduring contradiction of the mind! When you are being carried noisily away by steam-power as swift as the wind and as strong as the sea, you dream of the peace of a quiet house and a little garden, with your favourite books, the sun streaming through the window and the door closed to all but those who can say: Open Sesame!'[88]

But Gastineau and Du Camp were unusual in tempering their nostalgia with an expression of willingness to move with the times. If for them the view from

---

[87] 'Ah! Si l'on pouvait s'arrêter. Mais il n'y a pas de station. Il faut poursuivre sa route en emportant le regret de cette vision paradisiaque. Voir, regretter et s'en aller, c'est toute la vie. Il n'est donné qu'une minute à l'homme pour figurer dans le monde, et il passe fugitif, éperdu, proscrit et rapide comme la locomotive, projetant et promenant sur la lisière du champ l'ombre de ses wagons.' Gastineau, *Les Romans du voyage*, 28–29.

[88] '[L]'exclamation familière aux voyageurs: je voudrais vivre là!'; 'Quelle étrange et perpétuelle contradiction de l'esprit! Quand la vapeur vous emporte à grand fracas, rapide comme le vent et forte comme la mer, on pense au repos dans une maison tranquille, auprès d'un petit jardin, avec les livres aimés, le soleil à la fenêtre et la porte fermée pour tous, excepté pour ceux qui savent dire: Sésame, ouvre-toi!' Maxime Du Camp, *En Hollande. Lettres à un ami* (Paris: Poulet-Malassis et De Broise, 1859), 97–98. Cf. *L'Éducation sentimentale*, where Frédéric, on board a steamer, imagines walking with Madame Arnoux on the riverbank. 'The boat could stop, they only had to get off; and yet that simplest of things was no easier than changing the course of the sun.' ['Le bateau pouvait s'arrêter, ils n'avaient qu'à descendre; et cette chose bien simple n'était pas plus facile, cependant, que de remuer le soleil!'] *OC* II, 11.

the moving window represented mild regret for a vanishing way of life, for others it conveyed a more disturbing sense of disorientation or detachment. In fictional texts, the wish to stop the train and step back into a world that has slipped past more often communicates not nostalgia but deep unease about change, an unease that takes several different forms. Several writers articulate a sense of apprehension by focusing on the dislocation between the view outside the moving window and the passenger who sits passively in his or her own enclosed space, detached from the passing scene. That image of the disengaged traveller appealed to disillusioned writers who had turned their backs on the political process after the failure of the 1848 revolution. For them it was a means of evoking the social imperviousness of a 'progress' which seemed independent of any individual agency, and whose powerless 'passenger' can only gaze uncomprehendingly at a two-dimensional outside world. In *L'Éducation sentimentale*, for example, Frédéric stares blankly through his train window as 'the little station houses slid past like backdrops', just as the busy banks of the Seine had seemed to glide by 'like two broad ribbons being unwound' when viewed from the steamboat at the beginning of the novel.[89] The external world passes in a barely recognisable blur or flattens into an artificial backdrop, disconnected and somehow unreal.

The celebrated photographer, writer and balloonist Nadar used the most avant-garde form of conveyance to articulate a similar sense of alienation. Describing a balloon ascent over Paris, he finds he can no longer recognise the familiar capital beneath him, and feels he has no place there as the roar and bustle of the city fall away. 'But this is no longer Paris, the Paris that I know!' he cries. His estrangement increases the higher the balloon rises, until it is not only the city that is unrecognisable: everything, including himself, feels altered and alien, and all sense of belonging is lost. 'I can no longer find myself […] Everything has completely changed – ideas, things, even names. […] Native Parisian that I am, I cannot help but feel a bitter and infinite sadness as I search for myself in vain today in this place that once was mine. I no longer have a home.'[90]

---

89 '[L]es maisonnettes des stations glissaient comme des décors'; 'comme deux larges rubans que l'on déroule'. Flaubert, *L'Éducation sentimentale*, *OC* II, 77; II, 8. Flaubert toyed with a similar disjunction in his preparatory drafts of *Madame Bovary*, although there the terms are reversed: the viewer remains static as the train rushes by. In order to convey Charles's inability to understand the lectures at medical school, Flaubert uses an image of him watching a train full of people flash past in a cloud of smoke, leaving him behind. Transcriptions of the drafts are available online at www.flaubert.univ-rouen.fr. See L'Atelier Bovary, Brouillons vol. 2, fol. 18v.

90 'Mais quoi! Ce n'est plus Paris, mon Paris que je connais'; 'Je ne saurais plus me retrouver […] Tout est changé, bouleversé, idées, choses et jusqu'aux noms […] Je ne puis me défendre, vieux Parisien né, contre cette amère, infinie tristesse de me chercher vainement aujourd'hui dans ce pays qui fut pourtant le mien. Je n'ai plus de pays.' Nadar, 'Le Dessus et le dessous de Paris' in *Paris Guide*, II, 1580, 1582, 1584–5.

So fundamental was this sense of change that language itself was implicated. As Nadar said, everything had changed, even names – or words. In a poem he recited to the Académie française in 1855, Jean Viennet bemoaned the deterioration of the French language and blamed the railways for its decline, claiming that it had been contaminated by anglicisms that felt and sounded dreadful in the mouths of Frenchmen:

> One hears only words that could rip metal,
> *Railway, tunnel, ballast, tender,*
> *Express, trucks* and *waggons*...as if a French mouth
> Were crushing glass and chewing cinders.[91]

Nevertheless, trains had begun to infiltrate literary language in a different and more creative way. Writers gradually recognised that the 'new lines of communication' (as the railway system was often called)[92] communicated in more sense than one. Forms of transport came to be seen as vehicles of expression, akin to literature itself. If it was something of a commonplace to bemoan the vanishing 'poetry' of the meandering stagecoach and its replacement by the 'prosaic' railway with its straight lines,[93] many writers nevertheless identified the railway with powerful literary qualities. A list of the names of stations on the Western line takes on the rhythm of the train when sung by station workers in the opening scene of Jacques Offenbach's operetta *La Vie Parisienne*, for example:

> We are employees of the line for the West,
> Which runs to Saint-Malo, Batignolles and Brest,
> Conflans, Triel, Poissy,
> Barentin, Pavilly,
> Vernon, Bolbec, Nointot,
> Motteville, Yvetot,
> Saint-Aubin, Viroflay,

---

91 'On n'entend que des mots à déchirer le fer, / Le *railway*, le *tunnel*, le *ballast*, le *tender*, / *Express, trucks* et *wagons*... une bouche française / Semble broyer du verre et mâcher de la braise.' 'Epitre à Boileau', cit. in Marta Caraion, *Les Philosophes de la vapeur et des allumettes chimiques* (Paris: Droz, 2008), 282, n. 88.
92 '[N]ouvelles voies de communication'.
93 E. g. 'Travelling by train is as prosaic as can be. You cross the land in a straight line, which [...] is deeply inimical to the poetry of travel.' ['Le voyage en chemin de fer est on ne peut plus prosaïque. On franchit l'espace en ligne droite, ce qui [...] répugne essentiellement à la poésie du voyage.'] Larousse, *Grand dictionnaire universel*, 'Chemins de fer' entry, 1162. See also Gastineau, *Les Romans du voyage*, 40–41.

> Landerneau, Malaunay,
> Laval, Condé, Guingamp,
> Saint-Brieuc and Fécamp.[94]

Even Flaubert, no rail enthusiast, praised the vigour and drive of Louise Colet's epic poem, *La Paysanne*, by comparing it to a railway: 'It's superb', he wrote. 'It runs like a railway.'[95] He appreciated the stylistic directness of the straight line, and had commented that in *Madame Bovary* he was trying to create a new style stripped of lyricism and authorial reflection, which would instead follow a 'geometrically straight line'.[96] Gastineau disputed the railway's 'prosaic' label, arguing that the very speed of train travel created poetry from the countryside it passed through; it transformed nature into a theatre peopled with heroes and monsters, and turned passengers into a receptive audience.[97] Attributing dramatic creative powers to the railway, he even claimed that the dramas that unfolded within trains – the amorous encounters, infidelities, burlesque incidents and crimes – were more powerful than anything produced by Corneille or Racine.[98]

Nowhere is this transformation more evident than in Paul Verlaine's remarkable poem of 1870, 'Le Paysage dans le cadre des portières', ['Landscape framed by a train window'], which appropriates the alien features of rail travel and harnesses them to poetic ends so that they become identified with the creative process itself:

> In the window-frames, the countryside
> Races furiously by, and entire plains
> With water, cornfields, trees and sky
> Are swallowed up in the cruel whirlwind
> Into which fall slim telegraph poles
> Whose wires look strangely like the flourish of a pen.

---

94 'Nous sommes employés de la ligne de l'Ouest, / Qui dessert Saint-Malo, Batignolles et Brest, / Conflans, Triel, Poissy, / Barentin, Pavilly, / Vernon, Bolbec, Nointot, / Motteville, Yvetot, / Saint-Aubin, Viroflay, / Landerneau, Malaunay, / Laval, Condé, Guingamp, / Saint-Brieuc et Fécamp.' Henri Meilhac and Ludovic Halévy, *La Vie parisienne*. Musique de J. Offenbach (Paris: M. Lévy, 1866), Act 1, scene 1.
95 'C'est superbe […] Ça marche comme un chemin de fer.' Flaubert, *Corr.* II, 307 (L. Colet, 16.4.1853).
96 '[L]igne droite géométrique.' Flaubert, *Corr.* II, 40 (L. Colet, 31.1.1852).
97 Gastineau, *Les Romans du voyage*, 56–57. In *Le Tableau de Paris* (1852) Edmond Texier refers to the omnibus as a 'travelling theatre' ['théâtre ambulant'] whose passengers are both actors and audience.
98 Gastineau, *Les Romans du voyage*, 45–48.

A smell of burning coal and boiling water,
The racket that a thousand chains would make
Were they attached to a thousand giants howling under the lash;
And suddenly, the drawn-out screech of an owl.
What does all that matter to me, since in my eyes I have
The white vision that lifts my heart,
Since the soft voice still murmurs for me,
Since the Name that is so beautiful, so noble and so resonant
Is mingled – a pure pivot for all this whirling –
With the rhythm of the brutal carriage, smoothly.[99]

The familiar outside world of peaceful fields and trees and sky is swallowed up in an inferno of burning coals and steam and screeching metal as the train rushes onwards. But here the threatening strangeness of the new comes to symbolise not only the disorienting sense of a changing world, but also the dangerous excitement of a changing form of expression. As the telegraph wires running by the track appear to rise and fall, they constitute a strange form of writing. Taking on 'l'allure étrange d'un paraphe', they come to resemble 'the flourish of a pen', and so the poet is able to detach himself from the brutal sounds and smells of the train by losing himself in word and rhythm and in a joyous 'white vision' suggestive of the white page. Thus in a curious convolution, the alien railway is absorbed into writing, and the image of the railway tracing its line like an inscription across the landscape becomes more familiar. Like the strokes of a pen, the locomotive's curling plumes of smoke and steam are seen as inscribing their own traces and rhythms on the landscape as the jarring sounds and rhythms of the train are transformed, smoothly – 'suavement' – into poetry.

It is clear, then, that modern transport crystallised a variety of concerns for Second Empire writers, and the various ways in which they wrote about it reveal something of the psychic landscape of the period. Whether viewed

---

99 'Le paysage dans le cadre des portières / Court furieusement, et des plaines entières / Avec de l'eau, des blés, des arbres et du ciel / Vont s'engouffrant parmi le tourbillon cruel / Où tombent les poteaux minces du télégraphe / Dont les fils ont l'allure étrange d'un paraphe. / Une odeur de charbon qui brûle et d'eau qui bout, / Tout le bruit que feraient mille chaînes au bout / Desquelles hurleraient mille géants qu'on fouette; / Et tout à coup des cris prolongés de chouette. / Que me fait tout cela, puisque j'ai dans les yeux / La blanche vision qui fait mon cœur joyeux, / Puisque la douce voix pour moi murmure encore / Puisque le Nom si beau, si noble et si sonore / Se mêle, pur pivot de tout ce tournoiement, / Au rythme du wagon brutal, suavement.' Paul Verlaine, *La Bonne Chanson* (Paris: Alphonse Lemerre, 1870).

as a positive symbol of progress, a disturbing emblem of change, or a bleak projection of a frustrated and alienated society, the railway seeped into French literary consciousness until it became an integral part of the creative process. Dramatising its surroundings and its occupants, and embodying multiple responses to modernity, the new transport system helped reshape the literature of the age.

Chapter Four

FOOD

One of the indirect consequences of the coming of the railways was a transformation in French eating habits, particularly those of the middle classes. Before the railways were built, the availability of food was limited by the amount that horses or oxen could pull, but under the Second Empire the new rail network made it possible to move large quantities of food quickly from one part of France to another. For the first time, thanks to the steam train, serious famine could be averted, and the bad harvests of 1853, 1856 and 1861 passed without mass starvation. Peasants might still prepare the simple, traditional foodstuffs that had remained virtually unchanged for generations,[1] but in towns and cities things were very different. The new urban middle classes craved more variety in their diet, and a growing industrial population needed more provisions, and wanted them more cheaply. As Auguste Luchet noted in 1867, steam transport allowed fashion rather than necessity to dictate eating habits: 'Everything changed with the advent of the railway. Shortened distances made our heads swim with swiftly-satisfied pleasures.'[2] In Second Empire Paris, patterns of eating altered radically as new foodstuffs became available. Oysters, to take but one example, were consumed in huge quantities now that the *trains de marée* could deliver regular, fresh supplies from the coast; to meet growing demand producers began to farm oysters, and in 1866 more than 260 million of them were sold in the capital, mainly to cafés and restaurants, which flourished as never before.

Eating *en masse* became a new fashion – the main dining room of the Grand Hotel in Paris could seat six hundred guests – and according to Maxime Du Camp, by the end of the Second Empire there were 23,643 restaurants in Paris alone, many of them low-priced, popular eating-places catering for the

---

1 Marceline Michaux, *La Cuisine de la ferme* (Paris: Librairie agricole de la maison rustique, 1862), 1.
2 'Les chemins de fer naquirent, et tout changea. Le raccourcissement des distances donna le vertige des jouissances promptes.' Auguste Luchet, 'Les Grandes cuisines et les grandes caves', *Paris-Guide*, II, 1547.

growing working population.[3] Contemporary guidebooks proudly quoted statistics showing the vast quantities of food that passed through the newly-built Paris food market at Les Halles, which quickly became a symbol of the prosperity and materialism of the Second Empire. Sales figures for 1866 included 14 million kilos of fish, nearly 12.5 million kilos of grapes and over 232 million eggs;[4] figures for the following year were higher still because of the needs of visitors to the *exposition universelle*, and included over one million swallows and half-a-million partridges.[5] As Philibert Audebrand would later reminisce, for many this was the Golden Age of eating.[6]

It was also something of a Golden Age for writing about food. Writers were acutely conscious that food – and their relation to it – was changing. Food had, of course, featured in French literature before. Rabelais' influence lived on and gastronomy was a familiar theme in the first part of the nineteenth century,[7] but in the 1850s and 1860s food was written about far more prolifically and diversely than ever before.[8] In novels, plays, poetry, guidebooks, household manuals, recipe books and newspapers (where the Baron Brisse was the first to introduce a daily column of recipes), food was being turned into language.

Writing about food offered a way of thinking about issues that reached far beyond the kitchen. Authors realised how readily the preparation and consumption of food lent itself to interpretation, and their imagination was increasingly coloured by gastronomic analogies. The endless rituals that surrounded the preparation and presentation of food, and the fact that it could be transformed from the natural state into an elaborate confection designed to be enjoyed (or destroyed, depending on one's point of view), meant that food was an ideal form of symbolic expression; accounts of meals or foodstuffs provided new possibilities for articulating ideas, values,

---

3 Maxime Du Camp, *Paris, ses organes, ses fonctions et sa vie dans la seconde moitié du XIXe siècle* vol. 2, 6 vols. (1870; Paris: Hachette, 1869–1875), 190. Du Camp regrets the demise of picturesque open-air stalls selling grilled herring, boudin, meat or eggs cooked on the spot, but recognises that Paris has become more hygienic. Ibid., II, 196–97.
4 Victor Borie, 'Les Halles et les marchés', *Paris-Guide*, II, 1520–21.
5 Du Camp, *Paris, ses organes…*, II, 454.
6 Philibert Audebrand, *Un café de journalistes sous Napoléon III* (Paris: Dentu, 1888), 26.
7 See Christopher Prendergast, *Paris and the Nineteenth Century* (Oxford: Blackwell, 1995), 19.
8 A comparison with Balzac demonstrates the extent to which the literary representation of food changed in the Second Empire period. At the climax of his 1831 novel *La Peau de Chagrin* Balzac describes a spectacular banquet and creates a vivid impression of luxurious excess in a passage stretching over many pages, but he does so with barely a mention of the dishes served.

fantasies or aspirations. Like the railway, it became another polarising marker for views about changing values as attitudes to morality, social structures, politics, power, revolution and democracy emerged in culinary texts. Writers recognised that food was 'good to think with'.

Couching their musings in terms of nourishment, many writers used it to reflect on social and political developments. The historian Michelet, for example, used a culinary metaphor to convey historical change, tracing the major shifts in eighteenth-century France by comparing different types of coffee:

> The three ages of coffee [...] mark solemn stages in the brilliant century of the Enlightenment. Arabian coffee prepares the way [...] Soon (1710–1720) comes the reign of Indian (Bourbon) coffee, both plentiful and popular [...] coffee from volcanic soil makes the new Regency spirit with its subtle gaiety explode onto the scene [...] The strong, full-bodied coffee from Santo Domingo, rich and stimulating, nourished the century's age of maturity, the great era of the *Encyclopédie*... which [could see] the future of 1789 gleaming at the bottom of the dark brew.[9]

Nestor Roqueplan turned to culinary metaphors to express his distaste for the contemporary scene, commenting that 'all those little ingredients that used to add spice to the social stew have been done away with. The only food that is left for the intellect is the tasteless, indigestible roast beef of politics.'[10] And Victor Hugo used the vocabulary of consumption to lament the political conservatism of the bourgeoisie, conveying their lack of revolutionary zeal in terms of sated appetite: 'Yesterday they were hungry, today they are satisfied, tomorrow they will be satiated.'[11]

---

9 'Les trois âges du café...marquent les moments solennels du brillant siècle de l'esprit. Le café arabe [le] prépare...Bientôt (1710–1720) commence le règne du café indien [de Bourbon] abondant, populaire...le café de terre volcanique fait l'explosion de la Régence et de l'esprit nouveau, l'hilarité subtile...Celui de Saint-Domingue, plein, *corsé*, nourrissant aussi bien qu'excitant, a nourri l'âge adulte du siècle, l'âge fort de l'Encyclopédie...qui [vit] au fond du noir breuvage le futur rayon de '89.' J. Michelet, cit. in R. Barthes, 'Pour une psycho-sociologie de l'alimentation contemporaine' in J. J. Hémardinguer, *Pour une histoire de l'alimentation* (Paris: Colin, 1970), 315.

10 '[T]ous les petits ingrédients qui relevaient le ragoût social sont supprimés. L'intelligence n'a plus pour pâture que l'indigeste et insipide *roast-beef* de la politique.' Nestor Roqueplan, *Regain. La Vie parisienne* [1854], cit. in D. Oster and J. Goulemot, *La Vie parisienne: Anthologie des mœurs du XIXe siècle* (Paris: Sand/Corti, 1989), 52.

11 'Hier c'était l'appétit, aujourd'hui c'est la plénitude, demain ce sera la satiété.' Victor Hugo, *Les Misérables*, vol. 2, ed. Yves Gohin (1973; Paris: Gallimard, 1995), 131.

The most characteristic feature of the profusion of food writing, however, was its emphasis on order, an emphasis that betrays a concern for order in the broadest sense. In the household manuals that abound at this period the need for systematic organisation is stressed at every turn, from the categories into which the recipes are organised, to the detailed instructions about where and when each dish and dining accoutrement is to be placed on the table, and when and in what order they are to be removed.[12] Seating arrangements, too, were to be meticulously calculated: gentlemen were allowed sixty centimetres of table space, but a metre had to be allocated to ladies wearing 'billowing gowns'.[13] Several novels of the period introduce details of seating plans into their narrative as a means of suggesting order. The Comtesse de Ségur, for example, uses an account of seating arrangements at the wedding banquet that closes *L'Auberge de l'ange-gardien* as a way of indicating that order and harmony have been restored to the lives of the guests; the guests themselves represent the army, the church, the law and political authority, and so convey an image of social stability even as they sit down to dine:

> the general offered Elfy his arm and seated her on his right; on his left was the parish priest; next to Elfy sat her husband; next to the priest was the lawyer. Madame Blidot sat opposite the general; on her right were Dérigny and his children; on her left, the mayor and his deputy. Then the rest of the guests seated themselves where they pleased.[14]

French table rituals were far more strictly regulated than their English equivalents during the Second Empire. Manuals issued precise instructions

---

12 See, for example, Rosalie Blanquet, *La Cuisinière des ménages, ou manuel pratique de cuisine et d'économie domestique pour la ville et la campagne* (Paris: Théodore Lefèvre, 1863), chapter 5: 'Service de table'. Baron Brisse's book of recipes included a catalogue of meats, fish, fruit and vegetables in season for each month of the year, and he boasted that this 'real, unprecedented innovation' ['innovation réelle, sans précédents'] would help the housewife to achieve the 'order, cleanliness and economy' essential to the smooth running of her household. Baron Brisse, *Recettes à l'usage des ménages bourgeois et des petits ménages, comprenant la manière de servir à nouveau tous les restes*' (Paris: E. Donnaud, 1868), v–vi.

13 '[R]obes ballonnées'. L. E. Audot, *La Cuisinière de la campagne et de la ville*, 47th ed. (Paris: Audot, 1868), 84. Originally published in 1818, this was repeatedly revised and reissued and was said to be the most popular recipe book of the Second Empire.

14 'Le général donna le bras à Elfy, qu'il plaça à sa droite; à sa gauche, le curé; près d'Elfy, son mari; près du curé, le notaire. En face du général, Mme. Blidot; à sa droite, Dérigny et ses enfants; à sa gauche le maire et l'adjoint. Puis le reste des convives se placèrent à leur convenance.' Mme la Comtesse de Ségur, *L'Auberge de l'ange gardien* (Paris: Hachette, 1863), 368. Cf. a similar passage in Théophile Gautier, *Le Capitaine Fracasse* (1863; Paris: Garnier-Flammarion, 1967), 49.

about how to lay out a multitude of ornamental table accessories, including baskets of flowers, candlesticks, decorative centrepieces, butter dishes, oil bottles and sets of hors d'œuvre plates in a symmetrical and ordered pattern. They issued strict directions, too, about the order of service at table, and explained in minute detail and with accompanying diagrams the ostentatious *service à la française*.[15] Despite the fact that this elaborate and expensive ritual was highly impractical and was used only on the grandest of occasions by this period, detailed instructions were included even in manuals aimed at housewives who wanted to 'combine simplicity and well-being'.[16] To know, at least in theory, how to run such a tightly structured ritual satisfied a deep need for order and doubtless flattered the reader's fantasies of social elevation.[17]

At this period, food itself was subject to repeated classification.[18] Elaborate classificatory systems based on the action of nutrients on the body were devised, and distinctions were drawn between foodstuffs that were complete or incomplete, heavy or light, 'growth-promoting' or 'respiratory'.[19] Certain foods were classed as unhealthy, and advice was issued in authoritative tones: 'If you are unwell, avoid peas'; 'No lemonade, it exhausts the nervous system'; 'No barley water, it slows the digestion.'[20] This emphasis on order and control was apparent within recipes too, with writers insisting on balance of flavour and symmetry of presentation. For example, the Baron Brisse's recipe for Tête de Veau, (a dish that famously features in *L'Éducation sentimentale*),[21] stipulates that the brain and tongue must each be split in two lengthways and arranged symmetrically with the two ear sections on an oval platter.

---

15 See, for example, Audot, *La Cuisinière de la campagne et de la ville*, 86–92.
16 Audot, *La Cuisinière de la campagne et de la ville*, 86–92.
17 Cf. Emma Bovary's reaction to the elaborately served meal at La Vaubyessard. Flaubert, *Madame Bovary*, *OC* I, 590–91.
18 In *Vingt mille lieues sous les mers* (106), Verne subverts the classificatory urge when he has Ned Land dismiss Conseil's obsessive attempts to classify species of fish by observing that only two classes are needed: 'You class them as fish that are edible and fish that are not!' ['On les classe en poissons qui se mangent et en poissons qui ne se mangent pas!'] Timothy Unwin argues that in that novel Land and Conseil may be said to embody food and words respectively. See Timothy Unwin, 'Eat my words: Verne and Flaubert, or the Anxiety of the Culinary', in John West-Sooby, ed., *Consuming Culture: The Arts of the French Table* (Newark: University of Delaware Press, 2004), 125.
19 See Charles Reculet, 'La Division des substances alimentaires', in *Le Cuisinier praticien, ou la cuisine simple et pratique* (Paris: Dentu, 1859); or the 'Aliment' entry in the *Grand dictionnaire universel*.
20 'Si vous êtes malade, évitez les pois'; 'Point de limonade, elle active l'épuisement nerveux'; 'Point d'orgeat, il engourdit les facultés digestives.' Maurice Germa, in Charles Monselet, *La Cuisinière poétique* (1859; Paris: Michel Lévy, 1877), 116 and 118.
21 See Flaubert, *L'Éducation sentimentale*, *OC* II, 162. Here it is a banal and grotesquely misplaced symbol, used to 'prove that stupidity proliferates.' ['prouve que la bêtise est féconde.']

But food also served to conceptualise and categorise social class or nationality. Alfred Delvau's version was: 'Conger eels for the common people, sole for the middle-classes, turbot for duchesses, lobsters for literary men and women, pink prawns for the ladies, herring for rogues';[22] while in his posthumously published encyclopedia of gastronomy (which he saw as the crowning achievement of his literary career), Alexandre Dumas used culinary tastes to create ironic national stereotypes:

> In France the stew is more highly rated than anywhere else; we know that Spaniards live on nothing but chocolate, chick-peas and rancid bacon; Italians on macaroni; the English on roast beef and pudding; the Dutch on roast meat, potatoes and cheese; and the Germans on sauerkraut and smoked ham.[23]

A desire for order was expressed so insistently and urgently in relation to food that it seems to betray some deeper concern. Charles Reculet, the author of *Le Cuisinier praticien, ou la cuisine simple et pratique*, was revealingly outspoken in his demands for the restoration of order in culinary matters. Acknowledging that these were undergoing a fundamental change, he made an impassioned plea for an enlightened regime based on rationality and the rule of law, which would be capable of putting an end to the chaos and disruption of the past. Although writing about recipe books, Reculet's uncompromising language suggests that his recipe for the future was as political as it was culinary. In his preface he argues that in the past, cookery books were characterised by confusion and disorder – they were 'an incoherent jumble of unconnected formulae which they call recipes, randomly thrown together without principle or method'. To him, these books represent a benighted age. Referring to them as a dark labyrinth which offered the reader no guiding light for the way forward, and using terms more appropriate to a denunciation of the political and ideological turmoil in France in the first half of the century than to a discussion of food preparation, Reculet goes on to claim that culinary art has

---

22 'Congres bons pour le peuple, soles bonnes pour les bourgeois, turbots bons pour les duchesses, homards bons pour les gens de lettres, crevettes roses bonnes pour les petites dames, harengs bons pour les gueux.' Alfred Delvau, *Les Heures parisiennes* (1866), cit. in Oster and Goulemot, eds., *La Vie parisienne*, 69.

23 'En France la casserole est plus en honneur que partout ailleurs; on sait que les Espagnols ne vivent que de chocolat, de garbanços et de lard rance ; les Italiens de macaroni; les Anglais de roast beef et de pudding; les Hollandais de viande cuite au four, de pommes de terre et de fromage; les Allemands de choucroute et de lard fumé.' Alexandre Dumas, *Grand dictionnaire de cuisine* (Paris: Alphonse Lemerre, 1873), 378.

too long been subject to violent change – 'mutilated, corrected, distorted, and subject to every imaginable taste, whim and fluctuation because it was not based on solid foundations or enlightened by rational laws capable of revealing its true nature'.[24] Instead, the author wants to save cookery from 'chaos and confusion' and classify it as an exact science, based on clear rules and logical principles which will reveal its 'true nature'.[25] Behind Reculet's disquisition on French cooking one detects a wider plea for political stability and strong control.

Quite the opposite view, however, emerges from the work of Charles Monselet, who treats the art of cooking as if it were a radical political movement on the brink of a long anticipated revolution:

> Cooking awaits its revolution, even its Reign of Terror. It must renew and transform itself like everything else... To be strong and glorious, to dominate, to reign, it has to detach itself from outmoded traditions, move towards powerful revolutionary stomachs, and brandish the red flag of innovation over failing stoves.[26]

Whereas Reculet longs for order and control, Monselet is desperate for change. Calling on chefs to experiment with more exotic foods, he launches an attack on the dull predictability of restaurant menus, and claims to regret never having dined at a restaurant which sourced its meat from the Paris zoo and served fillet of zebra, leopard rib, hyena with mushrooms, and elephant's foot *à la poulette*. His enthusiasm for innovation is unbounded – he urges the reader to try grasshoppers, crickets, dragonflies, squirrels and canaries; he maintains that he has tried parrot and found it good, and asserts that rats are excellent when grilled and seasoned with herbs, salt, and a generous pinch of pepper. Underlying Monselet's argument is the desire for a great upheaval, and the belief that such a thing is inevitable. Culinary and political discourses merge as he writes of French cuisine's need for renewal in terms of revolutionary violence. Cookery, he says, will have to 'forge new paths, change the tablecloths, sharpen knives and

---

24 '[U]n amas décousu de formules, qu'ils appellent recettes, jetées pêle-mêle, sans liaison, sans méthode et sans loi'; 'mutilé, corrigé, altéré, soumis à tous les goûts, à tous les caprices, à tous les errements imaginables, faute d'être appuyé sur de bonnes bases, faute d'être éclairé par des lois raisonnées et propres à en démontrer le véritable caractère.' Reculet, *Le Cuisinier praticien*, 3.
25 Reculet, *Le Cuisinier praticien*, xii.
26 'La cuisine attend sa révolution, voire même sa terreur. Il faut qu'elle se renouvelle et se transforme comme toutes les choses... Pour être glorieuse et forte, pour dominer, pour régner, elle doit se dégager des traditions caduques, aller vers les estomacs révolutionnaires et puissants, agiter sur les fourneaux languissants le drapeau écarlate de l'innovation...' Monselet, *La Cuisinière poétique*, 24.

begin by immediately chopping off three hundred thousand sculpted heads of Abelards and chatelaines in Paris restaurants!' Although the severed heads of his text ostensibly refer to over-elaborate restaurant décor, by combining them with sharpened knives and the brandishing of red flags Monselet not only reminds the reader of past revolutions but implies that another upheaval is imminent: 'it is an inescapable law'.[27]

It therefore comes as no surprise to find an association between food and social order in the literature of the period. When the narrator of Nerval's *Les Nuits d'octobre* tells of a hallucination where he is blamed for 'drinking so much beer from March till October', the accusation acknowledges that drinks have their own seasons and implies that the season for beer, with its connotations of popular rebellion, should be well and truly over.[28] But the narrator carries on with his subtly subversive drinking. Texts such as these go against the grain of non-fictional food writing which seems to strive to introduce order into chaos; instead, literary texts more often adopt Monselet's standpoint. Exploiting the culinary to undermine order, they reveal it to be a tenuous and temporary state that will inevitably collapse into chaos. This is a familiar theme in Flaubert's novels, where descriptions of table scenes repeatedly evoke that process.[29] Flaubert was acutely aware of the metaphorical possibilities that lay in the process of preparing, displaying and destroying a culinary construct. In *Madame Bovary*, Emma's physical collapse and the impending disintegration of her life and that of her family is marked by a shattered meal: 'The table, with all the plates, was overturned; gravy, meat, knives, the salt-cellar and the oil and vinegar bottles were strewn across the room.'[30] Likewise in the early pages of *L'Éducation sentimentale*, the deck of the steamship, littered with empty nutshells, fruit peelings and discarded bits of charcuterie, offers a foretaste of that novel's central theme of disintegration, and as the novel continues, the sense of moral and political collapse is repeatedly conveyed by means of disintegrating meals. One such dinner provides a vivid metaphorical enactment

---

27 '[T]racer des voies, changer les nappes, aiguiser les couteaux et commencer par abattre tout de suite trois cent mille têtes sculptées d'Abeilard et de châtelaines dans les restaurants de Paris!'; 'c'est l'inévitable loi.' Monselet, *La Cuisinière poétique*, 24.
28 '[A]bsorber tant de bière de mars en octobre'. Nerval, *OC* III, 338. See Jean Fornasiero, 'Nerval se met à table: les aveux d'un buveur démocratique entre la République et le Second Empire', in John West-Sooby, ed., *Consuming Culture: The Arts of the French Table*, 109.
29 As J-P Richard famously noted, 'there is a lot of eating in Flaubert's novels'. ['On mange beaucoup dans les romans de Flaubert.'] *Stendhal et Flaubert. Littérature et sensation* (Paris: Seuil, 1954), 137.
30 'La table, avec toutes les assiettes, était renversée; de la sauce, de la viande, les couteaux, la salière et l'huilier jonchaient l'appartement.' Flaubert, *Madame Bovary, OC* I, 644.

of future civil unrest with spilt wine, spilt blood, a bombardment of oranges and corks, smashed plates and an exchange of hostilities.[31] The same pattern is taken to extremes in *Salammbô*'s opening feast, where the initial symmetry of the tables – aniseed-covered loaves alternate with large cheeses, and jugs of wine with jugs of water – soon turns to violence and chaos. By the end of the feast, the charred corpses of monkeys are dropping from burning trees onto the remains of a banquet that has come to resemble a battlefield, with drunken soldiers slumped on the blood-soaked ground alongside dead bodies that prefigure the carnage to come.[32]

In *Salammbô*, Flaubert also exploits the widely held view of food as a barometer of civilisation. The *Grand dictionnaire universel*'s 'Repas' entry stresses the idea that luxury, culinary variety and table-etiquette were the hallmark of civilised societies, whereas primitive man ate only in order to satisfy pressing physical needs, used his fingers to tear apart food served from a communal dish, and drank to excess. The food a man consumed was seen as affecting his imagination, judgement and courage, and a measured appreciation of fine food was held to be evidence of civilised behaviour and morality. The gluttonous, meat-eating English failed on this count. The French gourmet's approach to food, on the other hand, was taken as the sign of a finer nature and a more discriminating intellect: 'the gourmet links cause and effect, and analyses, discusses, researches, and seeks out all that is useful, agreeable, beautiful and good. He lives a dignified life and must possess sure senses, good judgment and delicacy.'[33] Flaubert's banquet scene at the beginning of *Salammbô* relies on such commonplace assumptions to guide the reader's initial response to the barbarian mercenaries and their more civilised Carthaginian hosts: the Barbarians are astonished by the sophisticated dishes set before them, even as they grab the unfamiliar food and gorge themselves.[34]

---

31 Flaubert, *L'Éducation sentimentale*, *OC* II, 53. Cf. the wedding meal in *Madame Bovary*, *OC* I, 583–84, where the food is laid out in careful symmetry but that orderliness soon disintegrates; the scene ends in a chaos of lurching, crashing, runaway carriages as replete and drunken wedding guests drive erratically home.
32 Flaubert, *Salammbô*, *OC* I, 694–700.
33 '[L]e gastronome remonte des effets aux causes, analyse, discute, recherche, poursuit l'utile et l'agréable, le beau et le bon. Il vit dignement et doit être doué de sens sûrs, de jugement et de tact.' Larousse, *Grand dictionnaire universel*, 'Gastronomie' entry.
34 Mlle Vatnaz, the unappealing spinster in *L'Éducation sentimentale*, has much in common with the Barbarians who tear their faces on the sharp spines of the lobsters they devour at the feast: 'Mlle Vatnaz ate almost the entire sheaf of crayfish by herself, and their shells sounded loudly against her long teeth.' 'Mlle Vatnaz mangea presque à elle seule le buisson d'écrevisses, et les carapaces sonnaient sous ses longues dents.' Flaubert, *L'Éducation sentimentale*, *OC* II, 53.

Yet as the novel progresses, the apparent distinction between barbarism and civilisation dissolves. In the final chapter, featuring a second great feast that echoes the opening one, the Carthaginian dishes are depicted as close to their original, raw state: boars with gaping jaws wallow in a dustbowl of spices, fur-covered hares appear to leap between flowers, and live doves fly up when dish-covers are removed.[35] Indicating the underlying barbarism of the supposedly civilised, the food seems to have undergone little culinary transformation, indeed seems still alive.

On the other hand, elaborate culinary effects could denote decadence. In *L'Éducation sentimentale* Flaubert shows the egregious Sénécal exploiting that position in an attempt to parade his moral superiority. Sénécal spurns the bourgeois wines, oysters, game, fruits and exotic delicacies on offer at M. Arnoux's house: 'These attentions were wasted on Sénécal. He began by asking for plain bread (as hard as possible), and following on from that, talked about the Buzançais murders and the food crisis'[36] – a reference to famine riots in the winter of 1846. Like Sénécal, many commentators took France's new eating habits to be symptomatic of the nation's moral and spiritual decline. As Destaminil wrote in *Le Cuisinier français perfectionné*, 'The cuisine of our forefathers produced robust bodies and stoutly-tested souls; our own produces only faint hearts and feeble constitutions.'[37] He particularly railed against the fashion for blancmange, which for him epitomised the lack of character of his enervated age, while for Flaubert the bourgeoisie's new reliance on the Baron Brisse's daily set menus perfectly illustrated the extent to which his contemporaries had lost the capacity to think for themselves.[38]

The multiple resonances of the word 'taste',[39] indicating aesthetic as well as gustatory preferences and with implications about social class, meant that food offered writers a particularly rich conceptual model for thinking about difference.[40] A reference to the Englishman's *rosbif*, for example, was

---

35 Flaubert, *Salammbô*, *OC* I, 795.
36 'Ces attentions furent perdues pour Sénécal. Il commença par demander du pain de ménage (le plus ferme possible), et, à ce propos, parla des meurtres de Buzançais et de la crise des subsistances.' Flaubert, *L'Éducation sentimentale*, *OC* II, 58.
37 'La cuisine de nos pères faisait des corps robustes et des âmes vigoureusement trempées; la nôtre ne fait que des constitutions frêles et des cœurs sans énergie.' M. Destaminil, *Le Cuisinier français perfectionné, contenant les meilleures prescriptions de la cuisine ancienne et moderne* (Paris: Renault, 1861), vi.
38 Flaubert, *Carnets de travail*, ed. P. M. de Biasi (Paris: Balland, 1988), 556 (Carnet 20, fol. 12v).
39 'Goût'.
40 The Goncourt brothers play with these resonances in *Manette Salomon* (148–49), where an artist's pet monkey is said to have developed 'a taste for painting' (or 'a taste for paint') ['le goût de la peinture'] as a result of eating tubes of paint.

shorthand for a wealth of cultural features that distinguished the French from their neighbours across the Channel.[41] Novelists could subtly convey class differences by describing the food their characters consumed, while eating preferences emphasised the gender difference, so graphically emphasised by costume at this period, for it was commonly held that male and female tastes were dissimilar. Michelet warned bridegrooms not to make their new wife switch suddenly from 'the fruit-eating existence which most girls prefer to a robust masculine diet. It would make her ill.'[42] It is this culinary gendering that Gautier teasingly exploits when he describes the ravenous hero of *Le Capitaine Fracasse* consuming partridge wings and slices of ham 'that vanish like snowflakes on a red-hot shovel', and comments that 'the display of voraciousness is inappropriate for young ladies, who are supposed to dine on dewdrops and nectar'.[43]

Food also marks the difference between wealth and poverty, between excess and deprivation. While *Salammbô*'s astonishing feasts display the most striking examples of excess, other Second Empire novels regularly feature scenes of disproportionate consumption. Even the Comtesse de Ségur, the author of popular children's books designed to be morally uplifting as well as entertaining, injects gross overindulgence into her accounts of meals. At the end of *L'Auberge de l'ange gardien*, for example, she describes a wedding breakfast given by a grateful general for a poor soldier and his bride. Although there are fifty-two guests, the chef is ordered to cater for a hundred and four hearty appetites and warned not to expect any leftovers. The description of the meal continues for many pages, and Ségur's account of the guests' relish of the food is punctuated by menu-like lists as the head waiter announces each new dish:

> 'Soups: crayfish bisque! Turtle soup! [...] Turbot with prawn sauce! Salmon with imperial sauce! Filets of venison in Madeira sauce! [...] Partridge wings with truffles!' 'Poultry supreme!' 'Roast pheasants! Capercaillies! Hazel grouse!' 'Wild boar hams! Lobster salad!'

---

41 See the articles on foreign meals in Monselet, *La Cuisinière poétique*. Hippolyte Taine discussed national food habits as a means of exploring national literary output; see his *Histoire de la littérature anglaise* (Paris: Hachette, 1864), e. g. I, xxvff.; I, 6–14.
42 '[L]a vie frugivore que préfèrent la plupart des filles à une forte nourriture d'homme. Elle en serait malade.' Jules Michelet, *L'Amour* (1858; Paris: Hachette, 1859), 92, 96. Michelet criticises English women for their inappropriately masculine diet (92).
43 '[A]ussitôt disparues que des flocons de neige sur une pelle rouge'; 'la montre de voracité ne sied point aux jeunes dames, lesquelles sont censées se repaître de rosée et suc de fleurs.' Gautier, *Le Capitaine Fracasse*, 55, 87.

These are followed by asparagus, peas, green beans, stuffed artichokes, and a profusion of desserts: 'whipped creams, unwhipped creams, ice-creams, set creams, sour creams. Then the pastries: babas, mont-blancs, Saint-Honoré cakes, cheesecakes, and mounds of profiteroles'; then comes a vast array of fruits, sweets and other delicacies. Madeira, Bordeaux-Laffite and wines from Burgundy and the Rhine have already been served before the pheasant arrives, by which time the general is on his tenth glass. Toasts are drunk in champagne, and when the meal is over the wedding party moves to a nearby inn where heavily laden tables offer further supplies of cold meats, fish, pastries, creams and jellies that are replenished until dawn. The text constantly insists on excess, the meal is a 'Belshazzar's feast', and the account ends with a detail not uncommon in Second Empire literary meals: near-fatal overindulgence. One guest comes close to death from overeating and another is barely able to move for three days.[44]

While they may be read as simple celebrations of plenty, these fictional feasts hint at more disturbing currents underlying Second Empire prosperity. Several novels of the period contrast massive banquets with extreme deprivation. Soon after *Salammbô*'s opening feast, Carthaginians starve to death when the city comes under siege, while the novel's closing feast is preceded by the death by starvation of the entire Barbarian army, trapped in the Défilé de la Hache. *L'Auberge de l'ange gardien* operates in a similarly contrastive mode, opening with a soldier giving his meagre ration of bread and cheese to two starving children, and ending, as we have seen, with the extraordinary excess of the wedding feast.[45] Gautier's *Le Capitaine Fracasse* follows the same pattern, opening with the Baron sitting alone with his starving cat in the kitchen of his ruined mansion and eating a frugal meal of thin soup, a scene which is immediately followed by a feast brought by a troupe of travelling players who pass by unexpectedly; and those scenes have their explicit counterpart at the end of the novel, when the Baron eats a similarly frugal, solitary meal which is followed by an even more sumptuous banquet.[46] (In this case the victim

---

44 '"Potages: bisques aux écrevisses! Potage à la tortue! [...] 'Turbot sauce crevette! saumon sauce impériale! filets de chevreuil sauce madère! [...] Ailes de perdreaux aux truffes! [...] Volailles à la suprême! [...] Faisans rôtis! coqs de bruyère! gélinottes! [...] Jambons de marcassin! homards en salade!'; 'crèmes fouettées, non fouettées, glacées, prises, tournées. Puis les pâtisseries, babas, mont-blanc, saint-honoré, talmouses, croque-en-bouche'; 'festin de Balthazar'. Ségur, *L'Auberge de l'ange gardien*, 368–379.
45 Cf. Baudelaire's prose-poem, 'Le Gâteau', *OC*, 157–58.
46 'It repeated the scene described at the start of this story so exactly that the Baron, struck by the similarity, thought that he had been dreaming and had never left his castle.' ['Il répétait si exactement la scène décrite au commencement de cette histoire que le Baron, frappé de cette ressemblance, s'imaginait avoir fait un rêve et n'être jamais sorti de son château.'] Gautier, *Le Capitaine Fracasse*, 465.

of excess is the Baron's hungry cat which gorges on pâté, fish and partridge, and dies, 'a victim of its greed'.)[47] Jules Verne's food-filled novels are similarly interspersed with scenes of starvation and surfeit – his *Voyage au centre de la terre*, for example, swings between evocations of the succulent meals prepared by the family cook, and the extreme privations Axel undergoes when he and his uncle are lost in the bowels of the earth.

Although famines were a thing of the past, the threat of starvation was still a living memory which may have left its trace in this recurrent pattern of fictional excess and starvation. Moreover, the alternation of hunger and plenty provided a convenient structuring device for novelists, and communal meals were useful narrative tools for bringing characters together, driving the plot and punctuating the storyline. But the insistence of such patternings in Second Empire writing suggests more than a simple reflection of memories of literal starvation, and points to underlying tensions beneath the apparent prosperity of French society. As is suggested by the iconic status that Géricault's famous 1819 painting *Le Radeau de la Méduse* achieved during this period, the representation of extreme hunger carried deeper resonance. Géricault's dying sailors adrift on their raft had, by the beginning of the Second Empire, come to be regarded as a symbol of France. In Michelet's words, 'he put France itself – the whole of our society – on that raft'.[48]

Food, or its absence, thus offered a means of tentatively exploring thoughts about social inequality, the struggle for survival, uncertainty about the future, and ambivalent attitudes towards change in the modern world. In his contribution to *Paris-Guide* Victor Borie celebrated the abundance of food that passed through the new Paris market, but alongside his mouth-watering account of prodigality is a paragraph evoking a poverty that can barely be expressed. He describes a corner of the Halles where every morning shops display plates covered with strange and mysterious foodstuffs 'whose name and origins one cannot discover at first sight'. Borie exploits the trope of excess in a long catalogue of these foods, only to produce revulsion in the reader instead of delight, for the dishes listed are in fact stale, half-eaten left-overs from restaurants and grand houses, sold on scraps of newspaper to the poorest of the poor:

> There are plates of bacon rind, a half-eaten leg of mutton whose bare bone points threateningly to the sky, a collapsed fragment of vol-au-vent, encrusted with congealed sauce; sweetbreads *à la poulette*; a plate of tapioca

---

47 '[V]ictime de son intempérance'. *Le Capitaine Fracasse*, chapters 1 and 2; and 504.
48 'C'est la France elle-même, c'est notre société toute entière qu'il embarqua sur ce radeau.' Cit. in Hugh Honour, *Romanticism* (Pelican Books, 1981), 41. Cf. Victor Hugo, 'Introduction', *Paris-Guide*, I, ix: 'Paris a été radeau de la Méduse; la famine y a agonisé.'

broth abandoned by an indisposed guest; a dish of macaroni that had been browned the week before; a *charlotte russe* with sodden biscuits swimming in rancid cream; and then some plain boiled beef; some leftover veal bourgeoise or beef *à la mode*; very stale wheaten rolls which a pretty mouth had nibbled disdainfully, mixtures of vegetables and meats accompanied by unimaginable sauces and things that have no name.[49]

Food descriptions elicit strong emotions in the reader, and Borie's list exploits this to the full in order to draw attention to a hidden underclass that has to survive on such disgusting remnants.

Writing about food was a means of provoking a range of reactions, from desire, envy or greed to anxiety, revulsion, horror or despair – reactions which writers were able to engage and direct towards other concerns. Ernest Capendu notably does this in his novel, *Mademoiselle la Ruine*. In one extraordinary scene he describes a dinner at the Café Anglais attended by financiers, celebrities and 'fashionable whores',[50] where the guests 'help' to clear away the dishes by flinging them though the window to shatter in the street below: 'a hail of dishes, plates and carafes smashed on to the asphalt, to the great delight and loud laughter of the participants and those watching this tasteful scene.'[51] But what starts as a display of destructive excess gradually turns into an act of charity. When Maryland, the courtesan who instigated the plate-throwing, realises there are poor people in the street below, she starts throwing down pâtés and terrines. As each dish sails through the window to the hungry crowd of coachmen,

---

49 '[D]ont on ne peut découvrir, par un premier coup d'oeil, ni l'origine ni le nom'; 'Ce sont des assiettes de couennes de lard, un gigot profondément entamé, et dont le manche décharné menace le ciel; un fragment de vol-au-vent, affaissé, incrusté dans la sauce figée; des ris de veau à la poulette; une assiette de consommé au tapioca, délaissée par un convive indisposé; un plat de macaroni gratiné la semaine précédente; une charlotte russe, dont les biscuits détrempés baignent dans la crème tournée; puis, du simple boeuf bouilli; un reste de veau bourgeoise ou de boeuf à la mode; des petits pains de gruau très rassis, qui furent grignotés par une jolie bouche dédaigneuse, des macédoines de légumes et de viandes, accompagnés de sauces impossibles et d'objets sans nom.' Victor Borie, 'Les Halles et les marchés', *Paris-Guide*, II, 1522.
50 '[P]écheresses en vogue'. Ernest Capendu, *Mademoiselle la Ruine* (Paris: Alexandre Cadot, 1861), 60.
51 '[U]ne grêle de plats, d'assiettes, de carafes, s'abbatit sur l'asphalte, à la grande joie et aux rires bruyants des acteurs et des spectateurs de cette scène de haut goût.' Capendu, *Mademoiselle la Ruine*, 90.

doorkeepers and cigar-scavengers gathered beneath, she recites its name in a parody of a waiter announcing the menu:

– Prawns and lobsters for you!' – shrieked Maryland as she sent the crustaceans flying out the window.
– And cold chicken!
– And galantines!
– And truffles with Champagne!
– And salmon trout!
– And pineapple salad! Mind the juice!
– Here come the hams!
– Here come the macaroons![52]

By the end of the scene she is tying bottles of Bordeaux Lafitte to a rope of napkins and tablecloths and carefully lowering them to the crowd below, and the diners at the nearby Maison d'Or restaurant have begun to follow suit. What started as arrogant destruction has turned into solidarity with the poor, and the impulse is spreading. Just as other writers exploited train and omnibus topoi, Capendu uses restaurant scenes to explore the breakdown of old social hierarchies. His narrator complains of 'the merging of all classes' whereby 'great lords and rich financiers go and sit down at table near lawyers' clerks or bank assistants enjoying their time off'. Maintaining that the working class is corrupted by coming into contact with the leisured classes, he considers their consumption of the same food to be symptomatic of this.[53]

Although such scenes draw attention to issues of social difference, the conventional concept of the shared meal is one of harmony – a nourishing ritual where families and friends unite around the table, and where the sharing of food represents a common bond. At one level is the emblematic and much-cited 'Dinner of the Three Emperors' held at the Café Anglais in 1867, which

---

52 '–A vous les écrevisses et les homards! – glapit Maryland en envoyant les crustacés par la fenêtre.
– Et les poulets froids!
– Et les galantines!
– Et les truffes au vin de Champagne!
– Et les truites saumonées!
– Et la salade d'ananas! – gare au sauce!
– En avant les jambons!
– En avant les macarons!' Capendu, *Mademoiselle la Ruine*, 90.
53 '[C]ette fusion entre toutes les classes'; 'grands seigneurs et grands financiers vont s'attabler dans le cabinet voisin de celui où s'émancipe le clerc de notaire ou le premier commis d'une maison de banque'. Capendu, *Mademoiselle la Ruine*, 59.

brought together Alexander II of Russia, his son, the future Alexander III, and Kaiser William I of Prussia, accompanied by Otto von Bismarck; at another is Michelet's rhapsodic celebration of domestic bliss as he describes a newly-married couple nourishing their love by sharing food:

> The communion of the table is very profound, particularly in the small household of a couple [...]. The man feeds the woman, each day bringing God's bread to his solitary beloved, like the bird in the fairy-tale. And the woman feeds the man. She suits the food to his needs, to his degree of fatigue and his known temperament; she humanises it with fire, salt and soul. She puts herself into it, adding to it the perfume of her beloved hands. Thus each is nourished by the other.[54]

Mealtime scenes which failed to conform to that association between shared food and shared values allowed authors further scope to use eating habits as a subtle means of conveying relationships. Thus Flaubert is able to communicate the gulf between Emma and Charles Bovary by showing how far they diverge from Michelet's ideal of nourishing exchange. He describes Charles slowly masticating his boiled beef while Emma merely nibbles a few nuts and draws on the oilcloth with the point of her knife as if inscribing her separateness and disaffection on the table. Emma's refusal of food becomes a cipher for her rejection of Charles and all he represents. Ordering dishes for herself alone and then rejecting them, she reflects that 'all life's bitterness seemed to have been served up on her plate, and in the steam of the broth it was as if other wafts of blandness were rising from the depths of her soul'.[55]

Writing about food thus offered ways of exploring and articulating misgivings about modern life. Anxiety and suspicion were frequently conveyed in terms of fears that modern food might be dangerously adulterated, and tales of falsification abounded. Small boys were said to go round wine-merchants selling spiders' webs to be glued over bottles and sprinkled with sawdust so that cheap, adulterated wine would look like vintage stock.[56] Maxime Du Camp

---

54 'Profonde, profonde communion que celle de la table, surtout dans le petit ménage où l'on est deux [...]. L'homme nourrit la femme, apporte chaque jour, comme l'oiseau des légendes, le pain de Dieu à sa bien-aimée solitaire. Et la femme nourrit l'homme. A son besoin, à sa fatigue, à son tempérament connu, elle approprie la nourriture, l'humanise par le feu, par le sel et par l'âme. Elle s'y mêle, y met le parfum de la main aimée. Donc, ils sont nourris l'un de l'autre.' Michelet, *L'Amour*, 95.
55 '[T]oute l'amertume de l'existence lui semblait servie sur son assiette, et, à la fumée du bouilli, il montait du fond de son âme comme d'autres bouffées d'affadissement.' Flaubert, *Madame Bovary*, *OC* I, 596.
56 Louis Noir, *Le Pavé de Paris* (s. d.) cit in D. Oster and J. Goulemot, eds., *La Vie parisienne*, 294–95.

details other examples of food fraud: it was common practice in Paris to skim and water down milk and to add bicarbonate of soda to prevent it from going sour, and milk was rumoured often to be laced with other substances such as plaster or horses' brains. Olive oil was regularly tampered with, as were roasted coffee beans which dishonest vendors mixed with barley, maize, oats, beetroot, carrots, acorns, chestnuts or chicory, and customers who bought fresh beans to roast at home in the hope of a purer product could be tricked by grocers adding fake beans moulded from clay.[57] There were worries, too, about artificial chemical concoctions being passed off as wine, butter or jam, and slowly but surely destroying the vital organs of those who consumed them. This is food as forgery, insidiously damaging while purporting to nourish. Seen in this light, food becomes emblematic not only of deceit and dishonesty, but also of the growing and possibly sinister power of science. The kitchen was becoming a laboratory in which traditional French cuisine was at the mercy of unscrupulous chemists.

Flaubert draws on this aspect of food's imaginative resonance in his depiction of Homais, *Madame Bovary*'s fraudulent pharmacist who epitomises everything the author detested about the Second Empire. Homais is as obsessed with domestic science as he is with pharmacology. Equally at home in his laboratory and his kitchen, his expertise in modern culinary methods is put to dubious use: 'he talked dazzlingly of aroma, osmazome, juice and gelatine. With his head more full of recipes than his pharmacy was of jars, Homais [...] also knew about all the latest inventions in economical cooking devices, and the art of preserving cheeses and doctoring bad wines.'[58] He has expertise in both jam-making and poisons, and talks of the lethal effects of over-processed boudin.[59] The poisonous falsehoods that he spreads may not emanate directly from his kitchen, but his laboratory provides the arsenic that Emma greedily swallows against the background noise of the Homais

---

57 Du Camp, *Paris, ses organes…*, II, 200–203. Cf. the precautions taken by Homais, when preparing coffee for Dr Larivière after Emma Bovary's death: 'Homais insisted on preparing his coffee at the table, having, moreover, roasted it himself, ground it himself, and blended it himself.' ['Homais tenait à faire son café sur la table, l'ayant, d'ailleurs, torréfié lui-même, porphyrisé lui-même, mixtionné lui-même.'] Flaubert, *Madame Bovary*, *OC* I, 683.

58 '[I]l parlait arome, osmazôme, suc et gélatine d'une façon à éblouir. La tête [...] plus remplie de recettes que sa pharmacie ne l'était de bocaux, Homais [...] connaissait aussi toutes les inventions nouvelles de caléfacteurs économiques, avec l'art de conserver les fromages et soigner les vins malades.' Flaubert, *Madame Bovary*, *OC* I, 607. Prosper Mérimée's *La Chambre bleue* features a head waiter who adds ratafia and eau-de-vie to cheap wine and serves it up as port to an English customer. *Romans et nouvelles* (Paris: Garnier, 1967), II, 505–06.

59 Flaubert, *Madame Bovary*, *OC* I, 683.

family eating in the dining room. In a further falsehood which reinforces the conflation of nourishment and poison, he reports in the local paper that Emma mistook the arsenic for sugar needed for her vanilla cream.[60] With this concatenation of meals, kitchen, laboratory, poison and falsehood, Flaubert underlines Homais's devious nature by drawing on the widespread perception of modern food as suspect and dangerous.

The corollary of such a suspicion of modern, processed food was a desire for simple, natural food, which betokened nostalgia for a simpler and more honest past. Although obviously aimed at city dwellers, a number of recipe books published during this period had titles with rural connotations such as *La Cuisine de la ferme*, or *La Cuisinière de la campagne et de la ville*, which exploited a common regret for a rural way of life that was rapidly vanishing as industrialisation drew more people into towns and cities. Second Empire novels regularly feature characters who are at their happiest when eating a simple meal of bread and cheese, often accompanied by fresh butter and freshly picked radishes, and usually washed down with cider; such meals conjured up images of honesty, virtue and authenticity.[61]

Foodstuffs in fact develop their own special mythology during the Second Empire. If radishes and butter evoke peasant wholesomeness, the truffle symbolises *nouveau-riche* wealth,[62] while the pot-au-feu is regularly deemed to be 'the national soup of the French'.[63] For many writers the pot-au-feu stood for the traditional values of honesty and solidity, which they felt were in danger of being eroded. (Ironically, a volume of Baron Brisse's recipes containing instructions for a *pot-au-feu* which had to be simmered for seven hours carries an advertisement for a one-franc instant stock cube on its

---

60 Flaubert, *Madame Bovary*, *OC* I, 685.
61 See, for example, Champfleury, *Les Aventures de Mlle Mariette, contes de printemps* (Paris: V. Lecou, 1853), 28: 'The lunch seemed the best meal of his life: bread that was better than cake, cutlets that actually tasted of lamb, butter and radishes bursting with fresh, delicate scents. Above all, the salad that Mlle Mariette had prepared made Gérard want to laugh, so joyous did the green herbs and red slices of beetroot seem to him.' ['C'est un déjeuner qui paraît le plus beau repas de la vie. Le pain est meilleur que du gâteau, les côtelettes ont un goût d'agneau, le beurre et les radis sont remplis d'odeurs fraîches et suaves; surtout la salade que mademoiselle Mariette avait accommodée donnait envie de rire à Gérard, tant il voyait de joie et de bonheur dans les herbes vertes et les tranches rouges de betterave.']
62 See for example Act II, scene viii of Eugène Labiche's play, *La Poudre aux yeux* in *Théâtre complet*, vol. 2, 10 vols. (1861; Paris : Calmann-Lévy, 1898), where a socially ambitious bourgeois seeks to impress by serving a dinner which includes truffles in virtually every dish, however inappropriate.
63 '[L]e potage national des Français'. See for example Brisse, *Recettes à l'usage des ménages bourgeois*, 16.

inside cover.) Others, however, uneasy at what they saw as a stifling of individualism in the name of bourgeois conformity, took the pot-au-feu as emblematic of that suppression. Flaubert devoted an entire tableau of his 1863 play, *Le Château des cœurs*, to the veneration that had grown up around the dish. Set in the Kingdom of the Pot-au-Feu, it portrays a gigantic beef stew as the focus of bourgeois worship: the 'thrice holy Pot-au-feu, the emblem of material interests' represents conservatism, conformity, and a refusal to look beyond the status quo. Flaubert's High Priest reminds the grocers, bureaucrats and men of letters who have gathered to worship the stew that 'happiness, both private and public, can be found only in the moderation of the spirit, in unalterable conventions, and in the glug-glug of the pot-au-feu', and when the hero, Paul, commits the ultimate sacrilege of refusing to partake of the broth, he is bound, gagged and imprisoned. This scene of bourgeois tyranny ends with a nightmarish vision of the giant cauldron raining down carrots, turnips and leeks as it rises high into the air, growing ever bigger until it envelops the whole city in darkness.[64] Eccentric though Flaubert's tableau may seem, the image of a world smothered by a gigantic cooking-pot crops up elsewhere in the writing of this period. It reappears, for example, in Baudelaire's poem 'Le Couvercle', where the whole of humanity is represented as simmering inside a huge pot with the dark sky pressing down like a lid.[65] By subverting the central emblem of the nation's culinary tradition, this Second Empire conceit makes its point subtly but powerfully, turning the stew pot into a symbol of oppressive conventionalism and stifled creativity.

But while most Second Empire writers who used food creatively did so in order to add a veiled, sometimes almost subliminally critical subtext to their writing, the exiled Victor Hugo felt free to give food a stronger voice. Like his contemporaries, he appreciated the transformative powers of the literary/culinary relationship, but he was forthright in exploiting their polemical possibilities. 'Reading is nourishment', he declared, likening the growth of literacy to the biblical miracle of feeding the five-thousand, and comparing the multiplying loaves to an outpouring of books that provided humanity with 'the food of enlightenment'. Still couching his objections in gastronomic terms, he complained that the poetry of his time was too sober and safe, and regretted

---

64 '[T]rois fois saint Pot-au-feu, emblème des intérêts matériels'; 'le bonheur particulier, comme le public, ne se trouve que dans la tempérance de l'esprit, l'immutabilité des usages et le glouglou du pot-au-feu.' Flaubert, *Le Château des cœurs*, *OC* II, 345.
65 'Le Ciel! Couvercle noir de la grande marmite / Où bout l'imperceptible et vaste Humanité.' Baudelaire, 'Le Couvercle', *OC*, 92. A similar image occurs in 'Spleen' (Ibid., 89).

the robust writing of old: 'It seems that everything is a question of sparing literature from indigestion. People used to talk about fecundity and power; nowadays they say: herbal tea.'⁶⁶ His own poetry, however, was no *tisane*. Under Hugo's pen the culinary metaphor becomes a powerful weapon for heaping contempt on Napoleon III and for openly challenging the new regime. In *Les Châtiments*, for example, the polemical impact of 'On Loge à la nuit' derives from the forceful image of a blazing hearth decorated with the imperial eagle, over which Napoleon III's closest allies are roasting the 'People-ox' so that it can be consumed by their filthy, bloodstained Emperor.⁶⁷

Elsewhere, however, a more positive relationship is established between the culinary and the creative as writers use food imagery to explore the literary imagination itself, and to reflect on their own creative processes. Nowhere is this more evident than in *Le Capitaine Fracasse*, where that relationship is strikingly deconstructed as Gautier plays with notions of imagination and creativity. A troupe of travelling players first conjures an illusion of food and drink on stage by means of cardboard chickens and wooden bottles; when they finish work they indulge in feasts of 'real' food, whose description in turn generates a vivid image of an imaginary military campaign:

> In the centre of the table the Pedant [...] triumphantly placed a fortress of a pie whose walls were glazed a golden brown, and whose flanks enclosed a whole garrison of pipits and partridges. He surrounded this gastronomic fort with six bottles, as outworks that had to be taken before the fort itself. A smoked ox-tongue and a slice of ham completed the symmetry.⁶⁸

Later, the actors encounter an eccentric innkeeper who recites endless descriptions of the mouth-watering dishes he says he would have offered them if only they had arrived earlier, and his words bring these so temptingly

---

66 'La lecture, c'est la nourrriture'; 'une alimentation de lumière'; 'Il semble que toute la question soit de préserver la littérature des indigestions. Autrefois on disait: fécondité et puissance; aujourd'hui l'on dit: tisane.' Victor Hugo, *William Shakespeare* (1864; Paris: Nelson, 1930), 93–95.

67 '[L]e boeuf Peuple' Victor Hugo, *Les Châtiments*, ed. René Journet (Paris: Gallimard, 1977), 150.

68 'Le Pédant [...] plaça triomphalement au milieu de la table une forteresse de pâté aux murailles blondes et dorées, qui renfermait dans ses flancs une garnison de becquefigues et de perdreaux. Il entoura ce fort gastronomique de six bouteilles, pour ouvrages avancés, qu'il fallait emporter avant de prendre la place. Une langue de boeuf fumée et une tranche de jambon complétèrent la symétrie.' Gautier, *Le Capitaine Fracasse*, 47–48.

to life that the players lick their lips and discuss their reactions to the imaginary food. Yet the fact that this food is a purely linguistic creation is insisted upon. These are not only 'imaginary delicacies' and 'deceptive dishes'; this is food that is purely grammar and tense and vocabulary, as the hungry actors indicate:

> Instead of those defunct dishes whose succulence cannot be doubted, but which are incapable of keeping body and soul together, recite the dishes of the day for us, for the past tense is particularly annoying in culinary matters, and hunger likes to have the present indicative at table. Enough of the past! It is all despair and fasting; at least the future tense allows the stomach to have some pleasant fantasies.

The innkeeper orders his kitchen staff to set to work, but they, too, turn out to be fantasies spun from his words – 'By dint of calling these illusory servants by their names, the *Soleil bleu*'s innkeeper had ended up believing in their existence.'[69] By drawing the reader's attention to the link between literary and culinary creativity in this way, Gautier is able to explore the relationship between reality and fiction: the innkeeper who uses language to conjure up a kitchen full of imaginary staff and succulent delicacies is the metaphorical counterpart of the author who peoples his novel with invented characters and situations, and who serves up a tempting confection to his readers. In this case, the innkeeper's imaginary meals act as a foil to the 'real' banquets that frame the novel – banquets which are of course themselves the products of Gautier's creative imagination and every bit as fictitious as those of the *Soleil bleu*'s innkeeper. Food here is thus a highly conscious means of drawing attention to the creative power of language, while at the same time calling into question any simplistic 'realist' reading that might assume a straightforward relation between an external object and its literary counterpart.[70]

---

69 '[D]élices imaginaires'; 'mets fallacieux'; 'Au lieu de ces plats défunts dont la succulence ne peut être révoquée en doute, mais qui ne sauraient nous sustenter, récitez-nous les plats du jour, car l'aoriste est principalement fâcheux en cuisine, et la faim aime à table l'indicatif présent. Foin du passé! C'est le désespoir et le jeûne; le futur, au moins, permet à l'estomac des rêveries agréables'; 'A force d'appeler par leurs noms ces serviteurs chimériques, l'aubergiste du *Soleil bleu* était parvenu à croire à leur existence.' Gautier, *Le Capitaine Fracasse*, 84–86.
70 Gautier again hints at the relation between food and writing in *Le Roman de la momie*, ed. G. van den Bogaert (1857; Paris: Garnier-Flammarion, 1966), 94–95, where the lengthy description of the dishes served at the Pharaoh's banquet includes references to papyrus and loaves marked with hieroglyphics.

Alert to analogies between the creative and transformative processes of cooking and writing, where the outcome is sampled and savoured on the tongue in each case, writers frequently used gustatory references as a tool for reflecting on their own art.⁷¹ Flaubert appreciated a certain bitter flavour in a book, but had a horror of the sly corruption of syrupy writing – 'sugary literature which is [swallowed] absorbed without distaste and which surreptitiously poisons'.⁷² On the other hand, he loved 'styles that really fill the mouth', as he told Louise Colet.⁷³ The processes of cooking and writing both took raw ingredients and aimed to transform them into something new, stimulating and satisfying, and cookery's transformative capacity was stressed. Both arts sought to surprise; and both worked by bringing together subtly different combinations of words or foods to produce a great range of sensations. It was in precisely these terms that Baudelaire saw his poetry, as he made clear in his projected preface for *Les Fleurs du mal*: 'May poetry be linked to the arts of painting, cooking and cosmetics through its ability to express every sensation of sweetness or bitterness, blessing or horror, by combining such and such a noun with such and such an adjective, similar or contrasting.'⁷⁴ In Baudelaire's view, the poet-chef could conjure up an infinite range of subtleties and surprises by creative combinations of ingredients, and the poet, like the chef, was driven by a desire for the new and unknown.

---

71 In an interview towards the end of his life, Jules Verne talked of the 'secrets of [his] literary cuisine' ['secrets de [sa] cuisine littéraire'.] See Timothy Unwin, 'Eat my words: Verne and Flaubert, or the Anxiety of the Culinary', in John West-Sooby, ed., *Consuming Culture*, 122. Unwin notes (124) that reading and eating become parallel activities in Verne's novels, and says that it is no coincidence that the symbolic centre of Captain Nemo's submarine in *Vingt mille lieues sous les mers* should be the dining room and the library, separated only by a partition, or that Emma Bovary should 'devour' books at her dining table.
72 '[L]es littératures doucereuses que l'on [avale] absorbe sans répugnance et qui empoisonnent sans scandale.' Flaubert, unpublished notes to M. Sénard, Feb. 1857, transcribed in *Bulletin Flaubert*-3 / 10 May 2001, 2.
73 '[L]es styles où l'on en a plein la bouche'. Flaubert, *Corr.* II, 247 (17.2.1853). Flaubert advised Mlle. Leroyer de Chantepie that the only way to make life bearable was to plunge into literature as if it were a perpetual orgy, for 'the wine of Art causes a long intoxication, and is inexhaustible'. [le vin de l'Art cause une longue ivresse et il est inépuisable'.] *Corr.* II, 832 (4.9.1858). The title of Charles Monselet's passionate work on gastronomy, *La Cuisinière poétique*, is further evidence of the common analogy between writing and cooking.
74 'Que la poésie se rattache aux arts de la peinture, de la cuisine et du cosmétique par la possibilité d'exprimer toute sensation de suavité ou d'amertume, de béatitude ou d'horreur, par l'accouplement de tel substantif avec tel adjectif, analogue ou contraire.' Baudelaire, 'Projets de préface', *OC*, 128.

As one commentator explained, 'we need dishes that have neither the name nor the look of what we are eating; and if there is no initial surprise for the eye, our appetite will not be stimulated enough. So our chefs go to great lengths to alter the appearance of everything they prepare.'[75]

That desire – encapsulated in the poet's desperate cry at the end of *Les Fleurs du mal*: 'We want [...] to plunge [...] To the depths of the Unknown to find something *new*!'[76] – finds its culinary counterpart in the urgent pleas of writers such as Monselet to venture into uncharted eating territory. Demands for gastronomic innovation betokened broader non-conformity: only by pushing back the boundaries of conventional foodstuffs would it be possible to escape the suffocating pot-au-feu mentality. Why not try woodlice, spiders, water-flea eggs, toad, smoked white ants, weevil larvae, or 'macaroni with cockchafer grubs', urged Clément Caraguel.[77] The search for gastronomic novelty went hand-in-hand with linguistic invention as writers readily acknowledged the close relationship between culinary and literary creativity. In *La Cuisinière poétique* Charles Monselet emphasised the connection: 'I have changed poems, or rather I have mastered yet another rhythm. In me, the wonders of nutrition now have a new bard [...] May your dinner be a poem.'[78] Following his advice to the letter, he produced a series of food poems with titles such as 'The Chitterling Sausage' or 'The Trout'.[79]

Théophile Gautier took the link between culinary and literary inventiveness even further when he accepted a dinner invitation by composing, in the innovative form of a 13-line octosyllabic monorhyme poem (where each line ends in '-ton'), a gloriously varied list of the dishes he might be served:

Whether it be chicken or duckling,
Partridge with cabbage or boiled beef with onions,
A pâté of cold veal or tuna,
Swallows' nests from Canton,

---

75 '[I]l faut des plats qui n'aient ni le nom ni l'apparence de ce qu'on mange; et si l'oeil n'est pas surpris d'abord, l'appétit n'est plus suffisamment excité. Nos cuisiniers s'exercent donc à faire changer de figure à tout ce qu'ils apprêtent.' See the *Grand dictionnaire universel*, 'Cuisine' entry.
76 'Nous voulons [...] / Plonger [...] / Au fond de l'Inconnu pour trouver du *nouveau!*' Baudelaire, *OC*, 124.
77 '[M]acaroni aux larves de hannetons'. Clément Caraguel, 'La Cuisine fantaisiste', in Monselet, *La Cuisinière poétique*, 190–194.
78 'J'ai changé de poésie, ou plutôt j'ai conquis un rhythme de plus. Les splendeurs de la nutrition ont désormais en moi un nouveau barde [...] Que votre dîner soit un poëme.' Charles Monselet, 'Lettres à Emilie sur la gastronomie', *La Cuisinière poétique*, 15–16.
79 'L'Andouillette'; 'La Truite'.

Or a clove of garlic on a croûton,
Pheasant or minced mutton,
Brown bread, brioche or pannetone,
Argenteuil or Brame-Mouton,
Cider or Burton's Pale Ale,
At Lucullus's or Cato's house,
I shall eat till I am full to the gills,
Swallowing everything like a glutton,
And leaving not a single crumb.[80]

Even writers coming from a quite different standpoint used the literary-culinary analogy to express their views. Destaminil, a reactionary who deplored innovation in literature as much as in cuisine, expressed his distaste for what he saw as the decadence of the age by denouncing one in terms of the other. 'We have done the same thing with our cuisine [...] as with our literature', he complained:

> Under the pretext of renewing or innovating, we have thrown ourselves headlong into a hotchpotch stew; every subject disappears under a mass of garnishes, nothing is full-flavoured, distinct, simple or perfectly clear; we are sinking into chaos; we pile on obscurities in an attempt at originality.[81]

On a purely linguistic level, that craving for originality manifests itself in the elaborate names given to dishes. Despite Monselet and Caraguel's complaints about conformism, the period was distinguished by the range of innovative ways of preparing and presenting basic foodstuffs, which in turn necessitated inventiveness in naming the new confections. Menus became

---

80 'Que ce soit poule ou canneton, / Perdrix aux choux ou miroton, / Pâté de veau froid ou de thon, / Nids d'hirondelles de Canton, / Ou gousse d'ail sur croûton, / Faisan ou hachis de mouton, / Pain bis, brioche ou panaton, / Argenteuil ou Brame-Mouton, / Cidre ou pale-ale de Burton, / Chez Lucullus ou chez Caton, / Je m'emplirai jusqu'au menton, /Avalant tout comme un glouton, / Sans laisser un seul rogaton.' 'Théophile Gautier à Charles Garnier', first published in *L'Univers illustré* of 18.1.1868.
81 'En cuisine, nous avons fait [...] comme en littérature. Sous le prétexte de la renaissance ou de l'innovation, nous nous sommes jetés à corps perdu dans le salmigondis; tout sujet disparaît sous la profusion des fioritures, il n'y a rien de corsé, de net, de simple et de parfaitement clair; on s'enfonce dans le chaos; on s'enveloppe d'obscurités pour être original.' Destaminil, *Le Cuisinier français perfectionné*, vii.

increasingly creative, often using historical and geographical metaphors to mythologise and disseminate new culinary conceits. Drawing up a menu was seen as the theoretical side of preparing a meal, and was recognised as a particularly difficult task because of the thousands of names recently invented for different soups, entrées, roasts and desserts.[82] The literary skills of a poet were needed to translate dishes into language, and this literary input was acknowledged in the name – *feuilletons* – given to the long, handwritten supplements added to the regular menu.[83] The very names given to dishes show evidence of the new relationship between writing and cooking: the designation 'epigrams of lamb', coined in 1858, contrived to associate an uninspiring dish of braised, breaded lamb cutlets with the idea of linguistic wit, and quickly passed into common usage. New appelations were devised to infuse the central (and often banal) ingredient with a further, mythical, often aspirational meaning, and like Chirriguirri in *Le Capitaine Fracasse*, a menu-writer had to be able 'to show insipid dishes off to best advantage by the spice of his words'.[84]

Flaubert shows the transformative but dishonest power of such names when he describes Emma Bovary charming her husband with 'the extraordinary name of a very simple dish', which Charles eats with pleasure even though it is badly cooked.[85] And in *L'Éducation sentimentale* he pokes fun at the linguistic excesses produced by the naming of dishes: 'The Maréchale began to run through the menu, stopping at strange names. What if we had, let's see, a turban of rabbit in the style of Richelieu, and a d'Orleans-style pudding?'[86] Thanks to a deftly applied word or two the everyday dish, the rabbit, is implicitly transformed into something oriental and exotic ('turban'), grand and powerful ('Richelieu'), while the humble pudding gains a royal attribution. Exploiting the linguistic inventiveness of the menu to the full, Flaubert playfully incorporates many of its features into his writing. In the same novel, for example, he depicts not only the profusion of dishes at Arnoux's dinner-party (where ten varieties of mustard are on offer), but also the strange, tongue-teasing names of the foods and wines which suggest exotic flavours and resound with their own musicality: 'He ate daspachio,

---

82 See *Grand dictionnaire universel*, 'Repas' entry.
83 Monselet, *La Cuisinière poétique*, 20.
84 '[A] faire valoir les mets insipides par les épices de sa parole.' Gautier, *Le Capitaine Fracasse*, 86.
85 '[L]e nom extraordinaire d'un mets bien simple.' Flaubert, *Madame Bovary*, OC I, 595.
86 'La Maréchale se mit à parcourir la carte en s'arrêtant aux noms bizarres. Si nous mangions, je suppose, un turban de lapin à la Richelieu et un pudding à la d'Orléans?' Flaubert, *L'Éducation sentimentale*, OC II, 85.

curry, ginger, Corsican blackbirds and Roman lasagne; he drank amazing wines, Lip-fraoli and Tokay.'[87]

Pleasure, revulsion, sensuality, pretentiousness – these were only a few of the effects that writers realised could be translated from food into fiction. The 'golden age for eating' thus spilled over into the literary domain as the novelist's craft was increasingly seen in terms of a master-chef choosing his ingredients and skilfully combining them to produce an end product that would satisfy the tongue and the senses. Recognising the new possibilities for expression that culinary imagery opened up for them, Second Empire writers exploited it to the full, for in it they had found a vehicle not only for exploring aspects of contemporary life and for quietly commenting on the changing world around them, but for reflecting on their own literary practice.

---

87 'Il mangea du daspachio, du cari, du gingembre, des merles de Corse, des lasagnes romaines; il but des vins extraordinaires, du lip-fraoli et du tokay.' Flaubert, *L'Éducation sentimentale*, *OC* II, 25. Flaubert frequently introduces menu-like descriptions into his novels – see, for example, his account of the food displayed at Emma Bovary's wedding, or the endless lists of exotic foods at the mercenaries' banquet in *Salammbô*. Cf. Eugène Labiche's play *La Poudre aux yeux* where an entire scene is given over to the composition of a preposterously pretentious dinner menu full of incongruously named dishes such as 'Rhine carp in the Chambord style' ['La carpe du Rhin à la Chambord']; the host insists that his chef add truffles to every course, and that he end the meal by serving his particular favourite – a nameless mint-flavoured dish which turns out to be the contents of a fingerbowl. *La Poudre aux yeux*, Act II, scene viii.

Chapter Five
PHOTOGRAPHY

Like the French railway system, photography had existed for over a decade before Napoleon III came to power. The French Academy of Science had been made aware of a completely new reprographic method – the daguerreotype – in 1839, but during the decade that followed only the most affluent could afford to own a daguerreotype or calotype. The early 1850s, however, saw a major turning point with the introduction of new, cheaper and faster processes which opened up photography to commercialisation on a vast scale, removing the medium from the exclusive preserve of scientists and specialists and ensuring its popularity. One of the period's most famous commercial photographers, André-Adolphe Disdéri, set up his hugely successful photographic studio in the centre of Paris in 1852, and over the following years the number of photographers and photographic societies expanded rapidly.[1] Demand for glass, paper and chemicals soared, egg-production had to be increased to meet the need for albumen, and it has been estimated that by 1860 33,000 people were making a living from photography in Paris alone.[2] Twenty years after the initial announcement of the discovery, photography had grown into a major industry and the Second Empire became the first period in French history to leave a photographic record of itself.

By the end of the Second Empire, photography had also left its own distinctive trace on the writing of the period. In the most obvious sense this is evident from the emergence of specialist journals dedicated to photography, in

---

1 The first French photographic society, La Société Héliographique, was founded in 1851, and in the same year the Bibliothèque Nationale in Paris established the obligatory legal deposit of photographs. See Michel Frizot, 'The Transparent Medium: From Industrial Product to the Salon des Beaux-Arts', in Michel Frizot, ed., *A New History of Photography* (Köln: Könemann, 1998), 93. The Société Héliographique (one of whose founding members was the painter Delacroix) was renamed the Société Française de Photographie in 1855.

2 Jean Sagne, 'All Kinds of Portraits. The Photographer's Studio', in Frizot, *A New History of Photography*, 105.

which experimenters and practitioners recorded and published the technical details of their processes, using a new specialised vocabulary of plates, exposures, developers, poses, lighting, screens and lenses which gradually filtered into common usage. But critics also sought ways to describe and evaluate the aesthetic qualities of the new medium, and in turn these aesthetic qualities subtly influenced their writing in many cases. Finally, writers of all kinds looked to the new medium of photography as a rich metaphor through which to articulate their ideas.

One of the exciting consequences of the new invention was that it offered a fresh way of seeing and representing the world. The public was fascinated by photographic images that allowed them to view far-off places or famous figures for the first time, but they were equally intrigued by images of the known and familiar which suddenly seemed strangely different. The renowned scientist Alexander von Humboldt, a member of the commission charged with assessing the importance of Daguerre's original discovery, had written to a fellow-scientist of his excitement on seeing that an early image had even captured a broken windowpane mended with gummed paper,[3] and much of that initial excitement at seeing familiar, trivial details reproduced in monochrome still remained. People marvelled at the detailed depiction of cracked plasterwork, drainpipes, roof-tiles and peeling advertising hoardings in early photographs of Paris streets. Portraits, too, seemed unnervingly accurate yet strangely unfamiliar – and not only because the sitter had to remain motionless, often clamped into position, for the long exposure-times needed in the early days of photography. Despite the photographic image's ability to reproduce its subject in minute detail, that elusive quality of familiarity-yet-strangeness focused attention, as we shall see, on the problematic nature of representation in all its forms.

Photography roused passionate feelings of hostility or enthusiasm and generated vigorous and sometimes acrimonious debate. As is evident from the terms in which it was couched, however, there was more at stake: the debate served as a catalyst for anxieties about wider ideological issues. The new medium was ripe for appropriation as a symbol, for being free of historical associations it allowed all kinds of values to be projected on to it. As Mary Warner Marien observes, 'photographic discourse provided a new way to explain transitions and to articulate anxiety about personal change as well as societal directions'.[4]

---

3 Michel Frizot, '1839–40: Photographic Developments', in Frizot, ed., *A New History of Photography*, 28.

4 Mary Warner Marien, *Photography and its Critics: A Cultural History, 1839–1900* (Cambridge: Cambridge University Press, 1997), xiv–xv.

One strand that runs particularly clearly through much of the Second Empire's photographic discourse emphasises the medium's role as a stabilising force. By recording images of the present and preserving them for the future, photography appeared to offer to fix and immobilise the external world, to protect it from further change. In an age of revolution and instability, photography was seen as providing continuity and permanence. One of its most eminent exponents, Ernest Lacan, stressed this when he described portrait photographers as being far more than simple camera-operators: the portraitist, he said, 'becomes the indispensable intermediary between the great figures of history and subsequent generations who will want to know what they looked like as well as what their names were'.[5] From this perspective, photography was perceived as mediating between past and future, and its very existence was associated with a guarantee of continuity. Throughout the 1850s the government-sponsored *Missions Héliographiques* produced a photographic record of France's ancient monuments that encapsulated not only their past grandeur but also the damage they had suffered at the hands of heretics and vandals. To photograph these monuments was in a sense to preserve them from further disintegration – to render them immortal, as Lacan put it. In terms that evoked France's recent civil disruptions, he wrote in 1856 that the photographic image resists 'time, revolutions and natural disasters that can destroy them to the last stone: from now on they live in the albums of our photographers'.[6]

Much Second Empire writing about photography emphasised the newness of the medium and identified it with hope for what lay ahead. Hippolyte Castille commented that its modernity and incalculable potential

---

5 '[D]evient l'intermédiare indispensable entre les grandes figures qui appartiennent à l'histoire, et la postérité qui voudra connaître leurs traits comme elle connaîtra leurs noms.' Ernest Lacan, *Esquisses photographiques à propos de l'Exposition universelle et de la guerre d'Orient* (Paris: Grassart et Gaudin, 1856), 215. Lacan, who launched the influential photographic journal, *La Lumière*, also wrote most of the articles on photography that appeared in the *Moniteur universel* and the *Journal officiel*.

6 '[L]e temps, les révolutions, les convulsions terrestres [qui] peuvent en détruire jusqu'à la dernière pierre: ils vivent désormais dans l'album de nos photographes.' Ernest Lacan, *Esquisses photographiques*, 29. Cf. the minutes of a photographic society meeting in August 1856: 'One of the most interesting applications of photography is the faithful and incontrovertible reproduction of historic or artistic monuments and documents, which time and revolutions always end up destroying.' ['Une des applications les plus intéressantes de la photographie est la reproduction fidèle et incontestable des monuments et documents historiques ou artistiques que le temps et les révolutions finissent toujours par détruire.'] *Bulletin de la société française de photographie*, August 1856, 214–229, cit. in André Rouillé, *La Photographie en France; textes et controverses: une anthologie 1816–1871* (Paris: Macula, 1989), 202.

exemplified change and pointed towards a future that was not yet clear: 'Like the electric telegraph, steam power and air travel – which is still undiscovered – [photography] is one of the agents of the great society of the future, whose approach we can all sense with a tightening of the chest, but whose complicated outline cannot be distinguished by even the most careful observer.'[7] Just as the universal exhibitions were described as 'new and unprecedented', as if they had sprung from nowhere, so photography's antecedents were denied. Commentators rarely acknowledged its precursors in the camera obscura or in the series of eighteenth-century drawing machines that used a combination of light and optics to produce an image.[8] Instead, they commonly wrote of photography as marking a profound rupture with the image-making of the past. It seemed to have come from nowhere; its arrival was frequently described as magical and mysterious, and commentators resorted to images of the supernatural to account for its sudden emergence.[9] Yet at the same time it was associated with nature and truth. Despite its dependence on chemicals and technology, the photographic image, as writers often pointed out, was produced by the sun itself, and the terms *héliographie* and *héliographique* reinforced this notion. Victor Hugo sent Flaubert a self-portrait with a note saying that his son Charles had taken it 'in collaboration with the sun'. This, for Hugo, was a guarantee of its accuracy, for how could the sun be wrong?: 'It must be a good likeness. *Solem quis dicere falsum audeat?*'[10] Photography thus lent itself to a range of interpretations. Seen as linking past and present yet also as the embodiment of the new, viewed as a natural phenomenon yet simultaneously representing

---

7 'Comme le télégraphe électrique, la vapeur et la navigation aérienne, non encore découverte, [la photographie] est un des agents de cette grande société future, dont chacun de nous peut sentir l'approche dans les oppressions de son cœur, mais dont l'ébauche complexe échappe aux regards les plus attentifs.' Hippolyte Castille, *Les Hommes et les mœurs en France sous le règne de Louis-Philippe* (Paris: Paul Henneton et cie, 1853), 337–8.

8 See Michel Frizot, 'Light machines', in Frizot, ed., *A New History of Photography*, 15–21.

9 There were many tales about a mysterious 'Stranger' or a mythical 'Professor Charles' having intervened at the process's inception. See Marien, *Photography and its Critics*, 6, 47–52.

10 '[E]n collaboration avec le soleil'; 'Il doit être ressemblant. *Solem quis dicere falsum audeat?*' Flaubert, *Corr.* II,1146, note 1. Intriguingly, in the same letter Hugo makes an indirect link between the sun and Bonapartism. The poet Lamartine, who had initially been hostile to photography on the grounds that it was merely a mechanical plagiarism of nature ('le plagiat de la nature par l'optique'), later changed his mind and used the same formulation as Hugo to write enthusiastically that 'it's a solar phenomenon in which the artist collaborates with the sun'. ['c'est un phénomène solaire où l'artiste collabore avec le soleil'] Cit. in Rouillé, *La Photographie en France*, 249–250.

technological progress, it could be identified with all the familiar attributes that proponents of the Second Empire were eager, as we have seen, to associate with the new regime.

Moreover, photography was also deemed capable of imposing its own order, presenting a differently perceived, much greater and more beautiful world than had seemed to exist before. 'How much beauty, and how many hitherto unnoticed marvels have been revealed by these splendid reproductions of cathedrals', was Ernest Lacan's reaction to a series of architectural images.[11] Wonderful things never before recognised could now be seen clearly. In the photographic discourse of the period this newly expanded vision was regularly associated with liberty: photography was seen as freeing the viewer from physical constraints and offering unprecedented access to the entire world. In Henri de Lacretelle's words, photography endowed mankind with a freedom and mobility formerly enjoyed only by birds, and Louis de Cormenin memorably celebrated photography's power to liberate man and enable him to explore the world with ease: 'man, who until now has been confined to a small space and unable to move, will be able to discover the form of his planet without exhausting himself [...] heliography, the preserve of a few intrepid souls, will go round the world for us and bring us back the universe in a portfolio, without our having to stir from our armchairs.'[12] (This attitude is echoed by the stay-at-homes in Baudelaire's poem 'Le Voyage', who beg the travellers to 'Show us your precious albums of rich memories [...] We want to travel without sails or steam!')[13] But Cormenin went further in his undeclared assimilation of photography to the ethos of the Second Empire. He not only associated it with a spirit of liberation and placed it firmly in a new technological age of rail, steam and electricity, but ascribed to it a colonising power that could dominate the Orient and bear

---

11 'Que de beautés, que de merveilles inaperçues jusque-là ont révélé les splendides reproductions des cathédrales.' Lacan, *Esquisses photographiques*, 30.
12 '[L]'homme, jusque-là confiné immobile dans un petit espace, pourra sans fatigue connaître la configuration de sa planète [...] l'héliographie, confiée à quelques intrépides, fera pour nous le tour du monde, et nous rapportera l'univers en portefeuille, sans que nous quittions notre fauteuil.' A propos de *Egypte, Nubie, Palestine et Syrie*, de Maxime Du Camp', *La Lumière* (12.6.1852), 98; cit. in Rouillé, *La Photographie en France*, 124. See also Louis Figuier, *La Photographie au salon de 1859* (Paris: Hachette, 1860), 35–36. In a similar vein, Philippe Burty noted in 1859 that the products of photography now covered the whole world. 'Exposition de la Société française de Photographie', *Gazette des Beaux-Arts*, May 1859, 209–21; cit. in *L'Art en France sous le Second Empire* (Paris: Editions de la réunion des musées nationaux, 1979), 461.
13 'Montrez-nous les écrins de vos riches mémoires [...] Nous voulons voyager sans vapeur et sans voile!' Baudelaire, *OC*, 123.

its bounty back to France in triumph.[14] Thus the new photographic order was framed by many commentators in terms that presented it as a force at once transformative yet stabilising, liberating yet dominating, a force that stretched far beyond the confines of France – like the Second Empire itself.

Much photographic discourse during this period links photography to a democratic and egalitarian order. As the number of photographic magazines and manuals increased, introducing new techniques to a wider public, so the number of practitioners grew. Writers repeatedly stressed that the new photographic societies brought people from different classes together on an equal footing; anyone could become a photographer.[15] As Ernest Lacan noted, 'Physically, the photographer looks like everyone else.'[16] Moreover, anyone could be photographed: the cheap and phenomenally successful small *carte de visite* format penetrated every level of society and blurred social distinctions.[17] To some writers this was a wonderful symbol of egalitarianism. Expressing strong approval of the way it broke down social barriers, they emphasised its capacity to educate and improve the masses. Among those who argued that photography produced social benefits by bringing about an improvement in popular taste were the eminent photographers Gustave Le Gray, Léon de Laborde and Francis Wey,[18] while an article in *La Revue photographique* of 1862 claimed that photography brought 'enlightenment to the masses in order to elevate and improve them'.[19]

To its opponents, however, it reeked of vulgarisation and decline. Among its harshest critics was Baudelaire, who commented in his famous article on photography that 'some democratic writer must have seen it as a cheap way of spreading distaste for history and painting among the masses'. According to Baudelaire, there was a natural alliance between photography and 'the stupidity of the masses', and he railed against it. For him, photography's

---

14 'A Propos de *Egypte, Nubie, Palestine et Syrie*, de Maxime Du Camp', *La Lumière* (12.6.52), 98; cit. in Rouillé, *La Photographie en France*, 124.
15 *L'Art en France sous le Second Empire*, 463, refers to photographic societies that brought together bohemian artists, socialists, members of the Institut de France, railway administrators, the sons of glovemakers and Spanish bankers, local archivists, Jockey-Club members, ichthyologists, authors of light comedies or books on electricity, lithographers, architects, sculpture restorers, porcelain painters and aeronauts.
16 'Au physique, le photographe ressemble à tout le monde.' Ernest Lacan, 'Le Photographe, esquisse physiologique: du photographe proprement dit', *La Lumière*, no. 2 (8.1.53), 7–8; cit. in Rouillé, *La Photographie en France*, 161.
17 Baudelaire, 'Salon de 1859: 2. Le Public contemporain et la photographie', *OC*, 395.
18 For Laborde, see Rouillé, *La Photographie en France*, 213ff.; for Le Gray and Wey see Marien, *Photography and its Critics*, 68.
19 '[L]es lumières dans les masses pour les élever et les rendre meilleures.' Cit. in Rouillé, *La Photographie en France*, 182.

popularity was evidence of the stupidity and superficiality of the common people, whom he describes as rushing forward like Narcissus to gaze at their own trivial image on the metal plate of the daguerreotype. The effect of photography was to coarsen taste and debase artistic discrimination, he argued. 'May we suppose', he asked, 'that a people whose eyes become accustomed to considering the products of a material science as things of beauty, do not, after a certain time, greatly diminish their ability to judge and feel that which is most ethereal and intangible?'[20] Baudelaire was not alone in objecting to photography's perceived tendency to vulgarise. In more down-to-earth mode, the writer and society illustrator Marcelin complained in a satirical article entitled 'Down with Photography!!!', that it was impossible to distinguish between members of different social classes by looking at their photographic images: captured by the lens, Delacroix could be mistaken for a ticket clerk and Ingres resembled a constipated grocer.[21]

Many writers also objected to what they regarded as the detached and mechanical nature of photography. Lamartine famously called it a plagiarism of nature by optics,[22] and for many others the mechanised accuracy of its reproduction resulted in images that were too exact and intractable. In particular the daguerreotype, with its hard, polished surface and its clarity of detail, was associated with the cruelty of uncompromising truth. Baudelaire wrote of the 'cruel and surprising charm of the daguerreotype';[23] the Goncourt brothers coined the expression 'to have the conscience of a daguerreotype' to convey the idea of being ruthlessly and painfully truthful;[24] and despite Nerval's active interest in the process during the early days of photography, he later described the daguerreotype as an 'instrument of patience aimed at tired minds, which destroys all illusions as it holds up the mirror of truth to each of its subjects'.[25]

---

20 'Quelque écrivain démocrate a dû voir là le moyen, à bon marché, de répandre dans le peuple le dégoût de l'histoire et de la peinture'; 'la sottise de la multitude'; 'Est-il permis de supposer qu'un peuple dont les yeux s'accoutument à considérer les résultats d'une science matérielle comme les produits du beau n'a pas singulièrement, au bout d'un certain temps, diminué la faculté de juger et de sentir ce qu'il y a de plus éthéré et de plus immatériel?' Baudelaire, 'Salon de 1859: 2. Le Public contemporain et la photographie', in *OC*, 395–6.
21 'A bas la photographie!!!' See Jean Sagne, 'All kinds of Portraits. The Photographer's studio', in Michel Frizot, ed., *A New History of Photography*, 111.
22 Cit. in Rouillé, *La Photographie en France*, 249–250.
23 '[L]e charme cruel et surprenant du daguerréotype'. Baudelaire, *OC*, 384.
24 '[A]voir la conscience du daguerréotype'. Edmond and Jules de Goncourt, *Renée Mauperin* (1864; Paris: Charpentier, 1876), 107.
25 '[U]n instrument de patience qui s'adresse aux esprits fatigués, et qui, détruisant les illusions, oppose à chaque figure le miroir de la vérité.' Nerval, *Les Nuits d'octobre*, *OC*, III, 322.

If for Nerval the daguerreotype was 'aimed at tired minds', other writers attributed that lack of vitality to the energy-sapping nature of the photographic process itself. In their *Journal* the Goncourt brothers record a visit they made in 1856 to the cluttered Paris studio of the photographer Thomson, where they were overwhelmed by a feeling that photographs drained all life from the subject: 'There is a kind of death in those embalmed likenesses; it is a funereal portrait of life, with all those different faces piled up and tidied away in boxes like coffins, all that flesh and those dead eyes, colourless and featureless.'[26] Champfleury dramatises that life-sapping quality in *La Légende du daguerréotype* (1863), where he exploits the medium both to question its ability to capture a genuine likeness and to convey the idea of contemporary man as feeble and enervated. Playing on the myth of the mysterious, supernatural aspects of photography, he tells how a barber's assistant sets himself up in Paris as a daguerreotypist and tries repeatedly to take a likeness of a M. Balandard, only to find that after fifty attempts, all that is left of the sitter is his voice; each successive shot has gradually worn away his body.[27]

---

26 'Il y a comme une mort dans cet embaumement de la ressemblance; un funèbre portrait de la vie, toutes ces faces diverses amoncelées et rangées dans des boîtes comme dans une bière, toutes ces chairs et ces yeux morts, sans couleur, ni physionomie.' Goncourt, *Journal*, I (21.12.1856), 224. In their fiction, the Goncourt brothers use references to daguerreotypes to contrast the medium's crudeness and lack of vitality with what they perceive as the colourful, life-enhancing, and essentially truthful attributes of real art: e. g. 'At a time when the theatre is no more than a moderately successful daguerreotype, let us return to the real theatre of imagination and the improbable, to poetry, to something that laughs and sways…' ['Dans un temps où le théâtre n'est plus qu'un daguerréotype plus ou moins réussi, remonter au vrai théâtre, au théâtre d'imagination, d'invraisemblance, à la poésie, à cette chose qui rit, se balance…'] Edmond and Jules de Goncourt, *Charles Demailly* (1860; Paris, Charpentier, 1876), 296. Cf. their comment about the photograph's inability to capture the changing complexity of a person's appearance: 'Your features do not look like the real you. Look at photographs of a man: no two are alike.' ['Vos traits ne vous ressemblent pas. Voyez les photographies d'un homme: pas une n'est pareille à l'autre.'] Goncourt, *Journal*, I (11.1.1863), 920.

27 See Jane M. Rabb, ed., *Literature and Photography: Interactions, 1840–1990* (Albuquerque: University of New Mexico Press, 1995), xxxix. In *Les Aventures de Mademoiselle Mariette*, Champfleury unsettles the daguerreotype's supposed ability to capture a true likeness. Wondering why a pretty girl has shown no interest in him, Gérard checks his appearance by scrutinising his reflection in the polished surface of a daguerreotype. The reader learns nothing about the daguerreotype image, which is literally overlooked by Gérard who sees only his own tight-lipped reflection. He wants to see himself as the girl has seen him – just as sitters wanted to see themselves as the camera captured them.

Photography thus became a touchstone for a range of attitudes and values. To its supporters, it symbolised social as well as technological progress. It educated the public by opening up a new vision of the world, viewed from unfamiliar vantage points and remote places, and accessible to all. It preserved the best aspects of the past for posterity, and it elevated public taste by bringing art to the masses. Identified with a new age of stability, democracy and egalitarianism, its 'natural' status enhanced by its solar origins, and associated with a heavily-freighted lexis of truth, freedom, light, vision and equality, to its followers photography was a mirror of all that was best about contemporary France. To its detractors, however, it represented unthinking conformity, artistic mediocrity, cliché; it was a purely mechanical process producing images that were soulless and cruel. Recording indiscriminately whatever came before the lens, it lacked colour and artistic sensibility and, crucially, it lowered and corrupted public taste. Vulgar and decadent, a shoddy substitute for the truth, to its critics it was, in short, a potent symbol of cultural decline.

But the debate also had another focus: the new medium served as a catalyst for conflicting views on the nature of artistic representation. Flaubert's *Dictionnaire des idées reçues* would later neatly caricature one of the commonly held positions of that time: 'DAGUERREOTYPE. Will replace painting.'[28] Others argued that, on the contrary, the photographer's cold, mechanical process could not begin to rival the subtlety and discrimination of a painter's artistry. Photographers, however, retorted that they, too, selected and harmonised their composition – that they, too, were artists – and to emphasise their affinity with *les artistes* several referred to themselves not as *photographes* but *photographistes*. Far from producing a soulless and indiscriminate record, they argued, they worked with the light to produce the desired effect, and to create a better likeness than most painters could hope to achieve. The pioneering photographer Blanquart-Evrard (who in 1851 introduced a new method for producing positive prints that allowed 200–300 prints per day to be made from a single negative), insisted that photographer and painter approached their subjects in the same fashion:

> In order to make a portrait, the 'photographist' must proceed like a painter. He has to have a strong sense of his model, and must vary the pose and the nature and colour of the model's clothing according to the

---

28 'DAGUERRÉOTYPE. Remplacera la peinture.' Flaubert, *Dictionnaire des idées reçues*, *OC* II, 306.

latter's character; and once he has fixed the composition of the picture in his mind, he must find appropriate ways of executing it.[29]

Reviewing the photographs exhibited at the Salon of 1859, Louis Figuier pointed out that photography was merely another process like drawing or engraving, and that it was sentiment, not process, that made an artist.[30] Théophile Gautier, who had tried taking daguerreotypes as early as 1840 on his journey to Spain with the photographer Eugène Piot, agreed that there was much more to photography than a mechanical reflection of what lay in front of the lens. For him it was an art – selective, creative and interpretative:

> Despite the bourgeois sentiments attributed to it, photography is turning into an artist and interprets the canvas exposed to its lens in its own way. It knows how to sacrifice unnecessary or over-intrusive details appropriately by casting them in shade, and how to save its brightest light for the face that interests it. It erases, blurs, flattens and accentuates with an artistry of which no one imagines it capable.[31]

Resistance to the idea of photography as 'art' remained strong, however. At the *exposition universelle* in 1855 the photography exhibit was relegated to the Industry pavilion to keep it firmly separate from the Salon where painting, sculpture and engravings were shown, and it was not until after a series of court cases in the early 1860s that the question of photography's

---

29 'Pour faire un portrait, le photographiste doit procéder comme le peintre. Il doit se pénétrer de son modèle, et varier, suivant le caractère de celui-là, la pose, la nature et la couleur des vêtements, et après avoir arrêté dans son esprit la composition du tableau, disposer ses moyens d'exécution en conséquence.' 'Des portraits', *Traité de photographie sur papier* (1851), 23–25. Cit. in Rouillé, *La Photographie en France*, 103. The same year, Francis Wey, editor of *La Lumière*, had questioned the concept of a 'true likeness': 'likeness is merely an interpretation subject to the tastes, fashions and prejudices of a period, and to the preconceived ideas of those who admire the artist's work.' ['la ressemblance n'est qu'une interprétation subordonnée au goût, à la mode, aux préjugés d'une époque, et aux idées préconçues des appréciateurs de l'oeuvre de l'artiste.'] 'Théorie du portrait, I' in *La Lumière*, 27.4.1851, 46–47, cit. in Rouillé, *La Photographie en France*. 117–120.)
30 Figuier, *La Photographie au salon de 1859*, 4.
31 'La photographie, malgré les sentiments bourgeois qu'on lui suppose, se fait artiste, et interprète à sa manière la toile exposée devant son objectif. Elle sait sacrifier à propos sous une teinte sombre tous les détails inutiles ou trop voyants, et réserver sa plus vive lumière pour la figure qui l'intéresse. Elle efface, elle estompe, elle assourdit et met en relief avec un art dont on ne la juge pas capable.' Cit. in Rouillé, *La Photographie en France*, 241.

status was finally decided. In a famous action brought by the photographers Mayer and Pierson against their competitors Bethéder and Schwabbe, the court ruled that photography should be officially recognised as an art form.[32]

Although this artistic dispute was conducted in terms of photography versus painting, it closely echoed contemporary literary controversies. The issues raised by the photographic debate were central to literary creativity, for the aims of Realist writers – their focus on detail, their widened range of subject matter, the desire to 'faire vrai', the impersonality of their narratives – coincided with the attributes of photography. Engaging with the photographic debate allowed writers to reflect further on aesthetic matters and on changing literary practices.

Many writers had taken a keen practical interest in photography almost from its inception. As we have seen, Gautier had carried daguerreotype equipment throughout his visit to Spain in 1840, and the images he brought back were among the earliest to be taken there.[33] Nerval had decided to equip himself with 'things to do with the daguerreotype' before setting off for Egypt in 1843, and stopped off at Malta to buy essential materials.[34] Maxime Du Camp took lessons in calotype photography from Gustave Le Gray in order to prepare himself for his photographic mission to Egypt with Flaubert in 1849–50, and was able to bring back the first photographs of the pyramids and the temple of Abu Simbel. Flaubert took an appreciative interest in Du Camp's photographic attempts, as his letters home from Egypt show; on at least one occasion he helped to take the photographs himself, writing to his mother that the experience had left his fingers stained

---

32 See Gisèle Freund, *Photographie et société* (Paris: Seuil, 1974), 84 and note 110. Cf. Louis Figuier, *La Photographie au salon de 1859*, i: 'In 1859, photography was allowed to be near the fine-arts exhibition for the first time, but not to become part of it.' ['En 1859, la photographie a été admise, pour la première fois, à se rapprocher de l'exposition des beaux-arts, sinon à s'y réunir.']
33 Rabb, ed., *Literature and Photography*, xxxvii.
34 '[D]es choses relatives au daguerréotype'. Nerval, *Correspondance*, *OC* I, 1390. Nerval's photographic attempts were not successful. He wrote to his father, Dr Labrunie, on his return: 'The daguerreotype came back in good condition, but I was unable to make much use of it. The chemical compounds that were needed decomposed in the hot weather; I took two or three views at most; fortunately I have painter friends such as Dauzats and Rogier, whose drawings are better than those done by daguerreotype.' ['Le daguerréotype est revenu en bon état, sans que j'aie pu en tirer grand parti. Les composés chimiques nécessaires se décomposaient dans les climats chauds; j'ai fait deux ou trois vues tout au plus; heureusement j'ai des peintres amis, comme Dauzats et Rogier, dont les dessins valent mieux que ceux du daguerréotype.'] Nerval, *Correspondance*, *OC* I, 1411.

black with silver nitrate.[35] Le Gray also shared his expertise with Alexandre Dumas *père*, who sailed with him to Greece and Turkey in 1861 with the intention of photographing ancient sites.[36] Like Gautier, Champfleury was a member of a photographic society, and Jules Verne, as one might expect of a writer fascinated by scientific discovery, was keenly interested in the new process and based his anagrammatically named character Ardan on his old friend, the photographer Nadar. Victor Hugo was also closely involved, corresponding with Hetzel about photography in 1853, supporting plans to publish an album of photographs of Jersey (though the volume never appeared), and willingly posing for his son Charles who was an enthusiastic early photographer.

Although intrigued at first by the practical possibilities of the new medium, however, most writers lost their initial zeal as the excitement and wonder of the early years of photography gave way to a debased, commercialised form of image. Despite their lack of enthusiasm for the medium, many nevertheless found themselves under attack for adopting 'photographic' methods as they experimented with new modes of literary composition. Realist writers regularly found themselves criticised for producing work that was akin to the objective and mechanically accurate methods of the photographer, and in particular to those of the daguerreotypist – for it was the precision and clarity of the daguerreotype that kept the strongest hold on the imagination of non-specialists. 'It is the jeering, trivialising fidelity of the daguerre method applied to the reproduction of the ridiculous and the odious', said one critic of Henry Monnier's realism, while another attacked Mérimée for his 'photographic method' and for 'daguerreotyping' his characters.[37] Realist fiction was accused of producing 'the brutal imitation of our manners, a kind of daguerreotyped reproduction of everyday life'.[38] Such critics complained that the realist writer, like the camera, gave equal emphasis to whatever passed before him and included irrelevant and undesirable details without applying any artistic discrimination. Thus Flaubert was denounced by Gustave Merlet for 'photographing' the farmyard scene as Charles Bovary arrives at Emma's father's farm, and for including an intrusive and irrelevant description of

---

35 Flaubert to his mother, 5.1.1850, *Corr.* I, 560; to Bouilhet, 13.3.1850, *Corr.* I, 605; to his mother, 3.5.1850, *Corr.* I, 618.
36 Rabb, ed., *Literature and Photography*, xxxvii.
37 Cit. in Linda Nochlin, *Realism* (London: Penguin Books, 1971), 44.
38 '[L]'imitation brutale de nos mœurs, une sorte de contr'épreuve daguérrienne de la vie de chaque jour.' Elme-Marie Caro in 1854, cit. in Jill Kelly, 'Photographic Reality and French Literary Reaction: Nineteenth-century synchronism and symbiosis', *French Review* 65, no. 2 (December 1991), 202.

poultry pecking in the manure, cows chewing the cud, and harnesses hanging in the dusty stable.[39] Writers were accused of being little more than photographic darkrooms where they developed their uncompromising image of the world. Reviewing one of Champfleury's novels, Merlet imagined the author boasting: 'my imagination is a darkroom. And God forbid that I should touch up the prints I run off.'[40]

The mechanical procedures of the photographer or daguerreotypist were thus seized on as a convenient and easily manipulable metaphor in the debate about changing literary practice. But the real problem at issue was not merely whether a writer or photographer had succeeded in capturing the essence of the subject. Although couched in such terms, the debate was not simply about representation or aesthetics – about whether what was represented was too true or not true enough. The photographic analogy allowed critics to query the suitability of a subject and to pronounce on what should have been glossed over or omitted; what was really at stake was what should or should not be seen. In effect, photography had become both a focus for conflicting attitudes towards a rapidly changing society, and a means of reflecting on how that new world should be shaped and represented.

At the same time, photography offered a new aesthetic, a new way of seeing the world, and despite all the protestations to the contrary, it had profound repercussions on literary practice. Photography recorded the surfaces of objects, providing information that was essentially superficial; devoid of metaphysical or theological speculation, it was a medium that privileged impassive observation and thus coincided with contemporary literary trends. Recognising that their increasing tendency towards an impersonal form of literature had its counterpart in the emotionally detached vision of the lens, writers began to think about literary practice in terms of the photographic process. While working on his novel *Daniel*, Ernest Feydeau was advised by Flaubert to draw back from his characters and point his lens at them from a distance:

> You will do me the favour, in future, of writing impersonal books and keeping your camera further away; you will see how well your characters speak once you stop talking through their mouths [...] It must be

---

39 Gustave Merlet, 'Le Roman physiologique: *Madame Bovary.*' *Portraits d'hier et d'aujourd'hui* (Paris: Didier, 1863), 107–08.
40 '[M]on imagination est une chambre obscure. Et Dieu me garde de retoucher les épreuves que je tire...' Cit. in Kelly, 'Photographic Reality and French Literary Reaction: Nineteenth-century synchronism and symbiosis', 201.

completely impersonal; [...] set your up lens a hundred leagues away from your life.[41]

Despite Merlet's cutting review of Champfleury, the creative imagination – that strange alchemy by which the external world was recorded and transformed by writers – came to be thought of in terms of the mysteries of the darkroom, as we see in Gautier's *Jettatura*, where the hero 'sees' a room in great detail in his mind's eye as he drops off to sleep. Its wood panelling, green hangings and English hunting prints are imprinted on his brain 'as in a darkroom', and later, as he sleeps, his unconscious fears are reshaped into vivid images 'in the darkroom of dreams'.[42]

Though literature was well able to produce panoramic sweeps or offer complex, nuanced analyses, it increasingly followed the camera's lead in focusing on significant moments or detailed fragments.[43] Increasingly, too, it adopted the photograph's aesthetic of immobilisation. By the mid 1850s it was technically possible to create 'instantaneous photography' with an exposure time of around one second, and as photographers vied with one other to find a way of capturing the movement of waves in a print, it is curious to note the emergence in fiction of verbal images of fixed, immobilized water – static sea or lake images, described in monochrome and often containing the image of a metallic plate. Gustave Le Gray caused great excitement when he exhibited his large-format (30 by 40cms.) photographic marine studies in London and Paris in 1856–57. He had tried to give the shifting seascape a sense of permanence, and critics used words such as 'meadow' or 'tombstone' to describe the apparent solidity of the water's surface. As the *Revue photographique* noted at the time:

> Sailing ships in motion, the swell of the sea, clouds floating in the air, and the sun itself with its long rays of glory are all reproduced and fixed, instantly and simultaneously, with no sleight of hand, no tricks. This time, the boundaries of the possible have been attained. We are not at all surprised that these enchanting pictures have caused such a stir.[44]

---

41 'Tu me feras le plaisir, désormais, d'écrire des livres impersonnels, de mettre ton objectif plus loin et tu verras comme tes personnages parleront bien du moment que tu ne parleras plus par leur bouche. [...] Il faudra que ce soit complètement impersonnel; [...] mets ton objectif à cent lieues de ta vie.' Flaubert, *Corr.* III, 12–13 (27.1.1859) and III, 27 (16.6.1859).

42 '[C]omme dans une chambre noire'; 'dans la chambre noire du rêve.' Gautier, *Jettatura*, in *Romans et contes*, 36, 88.

43 See Rabb, ed., *Literature and Photography*, xxxix.

44 *Revue photographique*, 5.2.1857. Cit. in Michel Frizot, 'The Transparent Medium', in Frizot, ed, *A New History of Photography*, 100.

In fact there had been considerable sleight of hand: although he denied it at the time, Le Gray had superimposed two separate negatives – one for the sea, one for the sky – to create a single print.

If we remember how writers contrived to subvert the speed of steam travel in order to express a sense of stagnation, we may perhaps better understand the appeal to them of such images of frozen movement. Fromentin's description of a seascape in *Dominique* is a good example:[45]

> Nothing stirred on board. The sea was as motionless as half-molten lead. The sky, pale and faded by the noonday glare, was reflected in it as though in a dull mirror. No fishing boat was in sight. But out at sea and already cut in half by the line of the horizon, a ship with all its sails unfurled was waiting for the off-shore breeze to return.'[46]

The utter stillness, the monochrome colouring, the emphasis on light, the daguerreotype resonance of the references to the motionless expanse of metal and the dull mirror-like surface in which the scene is reflected, all suggest that Fromentin, painter though he was, is here working to a photographic aesthetic. This example demonstrates the extraordinary richness of meaning that could be generated by an apparently innocent description. The effect is one of great subtlety and resonance, for the line of the horizon which appears to cut the ship in two not only reproduces the visual effect of many photographic seascapes but also echoes the theme of truncation which runs through the novel. Equally, the evocation of the motionless ship – in full sail, but going nowhere for the time being – taps into both the photographic aesthetic and the political resonance underlying those images of vehicles unable to progress which are such a feature of Second Empire fiction.

But perhaps the best way to illustrate the complex and evolving tensions surrounding the relationship between photography and literature at this period is to look at the case of Flaubert. Predictably, critics of *Madame*

---

45 Cf. *Salammbô*, where the sea 'seemed almost solidified in the cool of the morning' ['semblait comme figée dans la fraîcheur du matin'] (Flaubert, *OC* I, 699). Immobilisation is a constant figure in this novel, where the gulf of Carthage and the open sea 'looked as motionless as molten lead' ['semblaient immobiles comme du plomb fondu'] and the water is described as 'gigantic waves of a black ocean that had been turned to stone' ['flots gigantesques d'un océan noir pétrifié'.] Flaubert, *OC* I, 724.

46 'Rien ne bougeait à bord. La mer était figée comme du plomb à demi fondu. Le ciel, limpide et décoloré par l'éclat de midi, s'y reproduisait comme dans un miroir terni. Il n'y avait pas un bateau de pêche en vue. Seulement, au large et déjà coupé à demi par la ligne de l'horizon, un navire, toutes voiles déployées, attendait le retour de la brise de terre.' Fromentin, *Dominique*, 193.

Bovary complained that his writing smacked of the photographic method: soulless, undiscriminating, recording whatever happened to fall within its field of vision. Using the same analogy, Armand de Pontmartin accused Flaubert of setting a bad example to his followers, and argued that the school of *Madame Bovary* 'describes without love or preference, solely because the material objects are there and the camera is set up, and everything has to be reproduced'.[47] The novel also came under attack from Cuvillier-Fleury, who extended the hostile photographic metaphor even further:

> M. Flaubert has pointed his daguerreotype at a village in Normandy, and the over-accurate instrument has given him a certain number of likenesses, portraits, landscapes and little scenes in shades of grey which are unquestionably true, but which have that kind of dull, wan truth that seems, in copies of the physical world, to shut out the very light that produced them… Through that precision instrument which he manipulates with such dexterity, the material world is reproduced just as it is, no more, no less, but without poetry or ideal. In today's novel, written with the techniques of photographic reproduction, the painter is no longer a man: all that remains is a steel plate.[48]

It is particularly ironic that Flaubert should have been criticised for creating his own kind of cruel photographic realism, for he would probably have agreed with the objection that the daguerreotype reproduces the material world 'just as it is, no more, no less, but without poetry or ideal'. That was what he saw as photography's failure. Bemoaning the fact that he lived in a period which honoured photographers but sent poets into exile, he regarded photography as symptomatic of a contemporary mania for individualism that went hand

---

47 '[D]écrit sans amour, sans préférence, uniquement parce que les objets matériels sont là, que l'appareil photographique est dressé, et qu'il faut tout reproduire.' Cit. in Kelly, 'Photographic Reality and French Literary Reaction: Nineteenth-century synchronism and symbiosis', 201.

48 'M. Flaubert a braqué son daguerréotype sur un village de Normandie, et le trop fidèle instrument lui a rendu un certain nombre de ressemblances, portraits, paysages et petits tableaux en grisaille d'une vérité incontestable, de cette vérité terne et blafarde qui semble supprimer, dans les copies du monde physique, la lumière même qui les a produites… Sous cet instrument de précision qu'il manie d'un doigt si exercé, le monde matériel se reproduit comme il est, ni plus ni moins, mais sans poésie et sans idéal. Dans le roman tel qu'on l'écrit aujourd'hui, avec les procédés de la reproduction photographique, l'homme disparaît dans le peintre: il ne reste qu'une plaque d'acier.' *Journal des Débats*, 26.5.1857.

in hand with a weakening of character.⁴⁹ In 1853 he had forbidden his lover, Louise Colet, to send him her photograph, declaring that he himself would never consent to be photographed because photography could never get close enough to the truth: 'I detest photographs as much as I love the originals. I never find them *true*.'⁵⁰ Having wrestled with *Madame Bovary* for five years in order to achieve his desired effect, he would never have accepted that his novel fell into the same category as the photography he so despised.

Flaubert's response to photography, however, is more complex and interesting than has hitherto been recognised. In 1866, while he was working on *L'Éducation sentimentale*, Hippolyte Taine sent him a questionnaire about the relationship between memory and the literary imagination. Taine wanted to know how Flaubert remembered an object he had looked at closely some time before. Did Flaubert visualise it very precisely as a complete whole, with all its surface irregularities, or did he recall only a few fragments such as a gesture or an angle or an effect of light? Flaubert's reply shows him reflecting not only on memory, but on the nature of perception itself, and he uses the example of the inadequacy of photographic representation to articulate a problem that was crucial to a writer who had aspired to produce 'written reality'.⁵¹ 'I believe that (despite what people say) memory usually idealises – that is to say chooses. But perhaps the eye idealises too? Note how astonished we are by a photographic print. It's never *that* that we've seen.'⁵² If what the eye sees is different from what the camera reproduces – if we are surprised by a photographic version

---

49 Flaubert to Colet, 15.1.1853, *Corr.* II, 239; Flaubert, *Carnets de travail*, 556. The daguerreotype self-portrait which Charles Bovary thinks of ordering as a gift for Emma serves to convey his stupidity, cautiousness and conventionality (Flaubert, *Madame Bovary*, *OC* I, 613). In an early draft of the novel, Emma smashes a daguerreotype of her husband in a display of irritation. *Plans et scénarios de 'Madame Bovary'*, (presentation, transcription et notes par Yvan Leclerc), CNRS Editions Zulma, fol. 20 (1995), 41.
50 'Je déteste les photographies à proportion que j'aime les originaux. Jamais je ne trouve cela *vrai*.' To Colet, 14.8.1853, *Corr.* II, 394
51 '[D]u réel écrit'. Flaubert to Colet 7.7.1853, *Corr.* II, 376.
52 'Je crois que généralement (et quoi qu'on en dise), le souvenir idéalise, c'est à dire choisit? Mais peut-être l'oeil idéalise-t-il aussi? observez notre étonnement devant une épreuve photographique. Ce n'est jamais *ça* qu'on a vu.' To Taine, 20 ?.11.1866, *Corr.* III, 562. Cf. the long letter Zola wrote to Antony Valabrègue in August 1864, in which he reflects on the problematic relationship between reality and its artistic reproduction in terms of optical lenses. Émile Zola, *Correspondance*, ed. B. H. Bakker, vol 1, 10 vols. (Montreal-Paris: Presses de l'Université de Montréal – CNRS, 1978–95), 375–80; and the comment in Goncourt, *Charles Demailly*, 85: 'Realism is spreading and really taking off while daguerreotypes and photographs show just how much art differs from the real.' ['Le réalisme se répand et éclate alors que le daguerréotype et la photographie démontrent combien d'art diffère du vrai.']

of reality that is necessarily different from our immediate or remembered perception of that reality – what, Flaubert seems to be asking, is the nature of that difference? Is it simply that the eye and the memory are selective, whereas the camera is not? For Flaubert the photographic image is not merely the over-faithful and indiscriminate reproduction of reality that it was for other hostile commentators. Instead, its very inadequacy causes him to reflect on the nature of perception and on the ways in which external reality is mediated and re-mediated by the mind, the camera, the brush or the pen.[53]

These reflections are central to *L'Éducation sentimentale*, which offers the finest example of literature's interaction with photography during the Second Empire and so deserves close examination. Far from confirming his outright dismissal of photography, it reveals a reluctant fascination on Flaubert's part, and his complex engagement with the photographic aesthetic underlies the text and allows him to explore meaning in an entirely new way. The Paris of *L'Éducation sentimentale* is no longer the Paris of Balzac or Stendhal's novels. It is a grey, misty city whose representation derives less from 'the objective reality of things', as Flaubert said in his response to Taine,[54] than from one of the commonest genres of contemporary photography – the *vue de Paris*. The panoramic view of Paris from around the Pont Neuf was a photographic commonplace of the Second Empire, due in part to the fact that so many photographers had their studios near the river. These daguerreotypes and photographs capture a busy, working Seine, with barges, laundry boats, advertising signs, and a jumble of rooftops and pipework, and offer a very different picture from the more selective and tranquil images produced by painters and engravers. The images of the Seine and the bridges that recur throughout *L'Éducation sentimentale* clearly derive from – and refer to – the vision generated by early photographers who often set up their cameras on high window ledges or balconies. For example, the panoramic view from Frédéric's balcony over the river which flows 'between the greyish embankments, blackened here and there by sewage outlets, with a laundresses' floating platform moored by the bank where little urchins sometimes amused themselves in the mud by bathing a poodle,' evokes activity that would have been familiar to Flaubert's readers through a host of monochrome photographic images. The description continues, drawing the eye to the monuments and confused roofscapes that lie

---

53 Flaubert's *Carnets de Travail*, 478, contain notes on a painter who could recollect his model perfectly, and went insane. 'An over-exact memory, acting like a camera, damages the process of idealisation which is the only thing that can create the truth.' ['La mémoire trop exacte, agissant comme un appareil photographique, nuit à l'idéalisation qui seule fait vrai.']
54 '[L]a réalité objective des choses'. Flaubert to Taine, 20?.11.1866, *Corr.* III, 562.

further in the distance: 'Passing on from the stone bridge of Notre Dame on the left, and three suspension bridges, his gaze always moved towards the Quai aux Ormes, to a clump of old trees[...] The tower of St-Jacques, the Hotel de Ville, Saint-Gervais, Saint-Louis and Saint-Paul rose up opposite, among the jumble of rooftops.'[55] And the same buildings and bridges appear over and over again in the novel, seen from different angles and in different lights, just as they do in a profusion of photographic studies. Flaubert's referent is not so much Paris itself or indeed any one specific photographic representation of Paris, but rather a whole familiar photographic topos, a version of 'the objective reality of things' that had already been mediated many times by the camera, to the point of becoming, in both senses of the word, a *cliché*. (This photographic term took on its metaphorical meaning in the late 1860s as multiple photographic prints became commonplace.)[56]

By recreating in his novel the blurred, monochrome effect of early photographs as the subject merges into shadow or is viewed through grey films of mist,[57] Flaubert obliquely hints at the impoverished response to external reality that he feared typified the period. There is a particularly telling passage at the end of the fourth chapter of Part I. On his way home after an evening at the Arnoux's, Frédéric stops in the middle of the Pont Neuf, and suddenly feels as if he has been transported into another world: 'An extraordinary faculty whose purpose he did not know, had come to him.'[58] What seems to have generated this 'extraordinary faculty' is the dark monochrome and slightly blurred view across the river. The Seine 'was slate-coloured, while the sky, lighter in colour, seemed to be held up by the great masses of shadow that rose up on either side of the river. Buildings one could not make out intensified the darkness.

---

55 '[E]ntre les quais grisâtres, noircis, de place en place, par la bavure des égouts, avec un ponton de blanchisseuses amarré contre le bord, où des gamins quelquefois s'amusaient, dans la vase, à faire baigner un caniche. Ses yeux, délaissant à gauche le pont de pierre de Notre-Dame et trois ponts suspendus, se dirigeaient toujours vers le quai aux Ormes, sur un massif de vieux arbres [...] La tour Saint-Jacques, l'Hotel de Ville, Saint-Gervais, Saint-Louis, Saint-Paul se levaient en face, parmi les toits confondus.' Flaubert, *L'Éducation sentimentale*, *OC* II, 31.

56 During the lifetime of the Second Empire, the word *cliché*, which originally referred to a printing plate, came to mean a photographic negative, then a copy of a photographic print, and by the end of the 1860s, an overused commonplace.

57 Cf. Francis Wey, writing in *La Lumière* in 1851: 'One contemplates these direct positives as if through a fine curtain of mist. Very finished and accomplished, they unite the impression of reality with the fantasy of dreams: light grazes and shadow caresses them.' Cit. in André Jammes and Eugenia Parry Janis, *The Art of French Calotype* (Princeton: Princeton University Press, 1983), 4.

58 'Une faculté extraordinaire, dont il ne savait pas l'objet, lui était venue.' Flaubert, *L'Éducation sentimentale*, *OC* II, 26.

A luminous fog floated in the distance, above the rooftops.' It is at this precise moment that Frédéric decides that he will become a great painter, a decision implicitly undermined by the photographic nature of his perception of the view, and immediately mocked by the narrator with the ironic comment: 'The purpose of his existence was clear now, and the future guaranteed.' Of course Frédéric never does become a great painter, and his professional, political and sentimental future is far from 'guaranteed'; yet the strange few lines of text that immediately follow carry a hint of what the future may be:

> When he had closed his door, he heard someone snoring in the dark room near the bedroom. It was the other. He no longer thought about him.
> His face showed itself to him in the mirror. He thought he looked handsome – and paused for a minute to look at himself.[59]

There, in the 'cabinet noir' – the French term for the darkroom where photosensitive glass plates were prepared and prints developed – Frédéric stands motionless for a minute as his image is caught in the mirror. In this proto-Lacanian moment, issues of self-representation, doubling, imitation, perception and artistic ambition come together, subtly inscribed within a photographic context. That Frédéric should find the image of himself that forms within his 'darkroom' beautiful is surely Flaubert's ironic commentary on what the 'guaranteed future' of artistic representation will be.

Even when Frédéric and Rosanette escape from Paris to Fontainebleau, Flaubert still places them in surroundings that had already been pictured many times in many different ways. Although the Fontainebleau episode is normally interpreted in relation to the Barbizon painters, it also carries underlying photographic references, for the trees of Fontainebleau were a favourite subject for Second Empire photographers. In 1854 Paul Nibelle published an article in the photographic journal *La Lumière* celebrating the forest's photogenic qualities; and Gustave Le Gray took a highly acclaimed series of tree studies there, setting the criteria for a whole new genre.[60] In

---

59 '[E]tait de couleur ardoise, tandis que le ciel, plus clair, semblait soutenu par les grandes masses d'ombre qui se levaient de chaque côté du fleuve. Des édifices, que l'on n'apercevait pas, faisaient des redoublements d'obscurité. Un brouillard lumineux flottait au delà, sur les toits'; 'Le but de son existence était clair maintenant, et l'avenir infaillible. Quand il eut refermé sa porte, il entendit quelqu'un qui ronflait dans le cabinet noir, près de la chambre. C'était l'autre. Il n'y pensait plus. Son visage s'offrait à lui dans la glace. Il se trouva beau; et resta une minute à se regarder.' Flaubert, *L'Éducation sentimentale*, *OC* II, 26.
60 See Michel Frizot, 'Automated Drawing: The truthfulness of the calotype', in Frizot, ed., *A New History of Photography*, 71.

the Fontainebleau episode, Flaubert again draws our attention to problems of representation. Avoiding any simplistic contrast between raw nature and the city, he instead presents the reader with trees which, like the panoramic views of Paris, have already been mediated through countless previous representations. The coachman's recital of their fanciful names: 'Here are the Siamese Twins, Pharamond, the King's Bouquet...' shows one way in which they have been appropriated and monumentalised;[61] the silent presence of the painter with his box of colours points to another. The photographs by Le Gray and his imitators were a further, very different form, and Flaubert's inclusion of a telegraph pole in the background to his description of a wilderness not only indicates the impossibility of escaping from the modern world, but is perhaps a nod to a host of Fontainebleau images taken by less skilled practitioners of the indiscriminate and all-seeing lens.[62]

The cheapest and most common photographic genre at this time, the *carte de visite*, plays a crucial rôle in Flaubert's technique. Patented by Disdéri in 1854, the *carte de visite* was assured of success when the Emperor and his family posed for one, and the genre rapidly developed its own conventions which involved combining a dignified demeanour with a décor that reflected the sitter's social aspirations.[63] Flaubert particularly despised the genre, and once accused Ernest Feydeau of defiling his wife by sending him a *carte de visite* which made her look as if she were wearing a basin on her head. 'Any man who uses photography is guilty', he added. 'You have no principles!'[64]

But in *L'Éducation sentimentale*, where lack of principle is, after all, a central theme, the *carte de visite* is an essential referent. Throughout the novel, characters freeze into typical *carte-de-visite* poses, hold their position for a minute, often against a background of a few key props, then vanish. The reader's first sight of Frédéric establishes the pattern: 'A young man of eighteen with long hair and a sketchbook under his arm, stood motionless beside the tiller. He gazed through the mist at spires and buildings whose names he did not know.' In the classic pose of an artist, positioned by the tiller to indicate his

---

61 'Voici les frères-Siamois, le Pharamond, le Bouquet-du-Roi...' Flaubert, *L'Éducation sentimentale*, *OC* II, 125.
62 Flaubert, *L'Éducation sentimentale*, *OC* II, 126.
63 In Labiche's play, *La Poudre aux yeux*, a social climber buys an album full of *carte de visite* photographs for display on his table in order to impress visitors with his circle of friends; the photographs implausibly include Lord Palmerston and the acrobat, Jules Léotard. Conversely, Napoleon III cultivated the appearance of an approachable bourgeois rather than an imperial figure of authority in his *cartes de visite*, realising he could use photography to alter his public image.
64 'Tout homme qui se sert de la photographie est d'ailleurs coupable. Tu manques de principes!' Flaubert, 17.8.1861, *Corr.* III, 170.

political ambitions, and gazing into a misty distance, Frédéric is immobilised against a backdrop that has the artificial quality of a studio set: 'Like two large ribbons being unrolled'.[65] From that point on, the novel keeps freezing into photographic moments. The first description of Madame Arnoux on the boat has her sitting motionless in the standard *carte de visite* pose of the respectable bourgeoise, with her face in profile, a workbasket at her feet, and holding a piece of embroidery. Just as *carte de visite* images of contemporary celebrities invited close and speculative scrutiny, her immobility allows Frédéric (and hence the reader) to examine her in detail, and to speculate on her private life. Subsequently, Madame Arnoux repeatedly materialises suddenly yet without moving, often half hidden in shadow, dressed in the murky greys, blacks or sepias of a photographic print, sometimes with one detail fashionably retouched in colour: 'Madame Arnoux appeared. As she was enveloped in shade, he could only make out her head at first. She had a gown of black velvet, and in her hair a long Algerian hairnet in red silk was twisted round her comb and fell over her left shoulder.'[66] In another example the position of her hands suggests the techniques used by photographers to keep the sitter motionless during the long exposure, and her static pose is further emphasised by a reference to a sphinx: 'Madame Arnoux, motionless, had both hands resting on the arms of her chair; the wings of her bonnet hung down like the wrappings of a sphinx; her pure profile stood out in pale outline against the shadows.'[67] Later, Madame Dambreuse is caught, motionless, as if in a framed portrait: 'She stopped on the threshold (the door's lintel surrounded her like a frame)'[68] – just as Rosanette 'pauses for a minute' at Fontainebleau to look at her reflected image framed in the mirrors.[69] Time and again in this novel movement stops for a minute while a character strikes a conventional pose which exemplifies (and ridicules) notions of bourgeois respectability, the artistic

---

65 'Un jeune homme de dix-huit ans, à longs cheveux et qui tenait un album sous son bras, restait auprès du gouvernail, immobile. A travers le brouillard, il contemplait des clochers, des édifices dont il ne savait pas les noms'; 'comme deux larges rubans que l'on déroule'. Flaubert, *L'Éducation sentimentale*, *OC* II, 8.

66 'Madame Arnoux parut. Comme elle se trouvait enveloppée d'ombre, il ne distingua d'abord que sa tête. Elle avait une robe de velours noir et, dans les cheveux, une longue bourse algérienne en filet de soie rouge qui, s'entortillant à son peigne, lui tombait sur l'épaule gauche.' Flaubert, *L'Éducation sentimentale*, *OC* II, 24–25.

67 'Madame Arnoux, sans bouger, restait les deux mains sur les bras de son fauteuil; les pattes de son bonnet tombaient comme les bandelettes d'un sphinx; son profil pur se découpait en pâleur au milieu de l'ombre.' Flaubert, *L'Éducation sentimentale*, *OC* II, 80.

68 'Elle s'arrêtait sur le seuil (le linteau de la porte l'entourait comme un cadre).' Flaubert, *L'Éducation sentimentale*, *OC* II, 143.

69 '[S]'arrêtait une minute'. Flaubert, *L'Éducation sentimentale*, *OC* II, 125.

temperament, the actor, or the seductress; and at certain points entire groups freeze, caught in a conventional tableau such as at Monsieur Dambreuse's deathbed scene where 'everyone, for a minute, remained motionless'.[70] (Many photographers at this time, including Nadar, offered home visits to photograph deathbed scenes. The dead, like monuments, were ideally static subjects.) In all these cases Flaubert represents his characters representing themselves through their imitations of stereotypical images of how they wish to be seen – images of images which themselves stand in a problematic relation to any kind of 'objective reality of things'. And so in a delirium of representation that threatens to spiral on indefinitely, Flaubert manages, paradoxically, to convey a sense of his period as essentially posturing, inauthentic and derivative.

He even appears to make subliminal reference to the failed photographic print (of which there must have been many) immediately after the quarrel between Monsieur and Madame Arnoux that is witnessed by Frédéric. 'Then there was a great silence; and everything in the apartment seemed more motionless. A luminous circle above the oil-lamp whitened the ceiling, while shadows reached into the corners like layers of black gauze.'[71] Photographers record scenes of domestic harmony, not domestic quarrels. Far from offering a complete and faithful reproduction of the world in miniature, photography selects what it will record. The domestic quarrel had no conventionalised photographic image to which the text could refer, and so here we are referred instead to a botched print, a moment of time frozen in an image whose circular blank area at the top and layers of gauzy darkness at the corners deprive it of definition and seem to point to the limitations and failures of representation.[72]

One important sub-genre of the *carte de visite* which features explicitly in *L'Éducation sentimentale* is the pornographic photograph. This widespread form of *carte de visite* is evoked by the reference to the album of obscene images which Rosanette, as a young girl, found in the restaurant where she was

---

70 '[T]ous, pendant une minute, restèrent immobiles.' Flaubert, *L'Éducation sentimentale*, *OC* II, 144.

71 'Alors, il se fit un grand silence; et tout, dans l'appartement, sembla plus immobile. Un cercle lumineux, au-dessus de la carcel, blanchissait le plafond, tandis que, dans les coins, l'ombre s'étendait comme des gazes noires superposées.' Flaubert, *L'Éducation sentimentale*, *OC* II, 69.

72 Cf. the list of photographic defects in V. Cordier, *Traité des insuccès en photographie: Causes et remèdes* (Paris: Lieber, 1866), 27–37. These include 'Veiling which more or less obliterates the print'; 'Opaque black areas'; 'Uneven prints with high black and white contrast and no half-tone'; and 'Black streaks beneath the collodion.' ['Voiles effaçant plus ou moins l'épreuve'; 'Espaces noirs opaques'; 'Épreuve heurtée à contrastes vifs noirs et blancs sans demi-teintes'; and 'Traînées noires sous le collodion.']

violated. Yet here again, Flaubert seems to be using photography to challenge the idea of a straightforward relationship between representation, reception and reality.[73] The images may be obscene – we are told they are – but what they convey to the reader, paradoxically, is the very opposite of obscenity. The bewildered young girl, waiting alone in the restaurant and finally falling asleep with her head resting on the album, is a picture of innocence. That detail has its counterpart at the masked ball, when Rosanette makes an initial attempt to seduce Frédéric by striking a suggestively erotic pose: 'And, posing with her weight on one hip and with the other knee drawn back a little, stroking the mother-of-pearl knob of her sword with her left hand, she gazed at him for a minute, half entreatingly, half cheekily [...] Frédéric [...] not knowing what to do, wandered off into the ball.'[74] In this case Rosanette's pose refers the reader to a sub-text of erotic images, yet Frédéric fails to respond to its message and instead wanders off to listen to the painter Pellerin who, significantly, is talking about the relation between reality and representation. Pellerin blusters unconvincingly that the relationship is unproblematic: 'It's just a question of capturing the tone, that's all.'[75]

By the end of *L'Éducation sentimentale* Pellerin has become a photographer and the walls of Paris are plastered with identical copies of his photographic portrait, but the problem of representation has still not been resolved. Critics have tended to assume that Pellerin's move from painter to photographer symbolises the death of art, without noting that his photograph is not a straightforward representation. As if recognising, like his creator, that 'it's never *that* that we've seen',[76] he has manipulated his photographic image to represent himself with a tiny body and an enormous head.[77] Aesthetically unpleasing though this photograph may be, it shows that Pellerin resists the

---

73 Cf. the little 'médaillons' that edge Madame Arnoux's mirror. Deslauriers uses these family photographs to initiate a conversation with Madame Arnoux but he misinterprets them, saying that Mme Arnoux's mother 'looks like a splendid person, a real southerner.' ['a l'air d'une excellente personne, un type méridional.'] Mme. Arnoux replies that she came from Chartres (less than fifty miles from Paris). Flaubert, *L'Éducation sentimentale*, *OC* II, 97.
74 'Et, posée sur une seule hanche, l'autre genou un peu rentré, en caressant de la main gauche le pommeau de nacre de son épée, elle le considéra pendant une minute, d'un air moitié suppliant, moitié gouailleur [...] Frédéric [...] ne sachant que faire, se mit à errer dans le bal.' Flaubert, *L'Éducation sentimentale*, *OC* II, 50.
75 'Il s'agit seulement d'attraper la note, voilà.' Flaubert, *L'Éducation sentimentale*, *OC* II, 51.
76 Alison Fairlie calls Pellerin the 'echo' of his creator. See 'Pellerin et le thème de l'art dans *L'Éducation sentimentale*', in *Imagination and Language: Collected Essays on Constant, Baudelaire, Nerval and Flaubert* (Cambridge: Cambridge University Press, 1981), 412.
77 Flaubert, *L'Éducation sentimentale*, *OC* II, 162. The 'Photographie' entry in the *Grand dictionnaire universel*, XII, 889, gives precise instructions on how to do this.

notion of a mechanical reproduction of reality. He continues to struggle, however unsuccessfully, with the problems of perception, representation and creativity that preoccupied Flaubert and his contemporaries. Photography allows Flaubert to ask questions rather than find solutions. As he had once asked Louis Bouilhet: 'What does not look like itself, and what does? Do we ever see the same subject in exactly the same way?'[78]

One final aspect of Flaubert's photographic engagement is particularly intriguing. Whereas early Parisian daguerreotype studios had congregated mainly in the area around the Palais Royal, during the Second Empire many commercial photographers moved to new premises on the boulevards. In his memoirs, Nadar recalls that the large building on the corner of the Boulevard des Capucines which housed several of the most important photographic studios of the period, including those of Gustave Le Gray and the Bisson brothers, stood on the former site of the Ministry of Foreign Affairs, outside which, on 23 February 1848, the first shots of the revolution were fired.[79] So when Flaubert described that crucial episode in *L'Éducation sentimentale*, giving precise topographical references as the action shifts between the Boulevard des Capucines and the Palais Royal, he must have known that for his Parisian readers it would be overlaid by another image, an awareness of another and very different 'realité objective'. By the time the novel was published the site that marked the outburst of revolutionary idealism had been taken over by photographers' boutiques.

Disdainful though he was of photography, Flaubert, like many of his contemporaries, clearly saw it as a medium whose characteristics reflected the age. With more subtlety and imagination than most of his fellow writers, he drew on the photographic aesthetic not only in order to reflect on questions of representation, but also to convey his image of mid nineteenth-century France. Reaching into every social class, associated with the sapping of colour and energy, characterised by posturing, imitation, stasis and artistic mediocrity, photography was for him the perfect embodiment of the period.

---

78 'Qu'est-ce qui ne se ressemble pas et qu'est-ce qui se ressemble? Est-ce qu'on conçoit jamais le même sujet d'une façon identique.' Flaubert, 2.9.1850, *Corr.* I, 675–676.
79 See Nadar, *Quand j'étais photographe* (1900; Paris: Babel, 1998), 89.

Chapter Six
COSTUME

On coming to power, Napoleon III was determined to create an imperial court which would project a powerful image of affluence and prosperity. One way of achieving this was through ostentatious court costume, with the added aim of stimulating demand for fabrics and trimmings and so helping to regenerate France's failing clothing and textile industries. Thousands of officials were provided with specially designed, elaborately braided uniforms, and the Empress played her part by wearing what she called her 'political outfits'[1] – voluminous, richly decorated dresses – to encourage luxury and consumption and help revive the clothing industry. Her example caught on as fashionable women vied with one another in the conspicuous consumption of ornate dress,[2] and although Eugénie is said privately to have preferred simpler designs, the sumptuous dress code she imposed for her court receptions ensured a new lease of life for Lyons silk manufacturing. By the end of the Second Empire Paris was established as the fashion centre of the world.

During this period women's fashion changed at an ever-increasing speed. Skirts became fuller throughout the 1850s, supported at first by layers of petticoats made of stiff material such as the mixture of horsehair (*crin*) and linen (*lin*), which gave the crinoline its name. Waists were tightly laced to emphasise the skirts' flare, and as dresses grew more voluminous, technology came to the rescue with whalebone or steel skirt-hoops to support their weight. In 1856 the cage crinoline of steel ribs appeared, allowing the skirt to swing freely from the waist – a much lighter and less expensive solution than the petticoats. By 1860 the crinoline had puffed out to its widest circumference, before gradually deflating and becoming more oval over the following decade. A combination of aniline dyes (developed in the 1860s), new industrially-produced textiles, and increasing use of the recently invented sewing machine contributed to a radical shift in the way women dressed. Cheap, industrially-produced

---

1 '[T]oilettes politiques'.
2 The flamboyant Pauline Metternich brought eighteen trunks and as many hatboxes for a week's stay at the Imperial court at Compiègne. See Rupert Christiansen, *Tales of the New Babylon* (London: Minerva, 1994), 30.

garments allowed poorer women to imitate the styles of the wealthy, and they in turn adopted new, more exclusive designs to protect their 'distinction' in an ever-quickening pattern of changing fashion.

As the pace of change in the wider world increased, many writers came to see the rapid evolution of female fashion as a visible expression of social and cultural change.[3] 'Yesterday's fashion already seems very old-fashioned today', wrote a columnist in *Le Moniteur de la mode*, 'and what we admire today will be quite outdone by the fashion of tomorrow'. After using an image of horse-racing to convey the dizzy rate at which one fashion followed another, he continued: 'Fashions follow one another so rapidly that I was wrong to compare them to a race a moment ago; I would need a steam-engine, rather, to guide my pen through the thousand convolutions of that enticing labyrinth we call the vagaries of fashion.'[4] Another suggested that by bringing people from distant parts of the country into contact with one another, the railways were responsible for making people dress more carefully, and that this had in turn given rise to the new imperative to dress quickly and cheaply.[5] New needs were being created, with speed and economy as the driving force. The rapidity of change in contemporary dress was widely felt to be in keeping with the changing times, and even the names invented for the latest textiles and designs reflected the spirit of the age, with Zouave jackets, Garibaldi shirts, Malakoff skirts, and dresses in Empress blue, Imperial green, Magenta, Solferino, Crimean green or Bismarck brown.[6]

During this period, writing about clothes became all-pervasive. Fashion journals abounded, as did style manuals, clothing advertisements, books offering advice on how to dress, and specialist journals for the tailoring trade, all contributing to a great outpouring of writing about dress. In the discourse of fashion journals and dress manuals (which had a vested interest in describing the latest French fashions) one can clearly detect implicit support for the new Establishment, and the Empress (whom the British magazine *Punch* called

---

3 See for example the 'Costume' entry in the *Grand dictionnaire universel*. Its author is highly conscious of the way costume reflects and is modified by changes in economic, political, religious, moral and artistic conditions.

4 'La mode d'hier est déjà bien vieillie aujourd'hui, et celle que nous admirons en ce moment sera bien distanciée par celle de demain'; 'Les modes se succèdent avec une telle rapidité, que je me trompais tout à l'heure en parlant de course, c'est une locomotive à la vapeur qui deviendrait nécessaire pour guider notre plume à travers les mille sinuosités de cet attrayant labyrinthe appelé les caprices de la mode.' *Le Moniteur de la mode*, 15.2.1853, 157.

5 *Le Journal des tailleurs*, 1.8.1852. Cit. in Henriette Vanier, *La Mode et ses métiers, 1830–1870* (Paris: Colin, 1960), 128.

6 *Le Miroir parisien* (October 1962): 56; David Baguley, *Napoleon III and his Regime: An Extravaganza* (Baton Rouge: Louisiana State University Press, 2000), 309.

Queen of Fashion, Comtesse de la Crinoline, Goddess of the Bustles, and Impératrice de la Mode) was held up as a model of style.[7] Fashionable clothes adopted Spanish touches in celebration of her background.[8] Journals regularly offered their readers detailed descriptions of her gowns. Her visit to North Africa in 1855 resulted in a fashion for the burnous,[9] and when she wore a white tulle dress with diamond clasps at an Imperial reception in February 1863 and another floating white gown with diamonds at a Tuileries ball soon after, *Le Miroir parisien* could confidently state that 'we predict that white will be the favourite colour for elegant women this winter.'[10]

Delight in 'progress', admiration for the imperial family, pride in France's domination of the (fashion) world, and above all a belief in order shine through these reports, and many contributors suggested that to embrace changing fashions was to express willing endorsement of the way France was progressing. Even a practical fashion manual that aimed to instruct dressmakers in the art of creating different dress designs from a simple but adaptable dress pattern, felt the need to place its instructions within a moral and political context. For Pauline Mariette, the author of *L'Art de la toilette: Méthode nouvelle pour tailler, exécuter ou diriger avec économie et élégance tous les vêtements de dames et d'enfants* [*The Art of Dress: New Method for Economically and Elegantly Cutting, Making or Ordering all Clothes for Women and Children*], following fashion was a moral imperative, an expression of faith in social and economic progress, and indeed in French domination:

> Man must seek out progress and develop it, for to remain stationary is to move backwards. Women must progress too, and must vary their manners and dress according to the march of civilisation; and each nation should strive to walk ahead of the others, and impose its inventions and products on them.[11]

---

7 Baguley, *Napoleon III and his Regime*, 311.
8 In October 1862, *Le Miroir parisien* reported that the Spanish look was still very much in vogue: 'we see nothing but Figaro jackets, Almaviva collars, hair dressed with mantillas, Castilian hairnets, and Madrid fringes' ['on ne voit *que vestes Figaro, collets Almaviva, coiffures en mantille, résilles castillanes, franges madrilènes*'] (56).
9 Paul Louis de Giafferri, *L'Histoire du costume féminin français: Les Modes du Second Empire, 1852–1870* (Paris: Nilsson, 1922), 74.
10 '[O]n peut augurer que le blanc sera la couleur favorite des élégantes pour cet hiver.' *Le Miroir parisien* (February 1863): 155.
11 'Il faut que l'homme cherche le progrès et qu'il le développe, car l'état stationnaire est un recul. Il faut que la femme progresse aussi, et varie ses manières et ses vêtements suivant la marche de la civilisation; et chaque peuple doit faire ses efforts pour marcher à la tête des autres, et leur imposer ses inventions et ses produits.' Pauline Mariette, *L'Art de la toilette: Méthode nouvelle pour tailler, exécuter ou diriger avec économie et élégance tous les vêtements de dames et d'enfants* (Paris: Librairie centrale, 1866), 158–59. Cf. 'Must we not follow the march of progress in all things; and so let us say it again, dressing well in

Everything was for the best in the discourse that conveyed such a world-view – elegance was at its peak, the importance of being well-dressed was universally acknowledged, and all civilised nations looked to France for guidance in fashion and taste. By the 1860s, fashionable dress was represented as a force for peace, prosperity and civilisation: without it, readers were told, unemployment would be rife and France might well be forced to go to war.[12] As it was, however, France reigned supreme thanks to its clothing industry: 'in fashion, as in many other things, the French lead the world. The degree of civilisation, class distinctions, and industrial, commercial and cultural resources are all reflected in dress.'[13]

Such views are implicit in the utopian world depicted by Second Empire fashion magazines, dress manuals and catalogues. There, everyone dresses immaculately. Clothes and accessories are always new, fit perfectly, are worn with poise and elegance, and are never stained or crumpled or threadbare. The vocabulary of this perfect world deliberately identified itself with only the highest social levels, which were to be admired and if possible emulated. The Emperor and Empress, royalty past and present, and alluring royal mistresses were all evoked through costume; no hint of the rupture of 1848 troubled the world of the Second Empire fashion press. Instead, in a continuity of Monarchy and Empire, figures such as Mary Stuart, Madame de Pompadour, Madame de Maintenon, Marie-Antoinette and Queen Hortense as well as the Emperor and Empress themselves, gave their names to fashionable styles and colours.

Decreeing what the well-dressed lady will wear, these magazines set out what is and is not permissible. The tone may be light-hearted and teasing, but the authoritarian edge is clear: 'Everything we have just described must be followed and adopted, on pain of being caught out and punished by ridicule.'[14] Fashion was imperious, imposing censure and order – it must be followed to

---

the 19th century is much more than a profession; rather it is an arduous, difficult art, and we may say that many are called to it, but few are chosen.' ['Ne faut-il pas suivre la marche de nos progrès en toutes choses; aussi, répétons-le, bien s'habiller au XIXe siècle est plus qu'une profession, mais bien un art, ardu, difficile, dans l'exercice duquel nous pouvons dire qu'il y a beaucoup d'appelés, mais peu d'élus.'] *Histoire chronologique du vêtement (homme) suivie de l'art de se vêtir au XIXe siècle* (Paris: Vanier, 1867), 133.

12 Ernest Feydeau, *Du luxe, des femmes, des mœurs, de la littérature et de la vertu* (Paris: Clichy, 1866), 44–45, 53.

13 'En fait de modes, comme en beaucoup d'autres choses, le Français est le premier peuple de l'univers. Le degré de civilisation, la distinction des classes, les ressources de l'industrie, du commerce, de la culture, se reflètent dans les habits.' Rosine Delasalle, 'Jadis et aujourd'hui. Histoire de la mode', *Le Miroir parisien* (October 1862): 50. See also Ernest Feydeau, *Du luxe, des femmes, des mœurs, de la littérature et de la vertu*, 42–43; and *Histoire chronologique du vêtement (homme)*, 128.

14 'Tous les présents articles, que nous venons de décrire, devront être suivis et exécutés, sous peine d'être atteints et punis par le ridicule.' *Le Moniteur de la mode* (April 1852): 3.

the letter if the wearer was not to appear absurd (as Charles Bovary discovered when his unfortunate hat earned him the punishment of copying out *ridiculus sum* twenty times).[15] The magazines' rhetoric of *liberté*, *égalité* and *fraternité* might claim that everyone was free to dress as they pleased, but in reality the dictates of fashion and the threat of ridicule exercised a formidable constraint. Like the corsets widely advertised in these journals, which claim to imprison the wearer lightly and gracefully without her being aware of it ('one never feels uncomfortable in these charming prisons of twill and satin'),[16] the journals' discourse flattered the reader into conforming with authority and with clear social norms.

As in writings about transport or food, attitudes to changing class structures were embedded in writing about dress. Fashion commentators were in general agreement that male dress – and in particular the ubiquitous *habit noir*, the black tail-coat – reflected a new egalitarianism.[17] The *habit noir* was widely perceived as symptomatic of a society where class differences had all but vanished, and it was no longer considered to be in good taste for a Parisian to wear anything that would reveal his profession or rank. As Paul de Musset put it, 'The practice of going incognito is firmly entrenched in Parisian manners'; it was impossible to tell a senator from a clerk since both dressed alike.[18] To such commentators, contemporary clothing reflected a new freedom and prosperity that benefited everyone. As the anonymous author of one male

---

15 See e.g. Pauline Mariette, *L'Art de la toilette*, 158; or Flaubert's ironic version of such dictates in 'The Island of Dress' ['L'Ile de la toilette'] in *Le Chateau des cœurs*, where a choir announces the arrival of the King of Fashion: 'It is Couturin, King of Fashion. The only one who can methodically guide our fickle tastes [...] Mortals, [...] walk where his hand guides you. All his commands are to be taken seriously; defy them and you are lost; follow them and you are saved.' ['C'est Couturin, roi de la mode. / Le seul qui sache, avec méthode, / Diriger nos goûts inconstants [...] Mortels, [...], / Marchez où sa main vous conduit. / Tous ses ordres sont chose grave; On est perdu quand on les brave, / On est sauvé dès qu'on les suit.' Flaubert, *Le Chateau des cœurs*, *OC* II, 345.
16 'Jamais on ne se trouve gênée dans ces gracieuses prisons de coutil et de satin.' *Le Moniteur de la mode* (25.3.1853): 205; cf. *Le Miroir parisien* (June 1863): 280: 'Perfectly at ease in the corsets supplied by this firm [Richer], the woman who wears them feels no discomfort.' ['Parfaitement à l'aise dans les corsets de cette maison [Richer], la femme qui les porte ne ressent aucune gêne.']
17 E. g. 'An egalitarian idea created all our modern dress.' ['Une pensée égalitaire a créé tout notre costume moderne.'] Vicomte de Marennes, *Manuel de l'homme et de la femme comme il faut* (Paris: Librairie nouvelle, 1855), 68; 'The black tailcoat and white tie make all men equal.' ['L'habit noir et la cravate blanche rendent les hommes égaux.'] Octave Marilly in *La Semaine politique*, 5 July 1857, cit. in Vanier, *La Mode et ses métiers*, 198.
18 'L'usage de l'incognito est ancré dans les mœurs parisiens.' 'Parisiens et Parisiennes', in Dumas, Gautier et al, *Paris et les Parisiens au XIXe siècle. Mœurs, arts et monuments*, 406–407.

dress manual observed, 'Nowadays, everyone is free to dress as they wish [...]; from the wealthiest to the most humble, everyone, whatever their means, can be well-dressed. This happy indulgence brings a general air of ease and well-being to thousands of workers, and they too can dress as they like.'[19]

By deeming workers to share bourgeois values in aspiring to dress and behave like the middle classes, such an analysis of dress conveniently glossed over awkward or threatening social divisions.[20] Indeed, for some commentators the working man's adoption of the *habit noir* was in itself a significant force for moral good, since a feckless worker would soon start to exhibit proper middle-class values if he dressed like a bourgeois: 'The clothing industry helps to improve the morals of the masses. Nowadays a worker may wear a tailcoat; he has become used to this form of dress, which sets him up and obliges him to show self-respect. Drunkenness has lost much of its hold as a taste for clothes has gained ground.'[21]

But there were many who hated the idea of the old class structure being eroded, and for them, too, writing about dress was a conveniently indirect way of venting their displeasure. Costume itself was perceived as wonderfully expressive: 'Costume can by turns express wealth, pretension, flirtatiousness, austerity, or modesty', noted the *Manuel de l'homme et de la femme comme il faut*,[22]

---

19 'Aujourd'hui, chacun est libre de s'habiller à sa fantaisie [...]; depuis le plus riche jusqu'au plus humble, tous peuvent, quels que soient leurs moyens, être mis avec soin. Cette heureuse fantaisie répand l'aisance et le bien-être parmi des milliers d'ouvriers qui, eux aussi, peuvent se vêtir comme ils l'entendent.' *Histoire chronologique du vêtement (homme)*, 128.

20 Similarly, fashion journals make frequent use of the passive voice to erase all sense of the workers who produce the goods described. E. g. *Le Miroir parisien* (January 1863): 116: 'The hats are mostly made half of crepe or white silk lace and half of velvet in light red, mexican blue, mauve, etc. Velvet flowers are placed beneath the crown which is always very high; the upper part is adorned with feathers of various colours arranged in a cluster, or with floating ostrich plumes. Felt-coloured velvet also makes pretty bonnets with a cluster of similar feathers.' ['Les chapeaux se font pour la plupart mi-partis crêpe ou blonde blanche et mi-partis en velours groseille, bleu mexico, mauve, etc. Des fleurs en velours se posent sous la passe toujours fort élevée; des têtes de plumes de diverses couleurs disposées en bouquet, ou des plumes d'autruche flottantes en ornent le dessus. Le velours couleur feutre fait aussi de jolies capotes avec bouquet de plumes pareilles.']

21 'La confection contribue à la moralisation des masses. L'ouvrier...peut aujourd'hui endosser l'habit; cette tenue qui lui est devenue familière, le relève et l'oblige à se respecter. L'ivrognerie a perdu d'autant plus de terrain que le goût de la toilette en gagnait davantage.' Lemann, *De l'industrie des vêtements confectionnés en France*...(Paris, 1857), cit. in Vanier, *La Mode et ses métiers*, 128–29.

22 'Le costume exprime tour à tour la richesse, la prétention, la coquetterie, l'austérité, la modestie.' Marennes, *Manuel de l'homme et de la femme*, 49–50.

and sartorial images helped many writers to put their point across. For Eugène Chapus, writing under the pseudonym of the Vicomte de Marennes, the cut of men's trousers was symptomatic of the way in which old-fashioned strengths and values had been suppressed and replaced by modern feebleness. The shape of the modern trouser, he complained, favoured weak, spindly (and, by implication, socially inferior) legs and prevented strong, graceful ones from being appreciated, and now that boots were worn by everyone, a gentleman could no longer distinguish himself by displaying expensive silk stockings. Nor could a gentleman mark himself out by his superior deportment since the plain, dark cloth of the coat or jacket effectively camouflaged deficiencies in bearing, and 'all classes, without exception' were expected to wear the same puritanically plain linen. But the 'Viscount''s greatest bile was reserved for the *paletot*, a loose overcoat that was frequently deplored as being emblematic of a dull, new, one-size-fits-all uniformity. In increasingly politicised language, Marennes complains that:

> Class distinctions, professional values and character hardly exist. And so what did we do? We adopted the *paletot*, which is not made to fit anyone and which doesn't suit anyone [...] the order went out to tailors: practicality, ease, comfort, vulgarity, anonymity; and the *paletot* was created. They tossed us the *paletot*, that absolute annihilation of dress, the ultimate egalitarian garment, a veritable uniform of the phalanstery.

For writers like this, the contemporary trend towards more loosely cut clothes for men spelled the triumph of mediocrity.[23] It was a view shared by Baudelaire, who famously mourned the demise under the Second Empire of the dandy with his 'burning need to be original' and his 'oppositional, rebellious nature'. Describing how the true dandy had vanished, swamped by a rising tide of democracy that had suppressed the last remnants of human pride and reduced everything to the same level, Baudelaire linked the dandy's impeccable dress to a final defiant flash of heroism as the country sank into decadence and debased uniformity.[24]

---

23 '[I]l n'y a guère ni classe, ni moule de profession, ni caractère. Aussi qu'avons-nous fait? Nous avons adopté le paletot, qui n'est fait pour personne et qui va mal à tout le monde.[...] [L]es tailleurs reçurent le mot d'ordre: commodité, aise, comfort, vulgarité, effacement; et le paletot fut créé. Ils nous jetèrent le paletot, ce perfectionnement de l'annihilation du costume, le plus ultra du vêtement égalitaire, véritable uniforme de phalanstère.' Marennes, *Manuel de l'homme et de la femme comme il faut*, 68–69.

24 '[B]esoin ardent de se faire une originalité'; 'caractère d'opposition et de révolte'. Baudelaire, *OC*, 560.

Philippe Hamon has argued that as men's clothing came to represent sameness, social signs and distinctions took refuge in the female body and in women's fashions,[25] but the reality was rather more complex. While some contemporary writers blithely emphasised the egalitarian symbolism of the undifferentiated *habit noir*, others made it clear that such egalitarianism was an illusion: differences did exist, but differently from before, and writing about costume was a means of exploring and analysing such differences, in the socio-political as well as the sartorial sense.

As the 'Mode' entry in Larousse's *Grand dictionnaire universel* noted, little serious consideration had previously been given to the question of why and how fashion changed. Balzac is generally acknowledged as the first French writer to include details of costume in his novels,[26] but under the Second Empire authors recognised its wider significance and creative potential. Moreover, many serious poets and novelists, including Baudelaire, Flaubert, Gautier, Léonie d'Aunet and Louise Colet, felt the subject was important enough for them to move outside their normal literary sphere and write directly about fashion in journals such as *Le Journal des dames et messager des dames et des demoiselles*, *La Chronique de la mode*, *La Gazette des femmes*, and *Les Modes parisiennes*.[27]

Throughout this period the imagery of dress seeps into the language, so that the boundaries between the rituals of reading, writing and dressing come to blur and merge. Ideas are clothed in language; costume generates meaning; dress can be read; and in the words of Baudelaire, 'fabrics speak a silent language'.[28] Writers increasingly recognise an analogy between language and dress – they talk of an individual's dress 'speaking', and even refer to different nationalities as speaking different sartorial languages which

---

25 Hamon, *Expositions*, 184.
26 Balzac (who died in 1850) had considered the subject of dress from a theoretical point of view in his *Traité de la vie élégante*, pubished in *La Mode* in 1830, but because it appeared only in journal form the *Traité*'s initial impact was ephemeral. In 1853, however, it was reissued posthumously in a single volume which brought his semiology of fashion to wider attention.
27 See Théophile Gautier, *De la Mode* (Paris: Poulet-Malassis et de Broise, 1858); and Baudelaire, *Le Peintre de la vie moderne*, *OC*, 547–65, especially sections 1, 4, 9, 10, 11 and 12. Louise Colet published regular fashion articles in journals such as *La Chronique de la mode*, *La Gazette des femmes* and *Les Modes parisiennes illustrées*, and persuaded Flaubert to contribute to the last of these. Anne Herschberg-Pierrot, 'Flaubert journaliste: présentation,' *Littérature*, no. 88 (Dec. 1992): 115–126, includes the complete text of Flaubert's 'Causerie sur la librairie nouvelle' written under the pseudonym 'Arthur'. Léonie d'Aunet replaced Louise Colet on *Les Modes parisiennes* at the end of 1856. See Flaubert, *Corr*. II, 1167–68.
28 '[L]es étoffes parlent une langue muette'. Baudelaire, 'La Chambre double', *Le Spleen de Paris*, *OC*, 149.

echo national linguistic differences. So, for example, in his *Manuel de l'homme et de la femme comme il faut* of 1855, the Vicomte de Marennes points to an 'abundance of superfluity' in the English way of both dressing and writing. He complains that the English overdo things in both respects: they wear too much jewellery and add too many trimmings and lace to their outfits, just as they pile too much imagery into their overlong sentences. French style, on the other hand, is as restrained and economical in words and ideas as it is in dress: the elegance of the French is characterised by sobriety, correctness and purity of line in both domains, he asserts.[29]

These are rather blatant examples, but the best writers recognise dress as an extraordinarily rich language in itself, a way of expressing thoughts that were not easily articulable in more direct ways. When Baudelaire wrote of the delights of 'a cleverly composed *toilette*', he was referring as much to the aesthetic principles of his poetry as to the elements of a woman's costume.[30] When Gautier articulated the principles of his poetic theory in his poem 'L'Art', he did so in terms of footwear: his poetic Muse must shun the easy rhythms of a comfortable shoe that slips on and off the foot, and instead adopt the more constraining 'tight buskin'.[31] And Mallarmé likened the pleasure he derived from the formal constraints of the sonnet form to the effects of a corset on the female body: 'But Heaven, for me as for my old friend Shakespeare, is a sonnet! – where the mind enjoys being tortured like Camargo's breast in its fine corset!'[32] Indeed several writers described the writing process in terms of dress-making. Frédéric Soulié, for example, said that women hold their pen like a sewing-needle and write as if they were mending trousers;[33] Gautier likened the workings of his poetic imagination to the weaving of silken threads;[34] and Flaubert compared the literary process to embroidery: 'I would like to write everything I see, not as it is, but transfigured. I need to embroider it more.'[35]

---

29 Marennes, *Manuel de l'homme et de la femme comme il faut*, 64–65. The author adds that the same is true of English meals – 'one finds everything there in profusion, profusion substitutes for choice.' ['tout s'y trouve avec profusion, la profusion tient lieu du choix.']
30 '[U]ne toilette savamment composée'. Baudelaire, *Le Peintre de la vie moderne*, *OC*, 561.
31 '[C]othurne étroit'. Gautier, *Émaux et camées*, 130.
32 'Mais le Ciel, c'est pour moi comme à mon vieux Shakespeare / Un sonnet! – où l'esprit jouit d'être au martyre / Comme en son fin corset le sein de Camargo!' Stéphane Mallarmé, 'Sonnet' (March 1859), *Œuvres complètes*, ed. Carl Barbier and Gordon Millan (Paris: Flammarion, 1983), 77.
33 Cit. in Francine Du Plessix Gray, *Rage and Fire. A Life of Louise Colet* (London: Hamish Hamilton, 1994), p. 222.
34 Gautier, 'Après le feuilleton', *Émaux et camées*, 100.
35 'Je voudrais écrire tout ce que je vois, non tel qu'il est, mais transfiguré [...] Il me faut le broder encore.' Flaubert to Louise Colet, 26.8.1853, *Corr.* II, 416.

Resorting again to the imagery of dress to convey the mediocrity and lack of originality of contemporary literature, he complained of living in a world of ready-made clothes that come in only one size.[36]

Gautier takes the identification between writing and dress a step further in the prologue to his *Roman de la momie*, where he describes the clothes of the Egyptologist Dr. Rumphius in some detail. As is the case in many novels of this period,[37] Rumphius's costume tells the story of its past. Limp, crumpled and threadbare, his clothes display their owner's history to the observer/reader, while the pattern of inky pen-strokes that have left their trace on the fabric of his trousers evoke text as much as texture. Written about and written on, Rumphius' clothes signal to the reader that he, the writer, will transcribe the papyrus document that will turn out to be *Le Roman de la momie*. But Rumphius' costume, like the text, needs a 'careful observer' to decipher its meaning.[38]

The language of clothes is problematic, even to a careful observer. How to decipher dress comes to be a central concern at this period, reflecting a wider uncertainty about how to understand and make sense of the world at large. As the Vicomte de Marennes put it: 'Nowadays confusion reigns in ideas as much as in things.'[39] Deciphering the language of clothes is a central theme in *Les Toilettes tapageuses*, an 1856 comedy by Dumanoir and Barrière whose title could be translated as *Flashy Dressing*.[40] An aptly-named character, Couturier, is informed that in Paris there are two kinds of women who can be told apart by 'reading' their dress: 'dress is a woman's signboard...and some dresses are so eloquent that it is exactly as if you were to read on the first layer of their flounces: furnished flat to rent!'[41] In this play, costume is a text to be

---

36 Flaubert to Louis Bouilhet, 30.9.1855, *Corr.* II, 597.
37 Cf. Fromentin, *Dominique*, 85, where the first description of Madeleine inscribes her convent education in her dress: 'she was wearing its modest uniform; at the time I am speaking of, she was still wearing out a series of dismal dresses – tight, high-necked, worn away at the bodice from rubbing on desks, and threadbare at the knee from genuflecting on the paving-stones of the chapel.' ['elle en portait la livrée modeste; elle usait encore, au moment dont je vous parle, une série de robes tristes, étroites, montantes, limées au corsage par le frottement des pupitres, et fripées aux genoux par les génuflexions sur le pavé de la chapelle.'] Flaubert uses a similar effect in *L'Éducation sentimentale*, where the wear and tear of the boat-passengers' old clothes reveal something of their owners' past – office or shop work, a hasty breakfast, and so on. *OC* II, 9.
38 .'Observateur attentif'. Gautier, *Le Roman de la momie*, 29.
39 'Aujourd'hui la confusion règne encore dans les idées comme dans les choses.' Marennes, *Manuel de l'homme et de la femme comme il faut*, 14.
40 Dumanoir and Théodore Barrière, *Les Toilettes tapageuses: Le Théâtre contemporain illustré* (Paris: Levy, 1857).
41 '[L]a toilette, c'est l'enseigne de la femme...et il y a des toilettes tellement parlantes, que c'est absolument comme si vous lisiez sur le premier étage des volants: appartement meublé à louer!' *Les Toilettes tapageuses*, n. p.

read or misread. Sometimes its meaning is easily deciphered: the husband is flabbergasted when his wife proposes spending a thousand francs on a lace handkerchief, and he comments that she might as well wave a large bank note for all to see. His remark cuts through any argument about utility or elegance: to him the handkerchief is a blatant signifier of wealth, and will be read as such.[42] Elsewhere dress is literally read: the wife attends the opera wearing a gown of such extraordinarily lavish design that *Le Figaro* publishes a detailed description the next day. When her husband balks at buying her yet another extravagant outfit and comments that he can happily wear the same suit for three months, she retorts that no one writes about his suit in the newspaper. More often in this play, however, dress is misread, or its message is wrongly spelled out, as the female lead discovers when her extraordinary new gown, made from twenty metres of silk with twenty-four flounces and run up in a couple of hours for the outrageous price of eight thousand francs, is taken to be the 'advertising sign' of a prostitute. (It is particularly ironic that many women in the audience misread the authors' satirical intention and begged the actress playing the leading role to lend her exaggerated dress as a model. According to Maxime Du Camp, crinolines doubled in size within eight days of the play's opening night.)[43]

Problems raised by misinterpreting the messages of dress – or of unintentionally conveying the wrong message through dress – are commonplace in the writing of the period, and we shall return to them later. Problems of a different order arise, however, when dress – and language – lose their meaning altogether. Language itself is recognised as problematic, and despite all its 'embroidery' it may fail to communicate meaning as Flaubert's famous description of Charles Bovary's hat makes clear. As detail heaps upon detail, the hat fails to materialise in our mind's eye and so acts as a warning to the reader about the limitations of realist description.[44]

If Flaubert used the description of Charles' hat to draw attention to problems of language and representation, he was also keenly aware that costume was akin to poetry in its capacity to compress and convey meaning. The sight of Charles' coat, for example, sums up Emma Bovary's feelings about her husband: 'she saw all the mediocrity of his character displayed right there on his frock coat.'[45] Nowhere, however, is Flaubert's awareness

---

42 Earlier, the wife successfully argues that if she appears in an outfit she has worn before, everyone will think her husband has lost on the stock market.
43 Du Camp, *Paris, ses organes...*, VI, 192, cit. in Benjamin, *The Arcades Project*, 67.
44 See Tony Tanner, *Adultery in the Novel: Contract and transgression* (Baltimore and London: Johns Hopkins University Press, 1979), 238.
45 '[E]lle y trouvait étalée sur la redingote toute la platitude du personnage.' Flaubert, *Madame Bovary, OC* I, 608.

of the communicative power of clothing and its kinship with literature more evident than in his extraordinary rhapsody on the shoe. Writing to Louise Colet, he elaborates an ebullient history of French literary style from the Middle Ages to the present solely by evoking different types of footwear. His delight in visualising literary change through an optic of sartorial change is evident:

> Is there not an *obvious* relationship between the hard poems of the Middle Ages (often in monorhyme) and those iron shoes made all in one piece which men-at-arms wore in those days; between six-inch long spurs with fearsome rowels, and long, cumbersome, bristling sentences [...] In Louis XIV's day, literature had its stockings pulled well up! They were brown in colour. You could see the calf. Shoes had square toes (La Bruyère, Boileau), and there were also some strong riding boots, stout shoes of imposing cut (Bossuet, Molière). Then the toe becomes pointed, Regency literature (*Gil Blas*). They economise on leather and the *form* (another play on words!) is taken to such an exaggeration of *antinaturalism* that you would almost think you were in China (except where the imagination is concerned, at least). It's all pretty-pretty, light, over-elaborate. The heel is so high that balance is lost; there is no longer any solid basis. Moreover the calf is padded out: flabby philosophical padding (Raynal, Marmontel, etc.). Academic style puts paid to poetry; the reign of the *buckle* (the pontificate of Monseigneur de La Harpe). And now we are delivered up to the anarchy of *cobblers*. We have had greaves, mocassins and *poulaines*. In the weighty sentences of Messieurs Pitre-Chevalier and Emile Souvestre, both Bretons, I can hear the heavy thud of Celtic clogs. Béranger has worn the grisette's little ankle boot right down to the laces, and Eugène Sue makes excessive show of the vile down-at-heel boots of the murderer. The one reeks of burnt fat and the other of the sewer. There are grease stains on the sentences of the one, and trails of shit all through the style of the other [...] Sainte-Beuve picks up the most useless cast-offs, patches up those rags, disdains the familiar, and with the help of thread and glue, continues his petty trade (resurgence of scarlet heels, imitation Pompadour and Arsène Houssaye, etc.). So we must jettison all this rubbish and return to stout boots or bare feet, and above all put an end to my shoemaker's digression. Where the devil did it come from?[46]

---

46 'N'y a-t-il pas un rapport *évident* entre les durs poèmes du moyen âge (monorimes souvent) et les souliers de fer, tout d'une pièce, que les gens d'armes portaient alors, éperons de six pouces de longueur à molettes formidables, périodes embarrassantes et hérissées [...] Du temps de Louis XIV, la littérature avait les bas bien tirés! Ils étaient

Flaubert may have wondered what triggered his 'shoemaker's digression', but it was in keeping with a widespread sense among writers that costume was an important, flexible and supremely articulate form of expression, even if few were as exuberant as he in exploiting it.

It was, however, in fiction that costume's potential as a vehicle for expression was most thoroughly explored, and often in surprising ways. Conscious of the seductive power of the fashion journal, several authors explicitly associated the reading of these magazines with courtship of a rather suspect kind. (Léon sitting very close to Emma Bovary as they leaf through her fashion magazine together is possibly the most familiar example, but there are many others.)[47] In contrast to fashion journalists, however, fiction writers frequently convey a tension between the seductiveness of dress, and unease about what it might imply. Monpont wrote that to tempt Eve a modern-day Satan would take the form of a draper's assistant, a *commis en nouveautés* – an image also used by Flaubert in his portrayal of the shopkeeper Lheureux, whose displays of tempting fabrics and garments

---

de couleur brune. On voyait le mollet. Les souliers étaient carrés du bout (La Bruyère, Boileau), et il y avait aussi quelques fortes bottes à l'écuyère, robustes chaussures dont la coupe était grandiose (Bossuet, Molière). Puis on arrange en pointe le bout du pied, littérature de la Régence (*Gil Blas*). On économise le cuir et la *forme* (encore un calembour!) est poussée à une telle exaggération d'*antinaturalisme* qu'on en arrive presque à la Chine (sauf la fantaisie du moins). C'est mièvre, léger, contourné. Le talon est si haut que l'aplomb manque; plus de base. Et d'autre part on rembourre le mollet, emplissage philosophique flasque (Raynal, Marmontel, etc.). L'académique chasse le poétique; règne des *boucles* (pontificat de Monseigneur de La Harpe). Et maintenant nous sommes livrés à l'anarchie des *gnaffs*. Nous avons eu les jambarts, les mocassins et les souliers à la poulaine. J'entends dans les lourdes phrases de MM. Pitre-Chevalier et Emile Souvestre, Bretons, l'assommant bruit des galoches celtiques. Béranger a usé jusqu'au lacet la bottine de la grisette, et Eugène Sue montre outré mesure les ignobles bottes éculées du chourineur. L'un sent le graillon et l'autre l'égout. Il y a des taches de suif sur les phrases de l'un, des traînées de merde tout le long du style de l'autre [...] Sainte-Beuve ramasse les défroques les plus nulles, ravaude ces guenilles, dédaigne le connu et, ajoutant du fil et de la colle, continue son petit commerce (renaissance des talons rouges, genre Pompadour et Arsène Houssaye, etc.). Il faut donc jeter toutes ces ordures à l'eau, en revenir aux fortes bottes ou aux pieds nus, et surtout arrêter là ma digression de cordonnier. D'où diable vient-elle?' Flaubert, 26.8.1853, *Corr.* II, 419–420.

47 Emma reads *La Corbeille*, *Le Sylphe des salons* and *L'Illustration*. Cf. Ernest Feydeau, *La Comtesse de Châlis ou les mœurs du jour* (1867; Paris: M. Lévy, 1868), where the countess asks the narrator to read fashion magazines aloud to her in an attempt to seduce him. Cf. also Théophile Gautier, *L'Avatar* (1856), where the narrator is seduced by a passing beauty whose costume he describes at length before apologising for 'that fashion-journal description.' ['cette description de journal de mode.'] *Romans et contes*, 17–18.

lead to Emma Bovary's downfall.[48] It is, of course, a tension played out in the writing itself, where writer (and reader) take delight in descriptions of shimmering fabrics and rustling silks, while aware of their underlying message: what emerges with striking consistency from texts focusing on dress is anxiety about the breakdown of social structures. Plays and novels repeatedly associate a woman's obsessive interest in fashion with the break-up of the family. A typical example is Henri Tessier's 1858 play *La Mode*, where Clémentine leaves her husband working in Paris and travels alone to a spa resort. Drawn into a suspect 'fashionable' circle, she spends excessively on new outfits, is drawn into gambling and debt, and her exaggerated style of dress causes her to be mistaken for a prostitute. The play's explicit moral message is that fashionable clothes run counter to the laws of God and nature. Clementine's crinolines and corsets put at risk not only her health and reputation, but also her life and that of any future children; without the intervention of her devoted husband all family bonds would have been destroyed. The final message is that a woman's love for her husband renders her far more beautiful than anything the hypocrisy of fashionable dress can achieve. By focusing on costume and exploiting its on-stage visual impact to the full, Tessier thus raises wider concerns about gender relations and the stability of the family and of society at large.[49]

Les Toilettes tapageuses enacts a similar proposition. There, too, dress expresses anxieties about the integrity of family and social structures, and once again a middle-class wife's flamboyant costume causes her to be mistaken for a prostitute. Her long-suffering husband objects to her excessively wide skirts as 'fortifications' – physical barriers between man and wife which prevent intimacy. Voluminous dresses are represented as a threat not only to the institution of marriage and the perpetuation of the family line, but to society itself – 'flounces and crinolines are the ruin of a society'[50] – and the play ends

---

48 Monpont, *Les Femmes coquettes ou la ruine des maisons* (Paris: Ledoyen, 1857), 9–10. In *L'Éducation sentimentale*, Flaubert turns this cliché on its head by having Dussardier, the young idealist, work in a lace and drapery shop in the heart of the clothes and textiles area of Paris. *OC* II, 19.

49 Henri Tessier, *La Mode* (Paris: M. Lévy, 1858). Cf. Flaubert, *Dictionnaire des idées reçues*, *OC*, II, 306: 'Corset: prevents you having children'. ['Corset: Empêche d'avoir des enfants.'] The corset image is used by Alfred Delvau to describe the changes to Paris's expanding boundaries in 1859–60; he describes the city as a young girl growing into a woman and being encircled by a corset of stone. As she matures into 'a strapping woman' [une vigoureuse commère'], the first 'corset' becomes too tight for her, and she casts it off and has a larger one made. *Histoire anecdotique des barrières de Paris* (1865), cit. in D. Oster and J. Goulemot, eds., *La Vie parisienne*, 48.

50 '[L]es volants et la crinoline, c'est la ruine d'une société'. Dumanoir and Théodore Barrière, *Les Toilettes tapageuses*, n. p.

with a song attacking the crinoline. Calling for 'reform' and 'revolution', the authors make little attempt to conceal a political metaphor as they forecast the eventual overthrow of the crinoline's abusive reign of lies and artifice, and the establishment of an enlightened new order.[51]

So persistently do writers make the connection between women's overfondness for changing fashions and the collapse of social structures that it becomes something of a cliché. Flaubert, a past master at turning an *idée reçue* into a work of genius, exploits these connections in *Madame Bovary*, a novel where costume is all-pervasive.[52] His account of Emma's preoccupation with the latest Paris fashion that leads her into the debt and deceit which eventually destroy her and her family should be seen in the context of many inferior works which traced a similar trajectory. Flaubert avoids overt moralising, however, unlike his friend Ernest Feydeau, whose 1868 novel, *La Comtesse de Châlis ou les mœurs du jour*, develops a forceful moral message in a deliberately shocking narrative dominated by dress. Here the Countess's obsession with the latest fashions leads her into gaming and gambling, then on into sexual debauchery and perversion, family ruin and eventual madness (while giving Feydeau many opportunities to produce seductively detailed descriptions of her outfits). As in *La Mode*, the distinction between bourgeois respectability and prostitution becomes dangerously blurred. When the Countess visits the home of the courtesan Florence with the intention of viewing and possibly buying some of Florence's possessions, the two women discover they have much in common despite their difference in status. As the Countess says, 'She dresses tastefully, she talks decently, she's even witty. In short, there is almost no difference between her and...and us.'[53] It is only when the narrator,

---

51 'No more dresses that form a defensive wall, / Vast balloons / Often uninhabited! / Let us organise a holy crusade/ Against the abuse of tainted petticoats!/ Their reign continues in vain here/ One day the crinoline will collapse!... / On the ruins of falsehood / Truth will reappear! / [...] / War is declared on lies and artifice! Let us hit out merrily against the edifice of petticoats!' ['Plus de robes formant enceinte, / Vastes ballons, / Souvent inhabités! / Organisons une croisade sainte / Contre l'abus des jupons frelatés! / En vain, chez nous, leur règne se prolonge, / La crinoline un jour s'écroulera!... / Sur les ruines du mensonge / La vérité reparaîtra! [...] Guerre au mensonge, à l'artifice! / Gaîment frappons sur l'édifice / Des jupons!' Dumanoir and Barrière, *Les Toilettes tapageuses*, n. p.
52 Costume also underpins the narrative in Flaubert's *Salammbô*, where it acts as a subtle reminder of the relationship between the events of ancient Carthage and those of contemporary France. See Anne Green, 'Flaubert costumier: le rôle du vêtement', in D. Fauvel and Y. Leclerc, eds., *Salammbô de Flaubert: Histoire, fiction* (Paris: Champion, 1999), 121–128.
53 'Elle s'habille avec goût, elle s'exprime avec décence, elle a même de l'esprit. Enfin il n'y a presque pas de différence entre elle et...et nous autres.' Feydeau, *La Comtesse de Châlis*, 262.

one of the debauched Countess's lovers, sees the simple dress and natural colouring of the girl his father wishes him to marry, that he finally recognises the error of his ways. From the moment he set eyes on the Countess he had been literally caught up in the seduction of her dress – his feet became entangled in her train, he struggled in vain to free himself, falling madly in love in the process, and when she finally moved away he reflected, 'She had taken everything with her. She carried everything away behind her, in the undulating folds of her torn skirt.'[54] Unable to make sense of the confusing messages sent out by her different costumes (which range from the simple black dress she wears when sitting sewing at home with her husband, to the scandalously low-cut wisp of gauze that passes for a costume of Diana), he is torn between disapproval and desire. By the end of the novel he finally realises that he has been caught up in a situation representative of the perilous state of contemporary society. He now understands that French women's fixation with their appearance has made them the laughing-stock of Europe and has led to an erosion of patriotism. As he confesses to his father, 'I was thrashing about in the quagmire of modern society. This society is done for.'[55] Having liberated himself from the thrall of the Countess's costumes, the narrator ends with an uncompromising message: only freedom can bring about a regeneration of moral values, and 'Everything [...] must be changed in the old social structure.'[56] Beyond the political challenge of the novel's conclusion lies another, less explicit concern – a fear that women will escape from their proper place in society. It is primarily through his seductive and often titillating descriptions of their clothes that Feydeau manages to suggest that women are dangerously alluring, sometimes sinister and monstrous, and possibly insane: they embody the threat of disruption.

A remarkable number of texts of the period feature a moment when a man is engulfed by a woman's voluminous skirts as if eclipsed by her presence. Often the point is made jokingly – a husband complains that when he alights from a carriage he looks as if he is emerging from his wife's pocket, or that when he takes his seat at the theatre he vanishes completely, submerged in a sea of lace and silk.[57] But the situation arises too often in fiction for the

---

54 'Elle avait tout pris avec elle. Elle emportait tout derrière elle, dans les plis ondoyants de sa jupe déchirée.' Feydeau, *La Comtesse de Châlis*, 10–11.
55 'Je me débattais dans le bourbier de la société moderne. Cette société est perdue.' Feydeau, *La Comtesse de Châlis*, 330.
56 'Tout est [...] à remanier dans le vieil édifice social.' Feydeau, *La Comtesse de Châlis*, 335.
57 See for example *Les Toilettes tapageuses*; or Meilhac and Halévy, *La Vie parisienne*; or Taine, *Notes sur Paris*, 200, where the men sitting down at table find themselves half-buried by the dresses of the ladies seated on either side.

joke to be entirely innocent. Although it taps into archetypal male anxieties about being engulfed by a predatory woman, it also has other resonances; by momentarily reversing the sanctioned order of male dominance and making a joke of the woman's sudden supremacy, it uses dress to underscore a norm of female subservience.

Second Empire clothing strongly emphasised gender differences. While the ubiquitous *habit noir* may have played down class distinction, sexual difference was underlined to an unprecedented degree by the contrast between the monochrome uniformity of men's dress and the flamboyant colours and excessive size and ornamentation of women's gowns. The divergence between male and female dress is strikingly demonstrated by comparing a list of the essentials of a man's wardrobe published in the *Journal des tailleurs* with an inventory of a doll's trousseau in the Comtesse de Ségur's popular novel, *Les Petites filles modèles*. Even allowing for exaggeration on Ségur's part – she was, after all, writing to entertain young girls – the contrast is remarkable. The *Journal des tailleurs*, which had no incentive to underestimate sartorial demands, states that all a man requires is one black tailcoat, one pair of black trousers, one white and one black waistcoat, one white and one black cravat – 'and with that you will have all you need to go anywhere'.[58] The pretty wax doll, on the other hand, comes with a trousseau whose inventory runs over two pages of text:

1 round straw hat with a little white plume and black velvet ribbons;
1 blue taffeta bonnet with pompon roses;
1 green sunshade with ivory handle;
6 pairs of gloves;
4 pairs of laced boots;
2 silk scarves;
1 ermine muff and cape;
6 day dresses;
6 nightdresses;
6 pairs of drawers;
6 underskirts with fancy edging and trimmed with lace;
6 pairs of stockings;
6 handkerchiefs;
6 nightcaps;
6 collars;
6 pairs of sleeves;

---

58 '[E]t avec cela vous aurez de quoi vous présenter partout.' Cit. in Vanier, *La Mode et ses métiers*, 155.

2 corsets;
2 flannel petticoats; [...]
1 tartan merino wool gown;
1 pink poplin gown;
1 black taffeta gown;
1 gown in blue fabric;
1 white muslin gown;
1 nankeen gown;
1 black velvet gown;
1 lilac taffeta dressing-gown;
1 grey broadcloth overblouse
1 black velvet overblouse;
1 black silk talma;
1 blue corduroy mantelet;
1 embroidered white chiffon mantelet.[59]

Standing out from the rest of the novel by its length and distinctive typography, the Comtesse de Ségur's list serves several functions. On one level it operates like a fashion journal in its direct appeal to the fantasies of her young female readers, but it also sets costume at the centre of a text which weaves its didactic narrative around a series of incidents based on dress to convey notions of morality, charity, propriety and excess. The grotesquely over-ornamented gown of Mme Fichini, a pretentious and cruel stepmother, is contrasted with the plain, stained dress of her neglected little step-daughter Sophie, and with the simple elegance of the kind-hearted Mme de Fleurville and Mme de Rosbourg. Morality is clearly spelled out in dress: Mme Fichini has her come-uppance when her absurd crinoline overturns the chair on which she is about to sit, so that she falls to the floor, displaying her fat legs. The deserving poor have their rags replaced by simple, pleasing clothes; the undeserving poor remain as they are. Clothes here serve as reward or punishment, providing Ségur's young

---

[59] '1 chapeau rond en paille avec une petite plume blanche et des rubans de velours noir; 1 capote en taffetas bleu avec des roses pompons; 1 ombrelle verte à manche d'ivoire; 6 paires de gants; 4 paires de brodequins; 2 écharpes en soie; 1 manchon et une pèlerine en hermine; 6 chemises de jour; 6 chemises de nuit; 6 pantalons; 6 jupons festonnés et garnis de dentelle; 6 paires de bas; 6 mouchoirs; 6 bonnets de nuit; 6 cols; 6 paires de manches; 2 corsets; 2 jupons de flanelle; [...] 1 robe en merinos écossais; 1 robe en popeline rose; 1 robe en taffetas noire; 1 robe en étoffe bleue; 1 robe en mousseline blanche; 1 robe en nankin; 1 robe en velours noir; 1 robe de chambre en taffetas lilas; 1 casaque en drap gris; 1 casaque en velours noir; 1 talma en soie noire; 1 mantelet en velours gros bleu; 1 mantelet en mousseline blanche brodée.' Mme. la Comtesse de Ségur, *Les Petites filles modèles* (1858; Paris: Hachette, 1909), 93–95.

readers with an easily-read moral barometer. Mean-mindedness is conveyed by tatters or tasteless excess, while kindness and generosity of spirit go hand-in-hand with moderation and simple elegance.

Jules Michelet spoke for many of his contemporaries when he declared that 'dress is a great symbol'.[60] Like the authors of *Les Toilettes tapageuses*, he explored the relationship between husband and wife in *L'Amour* in terms of women's fashion, and wrote of his belief that woman represented a fixed point in a maelstrom of change. 'The current state of morals, the hectic giddiness, the blind turmoil we see around us must not deceive us as to the way things really are,' he wrote;[61] throughout history woman has been 'the element of fixity'.[62] Yet, writing in 1858, he saw women's new attitude to dress as indicative of a deeply worrying trend: women seemed to be losing their age-old place as the essential, still centre. Michelet writes of 'the astonishing spectacle of anxiety and restlessness which they offer us nowadays in their dress mania'.[63] These 'astonishing variations in costume and finery' are often a frantic and misguided attempt to retain their husband's love, he claims, warning that they are likely to fail.[64] The lover will be dismayed by continual change because he wants his woman to remain as she was when he first fell in love with her, rather than become a creature of disorienting variety. For Michelet there is something pathological about rapidly changing fashion, and he writes passionately of 'the follies, the transient epidemics of fashion and luxury' that run counter to the essential stability of woman's natural state.[65] Her 'dress mania' is seen as a disruptive force, destabilising family and social order. In direct contrast to the discourse of the fashion magazines of the period, which embrace the new and talk of the constant evolution of fashion in terms of progress and moral imperative, Michelet's attack on fashionable dress expresses, like that of many others at this period, a protest at the nature and dizzying speed of social change.

Jean Baudrillard has argued that fashion cannot exist in a society based on rank because in such a society there is no class mobility.[66] Each person keeps

---

60 'La toilette est un grand symbole.' Michelet, *L'Amour*, 33.
61 'Il ne faut pas que l'état des mœurs actuelles, l'effréné vertige, le tourbillonnement aveugle dont nous sommes les témoins, nous trompe sur le fond des choses.' Michelet, *L'Amour*, 31.
62 '[L]'élément de fixité.' Michelet, *L'Amour*, 32.
63 '[L]e spectacle étonnant qu'elles nous donnent aujourd'hui, d'inquiétude, d'agitation, dans leurs furies de toilette.' Michelet, *L'Amour*, 32.
64 '[V]ariations étonnantes dans la parure et la toilette'. Michelet, *L'Amour*, 32.
65 '[L]es folies, les épidémies passagères de luxe et de mode'. Michelet, *L'Amour*, 34.
66 Jean Baudrillard, *Symbolic Exchange and Death*, reprinted in Julie Rivkin and Michael Ryan, eds., *Literary Theory: an Anthology* (Oxford: Blackwell, 1998), 492–493.

to his or her station, which is confirmed by the wearing of appropriate dress. The corollary to this, of course, is that fashion will flourish in a society where class mobility is fluid, and the Second Empire, with its great movements of population from the countryside to the cities and its increasing numbers of *nouveaux riches*, undoubtedly saw fundamental changes in social hierarchies that were echoed by changing styles of dress in ways that many found troubling. The journalist Léon Gozlan was outraged by the brightly-coloured outfits worn by the congregation at a special church service for cooks, where the servants were presumptuous enough to dress in cashmere shawls and fancy ribbons like their mistresses:

> A passionate desire for luxury[...]plays a large part in corrupting and demoralizing Parisian domestic servants[...] When some poor fashionable ladies go so far as to sell their family's honour in order to have a 6,000 franc Indian cashmere shawl round their shoulders, is it any surprise that a servant should steal from her mistress so as to buy a French cashmere shawl for three hundred francs?[67]

A similar point is made more subtly and without moralising at the end of *Madame Bovary*, when Charles momentarily mistakes the servant Félicité for his dead wife, whose clothes the maid has appropriated.[68]

If apprehension at the loss of old social hierarchies often took the form of outbursts against the excesses of rapidly-changing fashion, this may in part explain why the clothes of peasants or of the very poor were rarely described in much detail – a smock, a ragged dress, or a pair of scuffed boots were usually enough to indicate a social rank perceived as unproblematic. It is when social hierarchies are challenged or disrupted that clothes receive closer attention from writers, for costume in this context acts as a particularly subtle vehicle for social comment. Often 'unreadable' to the characters within the text, to whom it conveys confusion and uncertainty, dress is more comprehensible to the reader, who is made to understand the wider significance of that confusion.[69] In *Germinie Lacerteux*, for example, Jupillon's over-tight trousers and white shirt

---

67 'La passion du luxe [...] est [...] un grand élément de corruption et de démoralisation pour la domesticité parisienne [...] Quand il y a des lionnes pauvres qui vendent jusqu'à l'honneur de leur maison pour avoir un cachemire indien de 6,000 francs sur les épaules, quoi de bien étonnant que la domestique vole la maîtresse pour acheter un cachemire français de trois cents francs?' *La Chronique parisienne* (31.3.1861), cit. in Vanier, *La Mode et ses métiers*, 200.
68 Flaubert, *Madame Bovary*, *OC* I, 689.
69 Cf. the popularity of the masked ball as a literary theme.

with its collar turned down to expose his neck are described by the narrator as being of dubious elegance; to the reader they are clear signs of his pretentious posturing, but Germinie misreads them as marks of distinction.[70] And in *Les Aventures de Mlle. Mariette*, Champfleury depicts a young man whose inadequate grasp of the elementary rules of dress highlights his anomalous social position and exposes him to ridicule. Far from allowing him to blend in with the crowd, his ultra-conventional clothes send out signals that set him apart and make him uncomfortable: 'he was ashamed of his white tie, which was a rather parliamentary emblem in the midst of the coloured scarves and fancy hats worn by the students. He felt awkward in his coat with its big tails, much too formal, and his long, slick black hair [...] seemed to him to make him look like a schoolmaster on a drunken night out [...] he was as unhappy in his clothes as a man whose boots are too tight.'[71] Although aware that he is sending out discordant and inappropriate signals, Champfleury's young man is unable to 'rewrite' himself and so is fated to be a misfit.

Interestingly, it is male rather than female characters who are shown to be uncomfortable in their clothes. In Second Empire fiction men's garments often rub and chafe and constrict, as if to demonstrate the violence that must be done to force the wearer into conformity, whereas women submit to the cumbersome volume of their skirts and the 'satin prisons' of their corsets without complaint, in keeping with expectations of female submissiveness. On the other hand, transgressive female behaviour is readily conveyed by wilful violation of those dress norms (as for example, when Emma Bovary unlaces her corset and lets her skirts slip to the floor). The trial of *Madame Bovary* for indecency, where the prosecutor repeatedly turned to this and other passages of costume description in order to argue that Flaubert's novel constituted an outrage to public morality, strikingly demonstrates the force of such contraventions – which of course were literary transgressions as much as moral or sartorial ones.[72]

As literary descriptions of dress at this period regularly encode social constructs of femininity, so fabrics take on a special significance of their own. Evocations of women's voluminous dresses emphasise their weightlessness

---

70 Goncourt, *Germinie Lacerteux*, 98.
71 '[I]l avait honte de sa cravate blanche, qui était un emblème un peu parlementaire au milieu des foulards de couleur et des chapeaux de fantaisie que portaient les étudiants. Il se sentait gêné dans son habit à grandes basques, par trop magistral, et ses longs cheveux plats et noirs, qui auraient pu s'allier avec tout autre costume, lui paraissaient lui donner des airs de ressemblance avec un maître d'études en goguette [...] il était aussi malheureux dans son costume qu'un homme dans des bottes trop étroites.' Champfleury, *Les Aventures de Mlle. Mariette*, 10.
72 See 'Le Procès de *Madame Bovary*', in Flaubert, *OC* II, 724–32.

(despite evidence to the contrary). Words such as 'filigree', 'lace', 'light', 'butterfly',' bubbles', 'floating' and 'flying' (*volant*, the French word for 'flounce' suggests flight) recur again and again in dress descriptions to create an effect of lightness and transparency that implies that the wearer is an airy creature devoid of substance.[73] Théophile Gautier writes of dresses with 'feathers as light as coloured vapour or rainbows';[74] Baudelaire describes 'the muslins, gauzes, and vast, shimmering clouds of fabric in which [a woman] envelops herself' and asserts that the wearer and her dress form 'an indivisible whole'.[75] The recurrent imagery of flying and floating, of clouds, rainbows and butterflies combine to create an image of woman as an unearthly being, a weightless creature whose ballooning skirts (*jupes ballonnées*) lift her above worldly cares and transport her into another realm. Dress description thus reinforces a view of women as insubstantial and volatile, unconcerned with weighty issues, ethereal rather than worldly.

There is an incongruity in writers' evident delight in producing lingering descriptions of sensual or filmy fabrics while preaching against the excesses of luxury, and no doubt the barely-suppressed eroticism of some of these descriptions was part of their appeal to readers. Although rainbow-coloured fabrics may have been intriguingly modern, and rustling silks readily denoted both luxury and seduction, writers found they could also exploit fabrics to tell a different story.

As often as not textiles were used to convey a bleaker vision of contemporary society, for certain fabrics evoked declining values and nostalgia for a lost way of life. Textiles, and the cotton industry in particular, were at the forefront of French industrialisation during the Second Empire. Use of the new power loom and the self-acting mule spread rapidly in the 1850s and cotton production soared, so that by 1861 France had the second-largest cotton industry in Europe. But in many Second Empire texts cotton becomes a byword for cheapness, shoddiness and falsity. Nestor Roqueplan, for example, saw cotton as encapsulating the defects of the period in general, and of the government in particular. Bemoaning the fact that it has become impossible to buy a fine woollen coat because fine woollen cloth is no longer manufactured, he complains that a new coat now starts to fade after a month because its fabric is one quarter cotton: 'Cotton sums up our age; cotton is trickery, it is sham, it is imitation, it is just a veneer of

---

73 '[F]iligrane', 'dentelles', 'légère', 'papillon', 'bulles', 'flottant', and 'volants'.
74 '[D]es plumes légères comme des vapeurs colorées, comme des arcs-en-ciel'. Gautier, *De la Mode*.
75 '[L]es mousselines, les gazes, les vastes et chatoyantes nuées d'étoffes dont [la femme] s'enveloppe'; 'une totalité indivisible.' Baudelaire, 'La Femme', *Le Peintre de la vie moderne*, *Œuvres completes*, 561.

goodness. Everything is cotton. Everything is cheap: the government as well as the shirts.'[76] In having *Madame Bovary* end with the orphaned Berthe working in a cotton mill, Flaubert indirectly makes the same point.

Many writers associate modern fabrics with lies and artifice, contrasting them with traditional fabrics which tell the truth. Roqueplan is not alone in mourning the disappearance of good old-fashioned linen, 'that fine luxury of our fathers',[77] and in doing so he evokes a cluster of regrets about social change. In the old days, he says, linen would be left out in the meadows for a month to strengthen and bleach naturally in the fresh air and dew, but the modern way is to bleach it for twenty-four hours with lime, which weakens the fabric so that it wears out quickly. (As a writer Roqueplan has a further regret: good linen-paper has become unobtainable, supplanted by poor-quality paper produced from cotton rags. Books, like fabrics, have deteriorated.) This change in textile production – faster, but resulting in a shoddy, weak product – sums up for Roqueplan all that is wrong with the age: 'It is our mania for cheap luxury, and this need to be equal not only before the law, but before everything, which is killing off high-quality manufacturing and levelling the price of all essential items.'[78]

He was not alone in making such associations. Nerval weaves the same connotations of fresh air and openness and nostalgia for better days through his use of fabrics in *Sylvie*, where the frothy lightness of lace is associated with Sylvie in her pre-Second-Empire youth. Lace as a fabric is open, penetrable, transparent, and in Nerval's tale it thus becomes linked with honesty and innocence. The delicate lacework that Sylvie makes by hand and the antique lace of the old wedding dress she finds in her aunt's attic convey a timeless, fairylike quality to the elusive country girl – 'the eternally young fairy of legend!', as the narrator exclaims.[79] But the young Sylvie with her frothy lace and floating hair and ribbons does not remain unchanged. When the narrator meets her again later, she is dressed in city fashions and tells him that lace is no longer in demand. Sylvie has moved with the times

---

76 'Le coton, c'est tout notre siècle; le coton, c'est l'attrape, c'est le semblant, l'imitation, c'est le plaqué des bonnes choses. Tout est coton. Tout est à bon marché: le gouvernement comme les chemises.' Nestor Roqueplan, *Regain*, *La Vie parisienne*, 1854. Cit. in Oster and Goulemot, *La Vie parisienne*, 52.
77 '[C]e beau luxe de nos pères'. Roqueplan, *Regain*, *La Vie parisienne*, 1854. Cit. in Oster and Goulemot, *La Vie parisienne*, 52.
78 'C'est notre rage de luxe à bon marché, c'est ce besoin d'être égaux, non seulement devant la loi, mais devant tout, qui tue les fabrications consciencieuses, et nivelle le prix de tous les objets nécessaires à la vie.' *Regain*, *La Vie parisienne*, 1854. Cit. Oster and Goulemot, *La Vie parisienne*, 52.
79 'La fée des légendes éternellement jeune!' Nerval, *Sylvie*, *OC* III, 550.

and become a glove-maker. Her green lace-pillow with its gently flicking bobbins has been replaced by a piece of engineering – 'la méchanique' – an unyielding, tong-like metal implement which grips the glove leather firmly while the pieces are stitched together.[80]

That contrast between transparency, lightness and airiness on the one hand, and a sinister, heavy, impenetrable and constricting uniformity on the other, is a characteristic tension that runs through Second Empire writing, subtly infusing apparently innocent descriptions with associations either of liberty, openness and honesty, or of constraint, concealment and control. Gloves were a favourite focus for conveying hypocrisy and restriction. It is no coincidence that the Goncourts should have made Jupillon, the deceitful lover in *Germinie Lacerteux*, a glove-cutter who puts on airs for the passers-by who pause to watch him at work. A commonplace view (which Flaubert later recorded in his *Dictionnaire des idées reçues*) was that gloves 'make people look respectable' – the implication being, of course, that they hide something less acceptable beneath a veneer of propriety.[81] It is a point to which Flaubert frequently returns, most notably in the 'Theory of the glove' he elaborated in one of his notebooks, highlighting the unsettling quality of 'this anti-natural thing' which is both like and unlike a hand:

> What it does is to idealise the hand by depriving it of its colour, just as rice flour does for the face; it makes it inexpressive (think of the unpleasant effect that gloves have on stage), but typical; only the shape is preserved and accentuated. That artificial colour, grey, white or yellow, blends in with the sleeve of the costume and [without] conveying the idea of something different (since the outline is preserved), introduces novelty into the known, and so makes this covered member resemble the limb of a statue. And yet this anti-natural thing can move (in this it differs from a mask, though a mask does have movement through the eyes). There is nothing more disturbing than a gloved hand.[82]

---

80 Nerval, *Sylvie*, *OC* III, 559.
81 '[D]onnent l'air comme il faut'. Flaubert, *Bouvard et Pécuchet*, ed. Claudine Gothot-Mersch (Paris: Gallimard, 1979), 522.
82 'C'est qu'il idéalise la main, en la privant de sa couleur, comme fait la poudre de riz pour le visage; il la rend inexpressive (voir le vilain effet des gants sur la scène), mais typique; la forme seule est conservée et plus accusée. Cette couleur factice, grise, blanche ou jaune, s'harmonise avec la manche du vêtement, et, [sans] donner l'idée d'une nature autre (puisque le dessin est conservé), met de la nouveauté dans le connu, et rapproche ainsi ce membre couvert, d'un membre de statue. Et cependant, cette chose anti-naturelle a du mouvement (différent en cela du masque, mais le masque a du mouvement par les yeux). Rien n'est plus troublant qu'une main gantée.' Flaubert, *Carnets de travail*, 234.

For Nerval, the shift from airy, open lacework to tight leather gloves reflected a melancholy distaste for the modern industrialised world, and that distaste was echoed by Flaubert, whose disillusion focused particularly on the mediocrity of contemporary literature for whose failings the gloved hand served as a perfect metaphor. Gloves blunt or suppress all expressivity, he argues, whereas what he wants is for the form – literary as well as physical – to speak and let the soul shine through. Contemporary literature, he writes elsewhere, is stifled and airless; it is 'barbarism in white gloves!' and desperately needs great breaths of fresh air.[83] The gloved hand imposes a false uniformity on what lies beneath, just as the crinoline disguises the true female form and offers an artificial construct in its place.[84] Suspicion of that artifice is compounded by a fear of what unspoken horrors may lie hidden beneath the woman's voluminous skirts or inside the smooth surface of her glove, both of which come to represent a society that thrives on pretence.

To reveal and exploit that pretence was to lay bare unpalatable truths. Gautier does this gently in his poem, 'La Bonne Soirée', where the poet disengages himself from formal society through a separation of body and clothes. The decision to remain comfortably at home instead of attending an ambassadorial ball is evoked by the empty garments that he will not wear:

> There's a ball at the British Embassy;
> My black suit is on the chair
> With its arms dangling;
> My waistcoat gapes open, and my shirt
> Seems to hold out its white cuffs
> To be put on.
> The tight, pointed boots
> Display their gleaming polish
> By the fireside;
> Next to the slim ties
> The glacé kid gloves stretch out
> Like flat hands.

The emptiness of these formal clothes denotes the poet's dissociation from the guests he imagines arriving eagerly at the ball in tailcoats and chiffon

---

83 '[B]arbarie en gants blancs!' Flaubert to Louise Colet, 19.3.1854, *Corr.* II, 538. See also *Corr.* II, 520, where Flaubert expresses disgust at the sight of opera singers performing William Tell while wearing gloves made by the fashionable glover Jouvin.

84 Cf. Baudelaire's poem 'Danse Macabre', *OC*, 103, where gloves, bonnet, pom-pommed shoes and an 'exaggerated dress in all its regal fullness' ['robe exagérée, en sa royale ampleur'], are worn by a skeleton.

gowns, for he sees beyond their attire to a vacant and deeply unattractive conformity:

> Backs on which a pustule blooms,
> Covering their reddened skin
> With airy tulle;
> Dandies and diplomats
> Whose dull-hued faces
> Display nothing.[85]

Clearly this is a far remove from the sphere of the fashion magazine where clothes fit beautiful bodies and where the gowns worn to society balls are discussed with reverence. But the fashion journals' idealised world, inhabited by modest yet charmingly seductive women whose desires are always in tune with the progress of a prosperous, harmonious and rapidly changing society, is repeatedly undermined by creative writers who use costume description to subvert the fantasy. In the world of Second Empire literature, clothes often misbehave. They are ripped, crumpled and soiled, their surface elegance is defiled, or their seams split open to reveal something disturbing or distasteful. At times they are misappropriated, for when worn by the wrong people even beautiful clothes express disorder, as Flaubert shows in *L'Éducation sentimentale* when the revolutionary mob sacks the royal palace: 'In a spirit of irony, the rabble donned lace and cashmere shawls. Gold fringes were wound round the sleeves of overalls, ostrich-plumed hats adorned the heads of blacksmiths, and ribbons of the Légion d'honneur were worn as belts by prostitutes.'[86]

Perhaps more than anyone, Emile Zola recognised the narrative potential of such a divorce between body and clothes, and he exploited it to the full in *Thérèse Raquin*. Dress in that novel takes on a deeply subversive role. Its importance is signalled from the outset, and it is immediately clear that it will be treated in a new way. Before introducing any of his main characters,

---

85 'C'est bal à l'ambassade anglaise; / Mon habit noir est sur la chaise, / Les bras ballants; / Mon gilet bâille et ma chemise / Semble dresser, pour être mise, / Ses poignets blancs. // Les brodequins à pointe étroite / Montrent leur vernis qui miroite, / Au feu placés; / A côté des minces cravates / S'allongent comme des mains plates /Les gants glacés [...] Les dos où fleurit la pustule, / Couvrant leur peau rouge d'un tulle / Aérien; / Les dandys et les diplomates, / Sur leurs faces à teintes mates, / Ne montrant rien.' Gautier, *Émaux et camées*, 127–29.
86 'La canaille s'affubla ironiquement de dentelles et de cachemires. Des crépines d'or s'enroulèrent aux manches des blouses, des chapeaux à plumes d'autruche ornaient la tête des forgerons, des rubans de la Légion d'honneur firent des ceintures aux prostituées.' Flaubert, *L'Éducation sentimentale*, OC II, 113.

Zola describes Thérèse's haberdashery shop in the damp and squalid Passage du Pont-Neuf. By means of a detailed enumeration of the contents of the window display, he deconstructs the image of the well-dressed woman purveyed by fashion writing of the period. Here the elements of fashion are dismantled and stripped of their allure; they assume an air of sinister foreboding. Separated from any central garment, the disembodied collars, sleeves, stockings, buttons and ribbons are displayed as disparate items that have lost their coherence as dress. Dusty and discoloured, impaled on metal hooks, metaphorically pierced by the sharp points of knitting needles and metal rod, muslin and tulle are detached from their conventional association with seductive softness and instead convey an atmosphere of cruelty, violence and despair:

> On one side there was some underwear; goffered tulle bonnets at two and three francs apiece, muslin sleeves and collars; then knitwear, stockings, socks, braces. Each object, yellowing and creased, was suspended pitifully from a wire hook. The shop window was thus filled from top to bottom with whitish rags which took on a mournful appearance in the transparent gloom. The new bonnets, more strikingly white, made glaring patches against the blue paper that lined the boards. And hanging from hooks along a metal rod, coloured socks added their sombre tones to the muslin's fading pallor.
>
> On the other side, in a narrower window, were piled big hanks of wool, black buttons sewn on white cards, boxes of all colours and sizes, hairnets with steel beads displayed on circles of bluish paper, sheaves of knitting needles, tapestry patterns, bobbins of ribbon, a heap of dull, faded objects which had no doubt languished there for five or six years. Every shade had turned a dirty grey in that cupboard, rotted by dust and damp.[87]

---

87 'D'un côté, il y avait un peu de lingerie; des bonnets de tulle tuyautés à deux et trois francs pièce, des manches et des cols de mousseline; puis des tricots, des bas, des chaussettes, des bretelles. Chaque objet, jauni et fripé, était lamentablement pendu à un crochet de fil de fer. La vitrine, de haut en bas, se trouvait ainsi emplie de loques blanchâtres qui prenaient un aspect lugubre dans l'obscurité transparente. Les bonnets neufs, d'un blanc plus éclatant faisaient des taches crues sur le papier bleu dont les planches étaient garnies. Et, accrochées le long d'une tringle, les chaussettes de couleur mettaient des notes sombres dans l'effacement blafard et vague de la mousseline [...] De l'autre côté, dans une vitrine plus étroite, s'étageaient de gros pelotons de laine verte, des boutons noirs cousus sur des cartes blanches, des boîtes de toutes les couleurs et de toutes les dimensions, des résilles à perles d'acier étalées sur des ronds de papier bleuâtre, des faisceaux d'aiguilles à tricoter, des modèles de tapisserie, des bobines de ruban, un entassement d'objets ternes et fanés qui dormaient sans doute en cet endroit depuis cinq ou six ans. Toutes les teintes avaient tourné au gris sale, dans cette armoire que la poussière et l'humidité pourrissaient.' Zola, *Thérèse Raquin*, 67.

Zola's window exhibits what appear to be dismal, hanging rags, the antithesis of the fashion magazines' presentation of dress as social aspiration (and the antithesis, too, of the idea of display promoted by the exhibitions). Instead, this display introduces a foretaste of doom. In a dehumanised premonitory vision of the mortuary window which plays a significant role later in the novel, it introduces an association between clothing and death. At the mortuary itself, passers-by stare through the window 'as if standing in front of a draper's window-display'; in an echo of the earlier passage, through the glass they see hanging a collection of 'awful rags' that have been removed from the disfigured corpses displayed on surrounding slabs.[88] Clothing in *Thérèse Raquin* is stripped of its normal functions and instead serves as a means of laying bare what lies beneath the surface.

In this novel about uncontrolled desire unmediated by morality or reason, clothes are never worn 'properly'. We see them crushed, soiled, ripped, covered with dead leaves, or discarded completely and left lying in crumpled heaps. Numerous displacements subvert or reverse the normal practice of dress. Laurent's mistress, an artist's model, undresses for work; Thérèse hides the naked Laurent beneath a pile of his clothes and tosses her own underskirt on top in order to prevent her mother-in-law discovering them in bed together; and conversely, Thérèse and Laurent spend two nights lying on their marriage bed, fully dressed, too terrified to remove their clothes or get under the sheets. In a particularly telling identification, the tattered skirts and trousers that hang on the mortuary wall are described as 'grimacing across the nakedness of the plaster', while the naked cadavers lying alongside appear to grimace back.[89]

Zola goes a step further than his contemporaries who hinted that something unpleasant lurked beneath the shimmering surface of the 'tainted petticoats'.[90] In *Thérèse Raquin* he has turned costume's function inside out: clothes become bodies, bodies become clothes, and nothing can be hidden any more. The rotting corpses in the mortuary are described as coloured rags, and their grotesquely swollen shapes echo the forms evoked by the distorting fashions of the day. The huge stomachs, bloated thighs and enormous arms of the corpses would fit unobtrusively beneath the skirts of a crinoline or into its puffed sleeves, while the mark of a rope around a hanged woman's throat is said to look like a necklace.[91] The dead bodies and their discarded clothes reflect one another perfectly: each is described in terms of the other, and

---

88 '[C]omme devant l'étalage d'un magasin de nouveautés'; 'loques lamentables'. Zola, *Thérèse Raquin*, 130.
89 '[G]rimaçaient sur la nudité du plâtre'. Zola, *Thérèse Raquin*, 130.
90 '[L]es jupons frelatés'.
91 Zola, *Thérèse Raquin*, 130–31.

in that identification there is a fundamental truth which contrasts with the surrounding dishonesty. Appropriately, the draper's shop suffers the same fate as the corpses. The abandoned shop is left to rot and the musty drapery starts to smell,[92] echoing the corruption which pervades the text.

Clothes and the body are violent antagonists in this novel, and in their struggle the flesh has to yield to its powerful tormentor. Laurent's immaculate new clothes are laid out neatly in preparation for his wedding, but they seize him in their grip when he puts them on. Unable to turn his head, he feels as if he is being stabbed and imagines his white waistcoat stained with blood as the starched collar cuts into his flesh.[93] By the end of the novel, Madame Raquin, the former draper, has succumbed to the same sinister forces; paralysed, her inert form looks 'like a bundle of clothes'.[94] In a knowing subversion of the Utopian world of the fashion journal, Zola's narrative deconstructs the customary associations of costume, and in doing so reveals the falsity of that idealised image of Second Empire France.

Costume in all its variety thus offered authors a subtle and flexible means of giving form to their views. Whether expressing confidence in the new regime or nostalgia for what had gone before; whether depicting a stable, egalitarian society or one whose very basis was under threat; whether celebrating progress and prosperity or hinting at unsavoury realities lurking beneath the surface, Second Empire writers found costume a rich new source of expression. As a means of evoking or challenging a changing world, it provided endless creative possibilities.

---

92 Zola, *Thérèse Raquin*, 236.
93 Zola, *Thérèse Raquin*, 168–69. Gautier imagines a similar effect in his poem 'Rondalla', but there the imagined bloodstain is transformed into a garnet stud: 'My knife stirs in its sheath; / Come now, who wants some incarnadine? / Who wants some red on his jabot / To make a garnet stud?' ['Dans sa gaine mon couteau bouge; /Allons, qui veut de l'incarnat? / A son jabot qui veut du rouge / Pour faire un bouton de grenat?'] *Émaux et camées*, 38.
94 '[C]omme un paquet de linge.' Zola, *Thérèse Raquin*, 213.

Chapter Seven

RUINS

It may seem incongruous to end this book with a chapter on ruins. The preceding chapters explored writers' responses to aspects of Second Empire France and examined the relationship between the period's social and technological innovations and its literature, but being neither new nor of recent interest, ruins hardly seem to fit this pattern. Yet each chapter has shown evidence of Second Empire writers' preoccupation with the idea of ruin in its broadest sense as they attempted to negotiate the changes taking place around them. The breakdown of order underlies many descriptions of display as writers dismantled the confident assurance of exhibition rhetoric, and that imagery of collapse is present throughout: in the recurrent evocations of disintegrating railway tracks and shattered carriages, in the frequent depiction of culinary confections destroyed not just by consumption but by acts of violence, in photographers' concern to record crumbling monuments in an attempt to preserve them from the ravages of time, and in the persistent association of fashionable costume with the idea of moral and financial ruin and social disintegration.

French writers' interest in the subject of ruins dates back at least as far as the Renaissance, when Du Bellay imported the Italian humanists' melancholy reflections on ruins into French culture. For Romantic writers, ruins had inspired sombre musings on the transience of existence and human endeavour. They offered visual evidence that nature eventually reasserts its domination over man's puny efforts by eroding his buildings and smothering them with lichen and bramble, in a reminder that even the hardest of marble ultimately turns to dust, like man himself. But by the mid-nineteenth century that response had become a platitude, like the entry in Flaubert's *Dictionnaire des idées reçues*: 'Ruins: make one think, and add a poetic touch to a landscape.'[1]

---

1 'Ruines: font rêver, et donnent de la poésie à un paysage.' Flaubert, *Dictionnaire des idées reçues*, *OC* II, 313. Roland Mortier, *La Poétique des ruines: Ses origines, ses variations de la Renaissance à Victor Hugo* (Geneva: Droz, 1974) traces the poetics of ruins since the Renaissance; Mortier takes the end of the Romantic period as his cut-off point.

Far from remaining a dead cliché, however, the ruin took on a new and urgent symbolism under the Second Empire as the imaginative resonance of the ruin underwent a fundamental shift. As a reminder of the ultimate folly of human enterprise, it represented a process that ran counter to the confident and forward-looking notions of progress, stability, novelty and prosperity that the regime sought to promote. Embedded in a cycle of ruin and reconstruction quite divorced from the melancholy aesthetic of the Romantics, the ruins that haunted the imagination of Second Empire writers were politicised and violent, and their reconstruction deeply suspect.

Second Empire literary ruins are brutal rather than contemplative. Their brutality is particularly evident in *Salammbô*, where destruction is depicted in the most violent terms. Whole cities are destroyed, and with them people and morals and beliefs, all with a ferocity and intensity that leaves nothing behind. All that remains of Tunis is a smoking heap of rubble spilling through breaches in the shattered city walls and spreading across the surrounding plain.[2] Hamilcar destroys even the ruins of ruins: 'He burned the ruins of ruins, leaving not a single tree or blade of grass.'[3] The whole novel is suffused with ruin imagery – even the tears trickling down Hannon's face are likened to 'wintry rain on a ruined wall'[4] – and although at the end of the novel the Carthaginians rebuild the ruins of their own city and believe that order has finally been restored, Flaubert's readers knew very well that the real Carthage would later be totally and utterly destroyed by Rome.

This over-determination of ruins, particularly marked in *Salammbô* but present in a striking number of Second Empire texts, has an obvious counterpart in the material world of Napoleon III's Paris where, under the direction of Baron Haussmann, thousands of homes were being torn down to make way for new streets, open spaces and public monuments. Crowded areas of housing that had clustered round networks of narrow, winding alleyways were demolished, former boundaries disappeared, and populations were displaced and social groupings disrupted. The demolition squads were widely accused not only of changing the face of Paris too radically, but of forcing workers to move out of the expensive new centre and fragmenting social cohesion by damaging the relationships between classes.

Although *Salammbô* purports to describe a distant and long-vanished civilisation, Flaubert politicises the destruction and rebuilding of Carthage

---

2 Flaubert, *Salammbô*, *OC* II, 791.
3 'Il brûla les ruines des ruines, il ne laissa pas un seul arbre, pas un brin d'herbe.' Flaubert, *Salammbô*, *OC* II, 789.
4 '[U]ne pluie d'hiver sur une muraille en ruine.' Flaubert, *Salammbô*, *OC* II, 731.

in ways that make parallels with Second Empire Paris inescapable. In both cities ancient walls are torn down so that their stones can be used to rebuild the ramparts. A short passage at the novel's centre describes the effects of such destruction on social hierarchies within the city, and hints at the emergence of dangerous new class tensions: once the old walls had gone, Flaubert writes, 'hierarchies based on race were replaced by differences in wealth, which continued to keep the sons of the vanquished separate from the sons of the conquerors; thus the patricians were annoyed to see the destruction of these ruins, while the common people, without really knowing why, were delighted.'[5] The violent and over-determined destruction of Carthage and its surroundings conveys intimations of changes which Flaubert's contemporaries would have recognised, with similarly divergent reactions.

Published a few years before *Salammbô*, Gautier's *Roman de la momie* also evokes a vanished civilisation of which few traces survive. The setting is a monumental Thebes at the height of its power – a city which seems immune to destruction. It is the antithesis of the ruin: 'the architecture [...] conveyed a sense of inescapable force, unyielding will and enduring persistence [...] The whole planet would have had to be shaken to its core to topple these pylons constructed from huge slabs of mountain; even fire could only have licked its tongue over these indestructible blocks.'[6] Yet the novel opens in the present, with a group of Egyptologists standing in the desert, studying the ruins that are all that remains of the great city, and it ends with the destruction of the Pharaoh and his army as the Red Sea engulfs them.

Such images of physical devastation clearly struck a chord with the Second Empire public. Crowds flocked to the Assyrian Museum in Paris to see fragments excavated from the ruins of the recently discovered city of Nineveh. As the author of *Les Ruines de Ninive* (1864) stressed, 'It was captured and destroyed, and destroyed so thoroughly that no visible trace of it remained. In the end no

---

5 '[L]a différence des fortunes, remplaçant la hiérarchie des races, continuait à maintenir séparés les fils des vaincus et ceux des conquérants; aussi les patriciens virent d'un oeil irrité la destruction de ces ruines, tandis que la plèbe, sans trop savoir pourquoi, s'en réjouissait.' Flaubert, *Salammbô*, *OC* I, 741. The 'hélépole' – the Barbarians' gigantic war machine designed to demolish a city – is itself demolished in the process, and Flaubert's description of it contains many common elements of accounts of half-demolished buildings in Paris: exposed beams, a series of floors shattered by the collapse, the plunge into the abyss. Flaubert, *Salammbô*, *OC* I, 776.

6 '[L]'architecture [...] présentait un caractère de force inéluctable, de volonté sans réplique, de persistance éternelle; [...] Pour faire tomber ces pylônes composés de quartiers de montagnes, il eût fallu que la planète s'agitât sur ses bases; l'incendie même n'eût fait que lécher de sa langue ces blocs indestructibles.' Gautier, *Le Roman de la momie*, 157.

one knew exactly where it had once stood.'⁷ The same was said of the Arènes de Lutèce, the extensive Gallo-Roman remains unexpectedly uncovered in the centre of Paris in the 1860s. This fascination with the destruction of the seemingly indestructible and with the total obliteration of ruins – even with the annihilation of the ruins of ruins – suggests an acute awareness that buildings were a repository of history, and that destroying them was tantamount to eradicating all trace of the past. Yet reconstructing them, as we shall see, was equally problematic. Writing about ruins was thus a way of reflecting on the eradication of a whole way of life. That such reflections were not confined to the distant past is indicated by the frequent presence of a solitary eagle – the emblem of Napoleon III – circling over the ruins of a once-great civilisation.

While *Salammbô* and *Le Roman de la momie* used ancient ruins to convey apocalyptic change and to show the *hubris* of power, many Second Empire texts focused instead on modern ruins. For classical writers, a ruin was by definition the remains of a monumental edifice such as a palace or a temple; the decay of humbler buildings had no affective resonance for them, and so was of no artistic interest.⁸ But with Napoleon III's *démolisseurs* reducing great swathes of Second Empire Paris to rubble, and with Haussmann's new buildings rising all around, the emotional impact of domestic ruins was evident to all.⁹ Writers were sensitive to the poignancy of half-demolished houses that exposed intimate details of the lives once lived there, and the image of torn wallpaper flapping on a newly revealed wall was much used to convey the pathos of shattered existences.¹⁰ Ruined lives were readily evoked by ruined buildings, as Flaubert well understood when he described Charles Bovary holding the hands of his dying wife, and 'flinching at her every heartbeat, as if at the aftershock of a collapsing ruin'.¹¹ (Earlier drafts of this passage refer to the aftershock of 'une démolition'.)

---

7 'Elle fut prise et détruite; et si bien détruite qu'il n'en resta plus aucune trace apparente. On finit même pas ne plus savoir à quel endroit précis elle avait existé.' H. L. Feer, *Les Ruines de Ninive* (Paris : Société des écoles du dimanche, 1864), 1. The site of Niniveh was discovered in 1842.
8 See Mortier, *La Poétique des ruines*, 9. Cf. Hippolyte Taine's comment, cit. in *Grand dictionnaire universel*, 'Ruines' entry: 'To be beautiful, ruins must be imposing or blackened by time.' ['Pour que les ruines soient belles, il faut qu'elles soient grandioses ou noircies par le temps.']
9 Ernest Blum and Alexandre Flan's 1862 review, *Voilà la chose!*, staged a procession of banner-waving demonstrators shouting 'Down with demolition men!' ['A bas les démolisseurs!'] See Maurice Allem, *La Vie quotidienne sous le Second Empire* (Paris: Hachette, 1948), 17.
10 E. g. Flaubert, *L'Éducation sentimentale*, *OC* II, 130: 'On apercevait l'intérieur des chambres avec leurs papiers en lambeaux; des choses délicates s'y étaient conservées, quelquefois. Frédéric observa une pendule, un bâton de perroquet, des gravures.' See also *OC* II, 99.
11 '[T]ressaillant à chaque battement de son cœur, comme au contre-coup d'une ruine qui tombe.' Flaubert, *Madame Bovary*, *OC* I, 684.

Poets, too, were sensitive to the symbolic resonance of the modern ruin. The emotional impact of seeing homes torn down conjured up images of death for Louis Bouilhet, and in his poem 'Démolitions' (1859) he represents rows of half-demolished houses as lines of corpses and pale ghosts rising from a winding-sheet of streets. Baudelaire finds expression for his own personal anguish by figuring himself trapped forever in a nightmarish ruin on the point of collapse, and wonders whether the mass of humanity that will be crushed when the ruin falls will leave any trace on the debris.[12] Evoking ruins was a way of articulating a sense that the past was being obliterated and history rewritten. As Pierre Véron shows in 'Le Vieux Paris', to demolish a house was to destroy an entire family history by erasing ancestral memories and severing precious connections with the past:

> For veneration adheres to these walls,
> And beneath the ashes of these dusty roofs is hidden
> All the past of our ancestors; [...]
> Then as it too vanishes, the old city takes with it
> A whole lost world, a whole dead age.[13]

In a poem entitled 'Paris nouveau', Anaïs Ségalas deplores, for similar reasons, the fact that buildings associated with major figures from France's cultural heritage have been torn down. Lamenting the destruction of buildings once inhabited by St. Louis, Charles V, Racine or Coligny, she points out that:

> To the antiquarian all these fine old houses
> Were urns filled with ancestors' ashes.[14]

In Gautier's words, 'The demolition of Paris [was] the topic of the day.'[15]

Gautier's own response was primarily aesthetic, however, and for him the changes were not unwelcome. He found a strange beauty in the half-demolished houses, delighting in the picturesque effects of light and shade on fallen timbers and piles of rubble. He admired the clean new buildings that

---

12 Baudelaire, 'Symptômes de ruines', *OC*, 189.
13 'Car il est à ces murs un culte qui s'attache, / Et de ces toits poudreux sous la cendre se cache / Tout le passé de nos aïeux; [...] / Puis en partant aussi la vieille ville emporte / Tout un monde perdu, toute une époque morte.' 'Le Vieux Paris' (1857). Cit. in Pierre Citron, *La Poésie de Paris dans la littérature française de Rousseau à Baudelaire*, I, 2 vols. (Paris: Editions de minuit, 1961), 335.
14 'Tous ces bons vieux logis étaient pour l'antiquaire / Des urnes qu'emplissaient les cendres des aïeux.' Cit. in Citron, *La Poésie de Paris*, I, 336.
15 'Paris démoli est une question à l'ordre du jour.' Gautier, 'Mosaïque de ruines', in Dumas, Gautier et al, *Paris et les Parisiens au XIXe siècle*, 38.

took their place once the ground had been cleared, and welcomed the festive air their ornamentation gave to the city.[16] For him, sweeping away the dust of the past was a necessary process, as essential to the city's hygiene as sweeping the filth from its streets. But for many others the effects of the demolition were disorienting, and the disappearance of familiar landmarks in a city under reconstruction forced even native Parisians to consult new maps to find their way around. Small wonder, then, that ruined buildings and routes blocked with rubble imprinted themselves on the Second Empire imagination, or that writers used that image to explore their uncertainty about the direction in which France was moving.

For the Goncourt brothers the disappearance of familiar surroundings echoed a profound sense of alienation, an acute malaise that ran much deeper than the physical changes wrought by demolition men. For them, the physical destruction of old buildings and the creation of new ones was a metaphor for the disappearance of familiar values and for the troubling uncertainty of the new. 'Our own Paris, the Paris where we were born, the Paris of 1830 to 1848, is vanishing', they wrote:

> [...] I am as estranged from what is to come and from what now exists, as I am from these new boulevards, which no longer have the feel of Balzac's world but seem like London or some future Babylon. It is stupid to come like this into a period that is under construction: the soul feels uneasy.[17]

Modern ruins were the perfect analogy to convey such unease in the face of 'a period that [was] under construction.' Whereas classical ruins had a massive solidity about them – great blocks of stone that had fallen centuries before and still lay half-embedded in the ground – the Second Empire ruin is presented as precarious and unstable, mirroring the society that produced it and the many vulnerable characters who feature in novels of the period.[18] The Goncourts' *Germinie Lacerteux* is a typical example of a character who is constantly on the

---

16 E. g. 'the old city dons a palace tunic all embroidered with sculpture.' ['la vielle ville revêt une tunique de palais toute brodée de sculpture.'] Gautier, 'Mosaïque de ruines', in Dumas, Gautier et al, *Paris et les Parisiens au XIXe siècle*, 39.

17 'Notre Paris, le Paris où nous sommes nés, le Paris des mœurs de 1830 à 1848, s'en va [...] Je suis étranger à ce qui vient, à ce qui est, comme à ces boulevards nouveaux, qui ne sentent plus le monde de Balzac, qui sentent Londres, quelque Babylone de l'avenir. Il est bête de venir ainsi dans un temps en construction: l'âme y a des malaises.' Goncourt, *Journal*, I (18 November 1860): 632.

18 Repeatedly, characters in Flaubert's novels cry out that they are ruined – 'ruined, stripped bare, done for!' ['ruiné, dépouillé, perdu!'], as Frédéric puts it (Flaubert, *L'Éducation sentimentale*, OC II, 41). In that novel (which is full of references to ruins)

verge of collapse until finally, echoing the capital's half-demolished buildings, 'with one fall after another, the wretched creature tumbled down into the street'.[19]

If the old Paris had gone, the new Paris had not yet arrived. As Charles Monselet wrote in *Les Ruines de Paris*, 'The Paris we have seen over the last few years is a Paris in transition [...] We stand between memory and promise.'[20] But literary texts of the time betray little confidence in that 'promise'. Poised between past and future, the Second Empire ruin is portrayed by writer after writer as on the point of crashing to the ground. Swaying in the breeze, ready to collapse at any sudden gust, it is exploited as the perfect metaphor for a society whose basic values have been eroded and which is in imminent danger of collapse. As Albert Angot put it:

Like a building with worn columns,
Society trembles at a breath of wind;
Its strongest pillars were the social mores of our past.[21]

---

the metaphor of ruin is also applied to Rosanette, Monsieur and Madame Arnoux, the Arnoux children, Madame Dambreuse and Dussardier, and significantly, a former writer is described as 'a ruin'. *OC* II, 139. In *Madame Bovary* the ruin metaphor is applied to Charles and Emma, while by the end of the novel the three doctors who succeed Charles are all 'demolished' ['battus en brèche'] by Homais.

19 '[D]e chute en chute, la misérable créature roula à la rue.' Goncourt, *Germinie Lacerteux*, 209. Earlier, the narrator says that 'The miracle of that life of disorder and heartbreak, that shameful and ruined life, was that it did not shatter.' ['Le miracle de cette vie de désordre et de déchirement, de cette vie honteuse et brisée, fut qu'elle n'éclatât pas.'] (155) Then Germinie is 'ready to fall' ['prête à tomber'] amidst 'shaking' and 'breakdown' ['ébranlement [...] défaillances']; the stones around her appear to dissolve and nothing seems solid any more. (200)

20 'Le Paris que nous avons sous les yeux depuis quelques années est un Paris de transition [...] Nous sommes placés entre le souvenir et la promesse.' Charles Monselet, *Les Ruines de Paris*, cit. in Oster and Goulemot, *La Vie parisienne*, 139.

21 'Pareille à l'édifice aux colonnes usées, / La société tremble à l'haleine du vent; / Ses plus fermes piliers étaient nos mœurs passées.' Albert Angot, *Nos ruines* (Paris: Ch. Douniol et cie., 1871), 3. Cf. La Jacressarde, one of the many ruined houses in Hugo's *Les Travailleurs de la mer*. 'The floor was covered with fallen plasterwork. No one knew how the house remained standing. It moved in the wind.' ['Les plâtrages tombés couvraient le plancher. On ne savait comment tenait la maison. Le vent la remuait.'] (p. 220). See also Flaubert's *La Tentation de saint Antoine* of 1856, at the end of which the Devil tells the Saint: 'Un vertige nouveau pousse à l'abîme l'humanité rassasiée! Entends-tu les civilisations pourries craquer dans les ténèbres, comme des palais qui s'écroulent?' [A new vertigo is pushing sated humanity towards the abyss! Can you hear the sound of rotten civilisations cracking in the darkness, like collapsing palaces?' Flaubert, *La Tentation de saint Antoine*, *OC* I, 521. De Tocqueville used the same image in 1856, writing of the Revolution of 1789: 'If it had not happened, the old edifice of society would nevertheless have fallen bit by bit instead of collapsing suddenly.'

Victor Hugo's famous pen and ink drawings of tottering edifices indicate the extent to which such imagery dominated his imagination, and his novels abound in ruined buildings charged with political metaphor. In *Les Travailleurs de la mer* – a novel teeming with ruins of every kind – he describes the 'Bû de la rue' with its ruined walls, rotting woodwork, cracked chimneys and collapsing roof in terms that leave no doubt about its symbolic meaning. Inside, old wallpaper peels from the walls in layers that inscribe a succession of France's past régimes – 'the griffins of the Empire, the crescent-shaped drapery of the Directoire, the balusters and cippi of Louis XVI'.[22] Like Bouilhet's ruins, this house is a 'corpse'. Moreover it is haunted by Satan; and in an oblique jibe at Napoleon III we are told that 'Satan is an emperor like another',[23] and that when the house has finally been destroyed, its stones will be appropriated to build a palace in the capital.[24] Although Hugo's novel is ostensibly set in the Channel Islands, the metaphors of ruin that run throughout conjure up a passionate image of a crumbling, collapsing, ill-governed France that will one day be salvaged by the genius and sacrifice of the outcast Gilliatt/Hugo. Hugo's Guernsey is a ruined fragment of France, eroded by the Atlantic;[25] the island is 'in mid-demolition';[26] and his St. Peter Port is a strange transformation of Paris with its resonant ruins and barricades: 'hovels, potholes, unpaved alleyways, burnt gables, dwellings that had collapsed, empty rooms with no doors or windows and with grass growing inside, beams that lay across roads, and ruins blocking the way'.[27] In a frenzy of demolition that is presented as blasphemous, everything is ruthlessly torn down and destroyed in the name of so-called progress:

> He disturbs, displaces, demolishes, pulls down, razes, digs, burrows, excavates, smashes, crushes, obliterates this, destroys that, and rebuilds with destruction. Nothing gives him pause, no mass, no block, no

---

['Si elle n'eût pas eu lieu, le vieil édifice social n'en serait pas moins tombé pièce à pièce au lieu de s'effondrer tout à coup.'] Alexis de Tocqueville, *L'Ancien régime et la révolution*, *Œuvres complètes*, (Paris: Gallimard, 1952), II, 96, cit. in Claudie Bernard, *Le Passé recomposé. Le roman historique français du dix-neuvième siècle* (Paris: Hachette, 1996), 184.

22 '[L]es griffons de l'Empire, les draperies en croissant du Directoire, les balustres et les cippes de Louis XVI.' Hugo, *Les Travailleurs de la mer*, 93.
23 'Satan est un empereur comme un autre.' Hugo, *Les Travailleurs de la mer*, 93–94.
24 Hugo, *Les Travailleurs de la mer*, 120. Although the 'capital' is supposedly London, the word inevitably evokes Paris.
25 Hugo, *Les Travailleurs de la mer*, 25–26.
26 '[E]n pleine démolition'. Hugo, *Les Travailleurs de la mer*, 82.
27 '[M]asures, fondrières, ruelles dépavées, pignons brûlés, logis effondrés, chambres désertes sans portes ni fenêtres où l'herbe pousse, des poutres traversant la rue, des ruines barrant le passage'. Hugo, *Les Travailleurs de la mer*, 39–40.

obstruction, no authority of magnificent materials or nature's majesty. If the vastness of creation is within his reach, he destroys it. He is tempted by that aspect of God that can be ruined, and he attacks its immensity, hammer in hand.[28]

This imagery of violent destruction also encompasses the wrecked steamship La Durande, whose humanised interior, like that of half-demolished Parisian houses, is ripped apart and exposed to view:

> it was an open trunk from which spilled a mass of debris, like entrails. Ropes and cables floated and quivered; chains swayed and shivered; the ship's nerves and fibres were laid bare and hung down. Anything that was not smashed was twisted; [...] everything had the form of a ruin.[29]

And like the archetypal Second Empire ruin, the grounded wreck is poised above the abyss, ready to collapse at the slightest tremor: 'Everything was collapsing, sinking, and a flood of planks, boards, metalwork, cables and beams had stopped right at the edge of the great split in the keel, from where the slightest shock could send it all plunging into the sea.'[30]

Despite the over-determined imagery of ruin that pervades *Les Travailleurs de la mer*, however, Hugo's vision is not one of terminal collapse. Like his wrecked ship which sails again, these ruins are presented as salvageable; something worthwhile can be constructed from the rubble. Thus for Hugo the image of the ruin can, as here, have a positive, creative side; the logic of his ruins is that destructive forces may be harnessed for beneficial ends. Although he rages at the satanic perpetrator of such destruction, his ruins also articulate the possibility of constructive revolution and social reintegration. The hamlets of Guernsey serve as a visible reminder of this process, for the

---

28 'Il dérange, déplace, supprime, abat, rase, mine, sape, creuse, fouille, casse, pulvérise, efface cela, abolit ceci, et reconstruit avec de la destruction. Rien ne le fait hésiter, nulle masse, nul bloc, nul encombrement, nulle autorité de la matière splendide, nulle majesté de la nature. Si les énormités de la création sont à sa portée, il les bat en brèche. Ce côté de Dieu qui peut être ruiné le tente, et il monte à l'assaut de l'immensité, le marteau à la main.' Hugo, *Les Travailleurs de la mer*, 80.
29 '[C]'était un tronc ouvert laissant échapper un fouillis de débris semblable à des entrailles. Des cordages flottaient et frissonnaient; des chaînes se balançaient en grelottant; les fibres et les nerfs du navire étaient à nu et pendaient. Ce qui n'était pas fracassé était désarticulé; [...] tout avait la forme de la ruine.' Hugo, *Les Travailleurs de la mer*, 310–11.
30 'Tout croulait, tout coulait, et un ruissellement de planches, de panneaux, de ferrailles, de câbles et de poutres s'était arrêté au bord de la grande fracture de la quille, d'où le moindre choc pouvait tout précipiter dans la mer.' Hugo, *Les Travailleurs de la mer*, 311.

walls of their cottages incorporate ornate pieces of masonry taken from the ruins of grander buildings. The recycled stones imply a self-regulating system of social evolution as old hierarchies break down and new ones form. Even the storm that threatens to engulf the wrecked ship is shown to follow this pattern: it subsides with a crash like that of collapsing timbers, the black clouds disintegrate, and a great crack splits open the darkness to reveal the blue sky of renewed hope.[31] Hugo's overarching vision in this novel is one of political optimism, and with characteristic daring he exploits the rhetoric of ruins to convey both violent destruction and a belief in the ultimate possibility of regeneration.

Gautier, too, appreciated the creative possibilities of the ruin. In particular, he was sensitive to its capacity to evoke human transformation, finding in its metaphorical resonance a way of exploring and conveying psychological change. He does this notably in his popular historical novel, *Le Capitaine Fracasse* (whose title already implies disintegration). The novel opens with a lengthy description of the dilapidated Château de Sigognac. As its destitute owner departs, Gautier shows how deeply his memories and personal history are embedded in the ruined building, and how ambivalent are his feelings about leaving the past behind:

> All these old, wretched, gloomy, disagreeable, dusty, dull things that had so bored and disgusted him, now seemed filled with a charm he had failed to recognise. He felt ungrateful to the poor old ruined castle which had nevertheless sheltered him as best it could, and which, despite its tumbledown state, had persisted in remaining standing so as not to crush him as it fell, like an octogenarian servant who stays standing on trembling legs for as long as his master is present.[32]

But by accepting change and moving on, the Baron opens himself up to a fuller and richer life. With his fortunes and happiness restored, at the

---

31 Hugo, *Les Travailleurs de la mer*, 427–28. Gilliatt has managed to bring order to the shattered wreck: 'Each piece of debris had its place. The entire shipwreck was there, classified and labelled.' ['Chaque débris avait sa place. Tout le naufrage était là, classé et étiqueté.'] (336).

32 '[T]outes ces choses vieilles, misérables, maussades, rechignées, poussiéreuses, somnolentes, qui lui avaient inspiré tant de dégoût et d'ennui, lui paraissaient maintenant pleines d'un charme qu'il avait méconnu. Il se trouvait ingrat envers ce pauvre vieux castel démantelé qui pourtant l'avait abrité de son mieux et s'était, malgré sa caducité, obstiné à rester debout pour ne pas l'écraser de sa chute, comme un serviteur octogénaire qui se tient sur ses jambes tremblantes tant que le maître est là.' Gautier, *Le Capitaine Fracasse*, 69.

end of the novel he returns to the castle whose transformation echoes his own:

> In place of the wretched hovel whose pitiful description you will remember, there stood a brand new castle, resembling the old one in the way a son resembles his father. Yet its form remained unchanged. It still had the same architectural layout; only, in the space of a few months, it had grown younger by several centuries.[33]

Such a buoyant approach to ruin and reconstruction comes as no surprise from an author who likened Haussmann's transformation of Paris to the old city donning a rich tunic 'embroidered with sculptures'.[34]

Few Second Empire writers shared such optimism in the face of change, however. The future they envisaged was more often a bleak one, and ruined buildings offered a vivid means of conveying the social and moral desolation they foresaw. Edmond About described watching demolition work in the capital, and warned that the buildings that would rise from the rubble would eventually be reduced to ruins in their turn.[35] Repeatedly, writers evoked the fate of the great cities of antiquity as a warning of what would happen to Paris. Gustave Claudin, for example, predicted that Paris would disappear as Babylon, Thebes, Syracuse, Carthage and Niniveh had done, leaving only a pile of overgrown ruins haunted by wolves.[36] Leconte de Lisle went further still: in his apocalyptic poem, 'La Dernière vision', he imagines a future devoid of life and even of the last traces of ruins:

> The surface of the earth is completely bare.
> No cities; their supports have been broken by age
> And collapse in a confusion of ivy-covered blocks of stone.

---

33 'Au lieu de la triste masure dont on se rappelle la description lamentable, s'élevait [...] un château tout neuf, ressemblant à l'ancien comme un fils ressemble à son père. Cependant rien n'avait été changé dans sa forme. Il présentait toujours la même disposition architecturale; seulement, en quelques mois, il avait rajeuni de plusieurs siècles.' Gautier, *Le Capitaine Fracasse*, 497.
34 '[T]oute brodée de sculpture'. Gautier, 'Mosaïque de ruines', in Dumas, Gautier et al, *Paris et les Parisiens au XIXe siècle*, 39.
35 Edmond About, 'Dans les Ruines', *Paris-Guide*, II, 917. Similar anxieties are expressed in the 'Ruines' entry in the *Grand dictionnaire universel*.
36 Claudin, *Paris*, 238–242. Claudin reinforces his desolate vision by reminding his readers that the ephemeral bustle of modern Paris overlays a grim and lasting reality – the rue Vivienne was once a vast Roman cemetery, and the Halles were built over 'le charnier des Innocents' where more than 1,400,000 Parisians lay buried.

Of places where the busy ant-hill used to swarm
There remains no trace that can speak and say: I existed!
[...] Time has run its course: things have fallen silent.
[...] All! All has vanished, without echo, without trace.[37]

Writers' fascination with ruins implies a need to distance themselves from the present, or at least to rethink their position in the temporal scheme: ruins allow them to project their imagination into the past or the future, or to dwell on a disintegrating present. But whereas Romantic ruins might prompt thoughts of a natural process of decay and the inevitable effects of time on even the most solid buildings, the ruins that feature in Second Empire texts suggest disturbance to the natural order. The expected cycle of construction, ruin and reconstruction is dislocated; these literary ruins no longer speak of a slow and picturesque decline, but instead suggest some violent cataclysm and a chronological process so fundamentally disrupted that time itself has been blocked or shattered. In *Arria Marcella*, as we have seen, Gautier delights in the incongruous juxtaposition of ancient and modern as his characters take the train to the ruins of Pompeii. There, traces of lettering on ruined walls cause them to wonder how the posters and advertisements of modern Paris might be viewed in two thousand years' time. Gautier's description of poignant domestic details that are still visible inside the ruined houses – 'all those domestic details that historians ignore and whose secrets vanish along with civilisations' – has clear echoes of literary responses to Haussmann's demolitions,[38] while his comparison between a gently smoking Vesuvius and the slopes of Montmartre seems to hint at some Parisian cataclysm yet to come. As the story unfolds among the ruins, the main protagonist

---

37 'La face de la terre est absolument nue. / Point de villes, dont l'âge a rompu les étais, / Qui s'effondrent par blocs confus que mord le lierre. / Des lieux où tournoyait l'active fourmilière / Pas un débris qui parle et qui dise: J'étais! / [...] Les temps sont accomplis: les choses se sont tues. / [...] Tout! Tout a disparu, sans échos et sans traces.' Charles Leconte de Lisle, 'La Dernière vision', in *Poèmes barbares*, ed. C. Gothot-Mersch (1866; Paris: Gallimard, 1985), 213–24. Cf. his description of a ruined palace in an equally bleak *poème barbare*, 'Le Barde de Temrah' (1859) (Ibid., 73–80). The second section (39–98) of Élise Gagne's *Omégar ou le dernier homme, proso-poésie dramatique de la fin du temps* (Paris: Didier, 1859), paints a destruction almost as complete as that of 'La Dernière vision'. Entitled 'Les Derniers habitants de Paris,' the scene is situated in a Paris of the year 2800 where everything but the Hôtel Dieu has been reduced to 'a heap of dust' ['un amas de poussière'] (40).

38 '[T]ous ces détails domestiques que négligent les historiens et dont les civilisations emportent le secret avec elles.' Gautier, *Arria Marcella*, *Romans et Contes*, 275–76.

experiences a sense of dislocated chronology: 'For him, the wheel of time was out of joint.'[39]

This sense of time being out of joint is present, too, in Flaubert's description in *L'Éducation sentimentale* of stonebreakers at work in the forest of Fontainebleau, where the newly-hewn stones 'became more and more numerous, finally filling the whole landscape; they were cube-shaped like houses, flat like paving-stones, propping each other up, overhanging one another, merging together like the monstrous, unrecognisable ruins of some vanished city.'[40] The hallucinatory landscape seems filled with the remains of a city ruined before it has even been built, just as a description of Paris earlier in the novel had evoked a wilderness littered with half-built shacks that had already been abandoned and resembled 'vague ruins'.[41] Like the linen factory under construction in *Madame Bovary* whose gear wheels already lie scattered and rusting on the surrounding wasteland,[42] or the unfinished temple in Nerval's *Sylvie* that is already an ivy-covered ruin,[43] construction and destruction are presented as indistinguishable as time collapses in on itself and progress is inconceivable.[44]

But the quintessential ruin of Second Empire writers is surely the barricade. Bringing together the shattered debris of modernity in a chaotic mass that resists forward movement, the literary barricade simultaneously denotes destructive change, resistance and blocked progress. Flaubert's description of barricades in *L'Éducation sentimentale* flows seamlessly into a description of the

---

39 'Pour lui, la roue du temps était sortie de son ornière'. Gautier, *Arria Marcella, Romans et Contes*, 303.
40 '[S]e multipliaient de plus en plus, et finissaient par emplir tout le paysage, cubiques comme des maisons, plates comme des dalles, s'étayant, se surplombant, se confondant, telles que les ruines méconnaissables et monstrueuses de quelque cité disparue.' Flaubert, *L'Éducation sentimentale, OC* II, 127. A similar chronological reversal occurs in *Les Travailleurs de la mer* where, instead of buildings being reduced to piles of stone, heaps of rock are described as ruined buildings: 'Here there is a fortress, here a crude temple, here a jumble of tumbledown houses and demolished walls – all the debris of a deserted town. There is no town, no temple, no fortress; it is the cliff.' ['Voici une forteresse, voici un temple fruste, voici un chaos de masures et de murs démantelés, tout l'arrachement d'une ville déserte. Il n'existe ni ville, ni temple, ni forteresse; c'est la falaise.'] (33).
41 '[D]e vagues ruines'. Flaubert, *L'Éducation sentimentale, OC* II, 45.
42 Flaubert, *Madame Bovary, OC* I, 608.
43 Nerval, *Sylvie, OC* III, 545.
44 This phenomenon crops up even in guidebooks to ruins. See, for example, Charles Marchal, *Les Ruines romaines de Champlieu (Campi locus)* (Paris: Dentu, 1860), 18–20, where the author discusses Roman remains in terms of modern achievements: the Roman road ('via ferrata') was a 'chemin de fer'; the Appenine Way had its own telegraph system; Thalès discovered electricity and Hieron of Alexandria made observations on steam power...

ruined houses that surround them, and his barricades are explicitly identified as ruins:

> Omnibuses, gas pipes and cart-wheels were still lying on the ruined barricades; small black puddles in some areas must have been blood. The houses were riddled with bullets, and their framework was visible beneath the chipped plaster. Blinds, held on by one nail, hung like rags. Staircases had collapsed and doors opened into space. The inside of rooms could be seen, with wallpaper in shreds; occasionally fragile things had survived. Frédéric noticed a clock, a parrot's perch and some engravings.[45]

Flaubert has here constructed a thoroughly modern and bloodstained ruin whose overturned buses, detached wheels and disconnected gas pipes spell out the barricade's function of impeding movement, just as the stopped clock and the doors that lead nowhere represent blocked progress.

A barricade again evokes a chaotic world in ruins in *Les Misérables*, where Hugo invests his description with bitterness at the cause of such turmoil:

> What was this barricade made of? The remains of three six-storey houses torn down for the purpose, some said [...] It had the woeful aspect of all works of hatred: ruin [...] Look! A door! A grating! An awning! A mantlepiece! A broken stove! A cracked cooking-pot! Bring everything! Throw everything on! Push, roll, dig, demolish, overturn, tear everything down! It was an amalgam of paving-stones, rubble, timber, iron bars, cloths, smashed window panes, old chairs, cabbage stalks, rags and tatters and malediction, [...] overturned carts [...] an omnibus [...] In that jumble full of despair, you could see rafters, bits of attic rooms with their wallpaper, window-frames with their glass panes still intact stuck in the debris awaiting the cannon-fire, ripped-out fireplaces, cupboards, tables, benches – a howling chaos.[46]

---

45 'Sur les barricades en ruine, il restait des omnibus, des tuyaux de gaz, des roues de charrettes; de petites flaques noires, en de certains endroits, devaient être du sang. Les maisons étaient criblées de projectiles, et leur charpente se montrait sous les écaillures du plâtre. Des jalousies, tenant par un clou, pendaient comme des haillons. Les escaliers ayant croulé, des portes s'ouvraient sur le vide. On apercevait l'intérieur des chambres avec leurs papiers en lambeaux; des choses délicates s'y étaient conservés, quelquefois. Frédéric observa une pendule, un bâton de perroquet, des gravures.' Flaubert, *L'Éducation sentimentale*, *OC* II, 130.

46 'De quoi était faite cette barricade? De l'écroulement de trois maisons à six étages, démolis exprès, disaient les uns [...] Elle avait l'aspect lamentable de toutes les constructions de la haine: la ruine [...] Tiens! cette porte! cette grille! cet auvent! ce

Like Flaubert's barricade, these politicised ruins absorb everything around them, and thus serve as the perfect metaphor for a society where everything – people, buildings, manners, hopes, reputations, fortunes, lives – was seen as tending to the ruined condition.[47] As the poet in Baudelaire's 'Le Cygne' reflects while he contemplates the confusion of rubble and building blocks that strew the Place du Carrousel and conjure up images of disintegration and loss even as they evoke the rebuilding of Paris, 'Everything [...] becomes allegory.'[48]

If the ubiquitous image of the ruin was an oblique means of commenting on social change, it also provided a way of reflecting on the very process of literary creation. Ruins were so richly expressive that some writers saw them as a kind of text, and in various ways the process of writing became bound up with the idea of ruin. Flaubert often talked of the business of writing a novel in terms of masonry. In a telling comment, he had noted that some of the stones of the Parthenon were the colour of ink;[49] he later compared literary production to the way in which the pyramids were laboriously constructed, block by block, and then abandoned in the desert to be pissed on by jackals and clambered over by bourgeois tourists.[50]

Flaubert frequently used the metaphor of a pyramid to explain how a novel is constructed, but as time went on he felt that structure loosen and

---

chambranle! ce réchaud brisé! cette marmite fêlée! Donnez tout! jetez tout! poussez, roulez, piochez, démantelez, bouleversez, écroulez tout! C'était la collaboration du pavé, du moellon, de la poutre, de la barre de fer, du chiffon, du carreau défoncé, de la chaise dépaillée, du trognon de chou, de la loque, de la guenille, et de la malédiction [...] des charrettes renversées [...] un omnibus [...] On y voyait, dans un pêle-mêle plein de désespoir, des chevrons de toits, des morceaux de mansardes avec leur papier peint, des châssis de fenêtres avec toutes leurs vitres plantées dans les décombres, attendant le canon, des cheminées descellées, des armoires, des tables, des bancs, un sens dessus dessous hurlant.' Hugo, *Les Misérables*, II, 543–44.

47 Cf. Gautier's comment that 'Of all the ruins in the world, the saddest sight is decidedly the ruin of man.' ['De toutes les ruines du monde, la ruine de l'homme est assurément la plus triste à contempler.'] *Grand dictionnaire universel*, 'Ruines' entry.

48 'Tout [...] devient allégorie'. Baudelaire, *OC*, 97.

49 Flaubert to L. Bouilhet, 10.2.1851, *Corr.* I, 752.

50 Flaubert to E. Feydeau, end of November 1857, *Corr.* II, 783. He chose a resonant phrase to announce his decision to abandon the beginning of *Salammbô* and start again: '*I'm demolishing everything.*' ['*Je démolis tout.*'] To Ernest Feydeau, 20.6.1858, *Corr.* II, 817. In 1867 he compared the process of writing *L'Éducation sentimentale* to hauling a waggonload of rubble. To George Sand, 12.6.1857, *Corr.* III, 653. See also Flaubert to Louise Colet, 2.7.1853, *Corr.* II, 373. He even likened himself to an ancient and unrestorable ruin (to Louise Colet, 6.6.1853, *Corr.* II, 347).

crumble as his writing style changed. The building blocks of text refused to stack firmly one upon the other, and his cry of 'it's not making a pyramid!'[51] no longer seemed to matter as his novels' structures developed from the neatly pyramidal *Madame Bovary* to the more amorphous *Éducation sentimentale*, and eventually to the unashamedly flattened form of *Bouvard et Pécuchet*.[52] With its narrative lacunae, missing explanations and temporal leaps, even his prose seems to mirror the ruin. Like the famous gap that occurs towards the end of *L'Éducation sentimentale* between the shooting of Dussardier during the coup d'état of 1851 and the continuation of the narrative in 1867, the numerous fragments of plot that break off and are never recovered are suggestive of an aesthetic that has absorbed the ruin's ruptures and fissures. Flaubert's text constantly forces the reader to turn back to try to make sense of the confusing mass of narrative with its gaps and dead-ends, just as his characters frequently find their paths blocked, either literally or metaphorically as they range across Paris and are obliged to retrace their steps. Although readers of *L'Éducation sentimentale* may feel 'dizzied by landscapes and ruins',[53] like Frédéric on his melancholy travels after the coup d'état, the sense of disorientation felt by Flaubert's earliest readers must have been greater still, for they would have been familiar with the many Parisian streets and buildings evoked in the text but demolished by the time the novel appeared in 1869.

If narrative structure often echoed the ruin form, so too did language, which was widely seen as subject to a process of semantic erosion – a point that Flaubert frequently demonstrated by showing how meaning and vitality were sapped from words as they degenerated into *idées reçues*. In *Madame Bovary*, the name of Yonville-l'Abbaye is all that remains of the former abbey – even its ruins have vanished, we are told, leaving only the empty words. And in *Les Travailleurs de la mer*, Hugo explicitly associates a loss of linguistic richness with the widespread quarrying and demolition work that has made Guernsey unrecognisable to its old inhabitants: the people of Guernsey once spoke French but now speak English. 'Another demolition', he comments.[54]

The physical ruins generated by the demolition men, together with the widespread sense that French society was becoming fragmented and familiar values eroded, raised questions about how to make sense of these changes. Writers recognised that ruins, whether or not they were inscribed

---

51 'Ça ne fait pas la pyramide!' Flaubert, 7.4.1863, *Corr.* III, 318, and 15.4.1863, III, 319.
52 See A. W. Raitt, '*L'Éducation sentimentale* et la pyramide' in *Histoire et langage dans 'L'Éducation sentimentale' de Flaubert* (Paris: CDE et SEDES, 1981), 129–142.
53 'L'étourdissement des paysages et des ruines.' Flaubert, *L'Éducation sentimentale, OC* II, 160.
54 'Autre démolition'. Hugo, *Les Travailleurs de la mer*, 82.

with ancient inscriptions or recent graffiti, were 'documents' that had to be 'read' to be understood. As with any text, their meaning needed to be completed by the imagination of the reader or observer if it was to be reconstructed in the mind – if an imaginary structure was to be created from the traces offered. The author of one guide to ruined French châteaux and abbeys referred to their ruins as pages of stone on which a complete record of the country's history could be read,[55] and there was a proliferation of guidebooks offering to help visitors understand the hidden significance of inert stones and translate them into a meaningful story. As Gautier pointed out, every stone that fell from a demolished building destroyed part of the text of history, for on each one 'the history of our forefathers could be read, written beneath the rust of time'.[56]

Yet much writing of the period is marked by a sense that ruins have undergone a semantic deterioration and no longer carry any hidden metaphysical truth, as they had done for the Romantic generation. When Second Empire ruins are 'read', their meaning is often said to be banal or indecipherable – they refuse to allow themselves to be reconstructed by the imagination – and the indecipherable ruin thus becomes a metaphor for the indecipherability of the past. Describing his failed attempts to uncover the early history of Paris, Hugo uses an extended image of digging through countless layers of ruined structures without ever arriving at a final truth, and concludes: 'It seems impossible to dissect this ruin thoroughly.'[57] Gustave Claudin, too, found himself unable to make sense of the Parisian ruins he examined 'without its being possible to discover or read anything at all in that dust',[58] while Maxime Du Camp wrote of the equally 'indecipherable debris' strewn across the site of ancient Thebes.[59] And in Jules Verne's *Vingt mille lieues sous les mers*, the impossibility of interpreting the breathtaking underwater spectacle of the ruined city of Atlantis mirrors the impenetrability of Captain Nemo himself:

> Captain Nemo, leaning on a mossy pillar, remained motionless as if turned to stone in mute ecstasy. Was he dreaming of those long-dead

---

55 Alexandre de Lavergne, *Ruines historiques de France. Châteaux et abbayes* (Paris: Amyot, 1860), vii.
56 '[S]e lisait, écrite sous la rouille du temps, l'histoire de nos aïeux.' Théophile Gautier, 'Mosaïque de ruines', in Dumas, Gautier et al, *Paris et les Parisiens au XIXe siècle*, 39.
57 'Disséquer cette ruine à fond semble impossible.' Hugo, 'Introduction' to *Paris-Guide*, I, vi.
58 '[S]ans qu'il fût possible de rien discerner ni de rien lire dans cette poussière.' Claudin, *Paris*, 241.
59 '[D]ébris indéchiffrables'. Maxime Du Camp, *Egypte, Nubie, Palestine et Syrie: dessins photographiques* (Paris: Gide et Baudry, 1852), 231.

generations, and asking them the secret of human destiny? Was it here this strange man came to steep himself in historical memory and live again this ancient life – he who wanted no modern one? What would I not have given to know his thoughts, to share them and to understand them!⁶⁰

A melancholy sense of the past as unfathomable and irrecuperable hangs over much Second Empire literature, and ruined stonework gave visual form to that feeling.

*   *   *

The end of the Second Empire was sudden and traumatic. On the morning of 2ⁿᵈ September 1870, Napoléon III capitulated to the Prussian army after a humiliating defeat at Sedan, and was taken prisoner. Two days later, on September 4ᵗʰ, a bloodless revolution in Paris swept away the Second Empire. 'Everything is falling at once', wrote Mérimée in an echo of the familiar image of the collapsing ruin,⁶¹ while Maxime Du Camp dramatised the comprehensiveness of the collapse by likening France to a man struck by lightning whose body crumbles to dust as soon as it is touched. France, he said, 'had just collapsed at the first shock'.⁶²

Shortly after the Second Empire finally fell (as so many images of tottering ruins on the brink of collapse had suggested it must), much of Paris lay quite literally in ruins. Entire streets were destroyed by fire or shelling during the

---

60 '[L]e capitaine Nemo, accoudé sur une stèle moussue, demeurait immobile et comme pétrifié dans une muette extase. Songeait-il à ces générations disparues et leur demandait-il le secret de la destinée humaine? Etait-ce à cette place que cet homme étrange venait se retremper dans les souvenirs de l'histoire, et revivre de cette vie antique, lui qui ne voulait pas de la vie moderne? Que n'aurais-je donné pour connaître ses pensées, pour les partager, pour les comprendre!' Verne, *Vingt mille lieues sous les mers*, 299.
The description of the underwater city – 'ruined, destroyed [...] its roofs open to the sky, its temples fallen, its arches dislocated, its columns lying on the ground' ['ruinée, abîmée, jetée bas, [...] ses toits effondrés, ses temples abbatus, ses arcs disloqués, ses colonnes gisant à terre'] (297) – is preceded by hints that it was destroyed by man, for the sea-creatures surrounding it are described in terms of a military campaign: 'enormous antennae blocking my road'; 'halberdiers'; 'metallic rattling sounds'; 'huge crabs pointing like guns on their carriages' ['une antenne énorme qui me barrait la route'; 'des hallebardiers'; un cliquetis de ferraille, des crabes titanesques, braqués comme des canons sur leurs affûts.'] (295).
61 '[T]out tombe à la fois'. Cit. in Du Camp, *Souvenirs littéraires*, 594.
62 '[V]enait de s'effondrer au premier choc.' Du Camp, *Souvenirs littéraires*, 387.

Commune, as were many public buildings including the Tuileries Palace and the Hôtel de Ville. At the end of a week when more than 20,000 Parisians were killed, Edmond de Goncourt set out through the still-smoking debris to view the destruction. He noted half-demolished barricades, the rue de Rivoli full of rubble that had fallen from the Ministry of Finance, and costumes salvaged from a theatre lying in charred piles of spangled silk. But above all it was the ruins of the Hôtel de Ville that captured his attention:

> The ruin is magnificent and splendid [...] With its empty niches, its smashed or broken statuettes, and the remains of its clock [...] it is a picturesque wonder – something to be preserved, if the country were not irrevocably condemned to M. Viollet-le-Duc's restorations. By an irony of fate, in the midst of all the damage the deceitful legend *Liberty, Equality, Fraternity* gleams in newly gilded letters on a still-intact marble slab.[63]

Goncourt was not alone in his appreciation of these ruins and in his jaundiced political reading of them. An image that had intrigued so many Second Empire writers – Paris suffering the fate of the great cities of antiquity – had become a reality, and travellers flocked from far and wide to view its ruins, and indeed to photograph them or to buy commercially produced souvenir photographs. Guidebooks to the Parisian ruins were quickly published so that visitors could 'finally visit Paris, as they visited the Ruins of Thebes, Palmyra and Carthage'.[64] The author of one guidebook wrote of sightseers 'going on a pilgrimage to the ruins of our monuments.'[65] The author of another went so far as to claim that the capital had been so obliterated that, as with Nineveh, 'there was nothing left to indicate to the traveller where the Queen of Cities once stood.'[66] But like Goncourt, the authors of these guides knew that Paris would soon be rebuilt, and in a curious reversal of the usual aim of

---

63 'La ruine est magnifique, splendide [...] Avec des niches vides, ses statuettes fracassées ou tronçonnées, son restant d'horloge [...] elle est une merveille de pittoresque, à garder, si le pays n'était pas condamné sans appel aux restaurations de M. Viollet-le-Duc. Ironie du hasard! Dans la dégradation de tout le monument brille, sur une plaque de marbre intacte, dans la nouveauté de sa dorure, la légende menteuse: *Liberté, Egalité, Fraternité.*' Goncourt, 26–27.5.1871, *Journal*, II, 450–51.

64 'Visiter enfin Paris, comme on visitait les Ruines de Thèbes, de Palmyre et de Carthage.' Timothée Trimm, [pseudonym of Léo Lespès], *Les Ruines de Paris. Chronique du Paris brûlé. Description des monuments, palais, maisons incendiées, scènes de dévastation, état actuel des ruines, etc.* (Paris: Librairie et imprimerie universelles, 1871), v.

65 '[V]ont en pèlerinage aux ruines de nos monuments.' *Itinéraire des ruines de Paris : notices historiques sur les monuments incendiés* (Paris: Librairie Madre, 1871), 6.

66 '[I]l ne restait rien pour indiquer au voyageur où fut la Reine des Cités.' Timothée Trimm, *Les Ruines de Paris*, iii.

guidebooks, they stressed the need to record and describe the ruins of Paris precisely so that later, when restoration had taken place, readers would be able to 'reconstruct in their minds the original state of things'.[67] Instead of guiding the reader to an imaginative reconstruction of the ruins, these writers do the exact opposite: they aim to preserve the ruins as they are, to prevent them from being erased from historical memory through rebuilding or removal, and to ensure that the destruction is not forgotten.

L. Hans and J. J. Blanc offer a particularly interesting account in their 1871 *Guide à travers les ruines: Paris et ses environs*. They are as steeped in the aesthetics of the ruin as writers had been under Napoleon III, and their version of the ruins of Paris echoes descriptions already seen in Second Empire fiction: they give details of houses whose façades have collapsed, and describe piles of rubble, the twisted metal of balconies, walls with chimney-pieces still attached, a picture-frame hanging by a nail with its canvas burned away, and shelves high in the air with little ornaments (a bronze lamp, a Chinese vase, a mirror, etc.) still in place. They delight, however, not only in the visual beauty of what lies before them, but also in its political significance.[68] For them, these ruins represent a vast change for the better. The Ministry of Finance, always in their view a mediocre building, has been transformed into 'a superb ruin'.[69] Like Flaubert using the demolition of walls in Carthage as a metaphor for changes in social compartmentalisation, Hans and Blanc read social significance into the Ministry's ruins: 'Fire is a workman of genius', they enthuse:

> Out of that uniform, geometric, insolently regular mass, it has created a lively, decorative, interesting building. The administration had divided the building into *management* and *offices*. The fire has simplified that classification, dividing its work into only three parts: a virgin forest, a screen, and a hive.[70]

---

67 '[R]econstituer dans leur cerveau l'état primitif des choses.' L. Hans and J. J. Blanc, *Guide à travers les ruines: Paris et ses environs*. (Paris: Lemerre, 1871), 1.

68 See Hans and Blanc, *Guide à travers les ruines*, 6.

69 'une ruine superbe'. Hans and Blanc, *Guide à travers les ruines*, 8. Théophile Gautier gives a vivid description of the roof of this building exploding into the sky like an erupting volcano and sending up showers of burnt paper like flakes of black snow. Théophile Gautier, 'Une Visite aux ruines', *Tableaux de siège, 1870–71* (Paris: Charpentier, 1871), II, 622. The fire could do little to improve the Palais Royal, however: according to Hans and Blanc it had always had a bourgeois look, and now made 'a mediocre ruin' ['une ruine médiocre.'] *Guide à travers les ruines*, 13.

70 'Le feu est un ouvrier de génie [...] De cette masse uniforme, géométrique, insolemment régulière, il a fait un édifice mouvementé, décoratif, intéressant. L'administration avait divisé ce bâtiment par *directions* et *bureaux*. Le feu, lui, a simplifié cette classification, partageant en trois seulement son oeuvre: une forêt vierge, un paravent, une ruche.' Hans and Blanc, *Guide à travers les ruines*, 12–13, 17.

Not only are the ruins of the Ministry seen as representing a structural transformation, but the undistinguished building has, in its ruined form, become a 'decorative' and 'interesting' monument. Even the Second Empire preoccupation with the image of the broken clock has been realised, for the authors note that all the civic clocks stopped as the fire reached them, allowing the spectator to chart its progress – ten to nine at the centre of the Place du Carousel, ten past one at the Palais Royal, and at the Hôtel de Ville (which they say resembles a shipwreck) the entire clock face has fallen out, exposing the twisted, rusty mechanism that lies behind.[71]

It may be tempting to see the events of May 1871 as an extraordinary realisation of the disordered visions of ruin and collapse and reconstruction that feature so prominently in Second Empire literature. The truth, however, is that writers viewed and interpreted the aftermath of Empire through a distinctive sensibility that had developed under Napoleon III's regime. After the Commune, the anticipated reconstruction of Paris's ruined centres of power was regarded with suspicion and was seen, paradoxically, as an attempt to obliterate rather than restore the past. Rebuilding the ruin thus becomes a metaphor for the rewriting of history – dishonest, hypocritical, untrue. During the Second Empire, writers such as Flaubert, Hugo, Gautier and Nerval had transformed conventional concepts of ruin and reconstruction and injected them with new resonance. It is testimony to the power of their vision that subsequent events in France came to be read through their altered and regenerated perspective.

---

71 Hans and Blanc, *Guide à travers les ruines*, 17.

Chapter Eight
CONCLUSION

The fall of Napoléon III's regime was widely regarded as a watershed in French history. 'A new world is about to begin, another France', Flaubert repeatedly told friends.[1] The sense that an era had come to an abrupt end was further marked by the disastrous siege of Paris and the bloodshed of the Commune that followed. Those harrowing events inevitably provoked reflections on the period that had gone, and prompted attempts to reappraise the Second Empire.

Over that twenty-year period, much about France had changed almost beyond recognition. As we have seen, its embryonic railway system had developed into a complete network, linking France to its neighbours and bringing immense economic growth. Increasing industrialisation had drawn thousands of workers to cities which swelled to accommodate them, while an expanding Paris underwent its own major transformation under the direction of Haussmann. New industrially-produced fabrics and dyes and cheaper machine-made garments had revolutionised the way people dressed and made fashionable clothes available to a far wider range of the population, with the result that dress fashions themselves changed with ever-increasing speed. Eating habits, too, had undergone change: with famine a thing of the past, a far greater variety of foodstuffs and preparation methods were available, though industrial processing had brought with it new fears of food adulteration. From being the preserve of the few, photography had become available to all, and by creating an unprecedented visual record of people and places, it helped to shape the way the Second Empire would be seen by subsequent generations. Writing, too, had developed new forms as writers absorbed and reflected on the world around them, and found that engaging with a changing material culture expanded their range of creative expression. Bringing these new phenomena into their work not only allowed them to reflect the modern world but offered a way of exploring, albeit tentatively and uncertainly, complex and often still unformed attitudes and ideas.

---

1 Flaubert, *Corr.* IV, 225, 231, 232, 242.

Although literature obviously did not change overnight at either the beginning or the end of this period, there is nevertheless something distinctive about Second Empire writing. Looking back over that time in his *Souvenirs littéraires*, Maxime Du Camp described its literature as indecisive, lacking in originality, and 'somewhat senile'.[2] He blamed the censorship laws for its enervation. But it is hard to agree with Du Camp's estimation of the literary output of a period during which writers such as Flaubert, Baudelaire and Nerval were at the height of their powers. On the contrary, the Second Empire is now recognised as having produced some of France's greatest literature, part of whose success lies in the new and imaginative ways in which it absorbed and used material culture. As we have seen, reactions to change were many and varied, and similarly there was no consensus about how the changing material world should be interpreted or transformed into writing. It allowed itself to be used subversively or supportively; it was capable of exploring the personal or the political; it could look outwards to the future, or allow writers to turn inwards and reflect on issues of literary creativity. Incorporating material change was a means of encapsulating social tensions and of expressing conflicting and sometimes contradictory ideas.

After the fall of the Second Empire, it is hardly surprising that writers such as Flaubert, Goncourt and Zola wanted to write novels set during the period. Indeed, if Maxime Du Camp is to be believed, Flaubert claimed that 'perhaps, in the great scheme of things, the only consequence of the coup d'état and its aftermath will have been to provide a few wordsmiths with interesting scenarios'.[3] Each of these novelists felt the urge to look back and try to understand the period that had come to such a decisive end, and all aimed to mediate their reflections through aspects of the material world with which this book has been concerned. Although Flaubert's great Second Empire novel, *Sous Napoléon III*, never went beyond the planning stage, its climax was to have taken place at the universal exhibition, and Flaubert's notes for it refer to menus, photography and dress as he attempts to distil the essence of the period.[4] Edmond de Goncourt noted in his *Journal* that if he were to write a novel about the social networking, gossip and intrigue of the Second Empire, it would have to feature elegant tea parties like those given by the Empress

---

[2] '[U]n peu sénile'. Du Camp, *Souvenirs littéraires*, 387.

[3] '[P]eut-être, après tout, le coup d'État et ce qui s'en est suivi n'aura d'autre résultat, dans l'harmonie universelle, que de fournir des scénarios intéressants à quelques bons manieurs de plume.' Du Camp, *Souvenirs littéraires*, 604.

[4] 'Le point culminant du livre est à la gde. exposition'. Bibliothèque nationale ms. n. a. fr 28278. See Anne Green, '*Sous Napoléon III* de Flaubert: ébauches abandonnées?' in Sonya Stephens, ed., *Esquisses/Ebauches: Projects and Pre-Texts in Nineteenth-Century French Culture* (New York: Peter Lang, 2007), 99.

and presided over by 'queens of fashion'.[5] But it was Zola who most fully exploited the possibilities of the Second Empire novel in his famous Rougon-Macquart series which charts the 'natural and social history of a family under the Second Empire',[6] and which occupied him until the early 1890s. In these novels, Zola frequently echoes commonplace associations of the period as he dramatises those elements of French material culture that writers of the time had found particularly resonant. In *La Bête humaine*, for example, he exploits the much-repeated image of the runaway locomotive; *Le Ventre de Paris* expands on the imagery of food; the momentum of rapidly changing fashion and its social and economic implications are spelled out in *Au Bonheur des dames*, while *La Curée* explores the import of ruin and reconstruction. By the time Zola embarked on his great series, however, the period's remarkable social and technological changes were no longer so novel and writers were no longer inhibited by censorship. Zola could adopt a more assured and openly polemical stance. But in doing so, he drew on visible aspects of French life that had already been moulded into conceptual tools by his predecessors as they experimented with turning the newly changing material world of the Second Empire into language.

---

5 '[D]es reines de la mode.' Goncourt, 21.4.1872, *Journal*, II, 508.
6 'Histoire naturelle et sociale d'une famille sous le Second Empire'.

Appendix
SECOND EMPIRE TIMELINE[1]

1852

Events

- Louis Napoleon becomes President following coup d'état of 2 December 1851.
- Press regime decreed.
- Paris-Strasbourg and Paris-Creil railway lines inaugurated.
- Gare de Lyon and Gare de Montparnasse completed.
- Work begins on the 'New Louvre'.
- Le Bon Marché founded.
- Plebiscite approves restoration of the Empire.
- Proclamation of Second Empire; on 2 December 1852 Louis Napoleon becomes Napoleon III.

Publications

Du Camp, *Egypte, Nubie, Palestine et Syrie: dessins photographiques*
Gautier, *Arria Marcella*
Gautier, *Émaux et camées*
Hugo, *Napoléon le petit*
Leconte de Lisle, *Poèmes antiques*.
Mérimée, *Nouvelles*
Nerval, *Les Nuits d'octobre*

1853

Events

- Marriage of Napoleon III and Eugénie.
- Napoleon III offers Britain an alliance against Russia.
- Subjugation of Kabylia (Algeria) completed.

---

1 Many of these entries are based on the much more extensive 'Chronology of the French Second Empire' in William E. Echard, ed., *Historical Dictionary of the French Second Empire, 1852–1870* (Westport, CT: Greenwood Press, 1985), 711–76.

- British and French fleets sail to Constantinople.
- Caisse Générale des Chemins de Fer formed.
- Concessions of the Lyons-Geneva and Paris-Mulhouse-Nancy railway lines.
- Poor harvest and food shortages.
- Haussmann named prefect of the Seine.
- In Paris Napoleon III inaugurates Boulevard de Strasbourg; construction of Rue des Ecoles and restoration of Tour Saint Jacques begin.
- Nadar opens his photographic studio.

Publications

Champfleury, *Les Aventures de Mlle Mariette, contes de printemps*.
Hugo, *Les Châtiments*.
Nerval, *Petits châteaux de Bohème*.
Roqueplan, *Regain: La Vie parisienne*.

1854

Events

- France and Britain declare war on Russia.
- French and British forces occupy Athens.
- Garde impériale reestablished.
- Allied war council decides on Crimea campaign.
- Siege of Sebastopol.
- Franco-Austrian-British treaty of alliance signed.
- Government takes over Crédit Foncier.
- 500 million franc war loan voted – first state loan to be issued direct to the public.
- Cholera epidemic.
- Construction of the Halles Centrales (new Paris market) begins.
- Completion of Rue de Rivoli.
- Reconstruction of Pont d'Austerlitz and Pont des Invalides.
- Macadam first used in Paris.
- Disdéri patents *carte de visite*.
- Telegraph opens between Paris and Bastia, Corsica.

Publications

Anon., *Les Petits Paris. Paris-en-omnibus*.
Augier, *Le Gendre de monsieur Poirier*.
Du Camp, *Les Chants modernes*.
Nerval, *Sylvie*.

1855

Events

- State visit to Britain by Napoleon III and Eugénie.
- Attempt on Napoleon III's life by Pianori.
- State visit to France by Queen Victoria and Prince Albert.
- Attempt on Napoleon III's life by Delmarre.
- Fall of Sebastopol
- Compagnie Générale Maritime established.
- Paris Compagnie Générale des Omnibus established.
- Concession of Paris-Lyon railway line; authorization of mergers to create Compagnie de l'Ouest.
- Commission of enquiry into railway accidents.
- Haussmann is authorized to prepare plans for Paris water supply.
- Universal exhibition in Paris.
- Courbet opens an independent 'Pavillon du réalisme' near the universal exhibition.
- Les Grands Magasins du Louvre opens.
- Completion of Pont de l'Alma and restoration of Saint Sulpice church.
- Napoleon III approves de Lesseps' Suez canal project.

Publications

Anon., *Les Douze expositions de l'industrie en France de 1798 à 1855.*
Anon., *Poésies des chemins de fer, par un chauffeur.*
Chapus, *Voyageur, prenez garde à vous!*
Exposition des produits de l'industrie de toutes les nations. Catalogue officiel.
Guénée, Potier and Mathieu, *Dzing! Boum! Boum! Revue de l'exposition.*
Marennes [pseudonym of Chapus], *Manuel de l'homme et de la femme comme il faut.*

1856

Events

- Congress of Paris.
- Birth of Prince Imperial.
- Treaty of Paris ending Crimean war is signed.
- Trade treaty with Siam.
- France and Britain break off relations with Naples.
- Franco-Spanish boundary treaty.
- Napoleon III donates 100,000 francs to set up soup kitchens.
- Population of Paris reaches 1,174,347.

- Pasteur develops germ theory of disease.
- Bessemer process patented.

Publications

Dumas, Gautier et al, *Paris et les Parisiens au XIXe siècle: Moeurs, arts et monuments*.
Duranty, *Le Réalisme* [published until May 1857].
Gautier, *Avatar*.
Gautier, *Émaux et camées* [expanded edition].
Lacan, *Esquisses photographiques à propos de l'exposition universelle et de la guerre d'Orient*.
Tocqueville, *L'Ancien régime et la révolution*.

1857

Events

- Flaubert prosecuted for obscenity in *Madame Bovary* and acquitted.
- Baudelaire prosecuted for obscenity in *Les Fleurs du mal* and convicted.
- Decree establishing a railway network for Algeria.
- France, Sardinia, Russia and Prussia break off relations with Turkey.
- Napoleon III and Eugénie make state visit to Britain.
- Anglo-French forces take Canton after blockade.
- Inauguration of railway lines: Paris-Chaumont, Paris-Rennes, Paris-Lyon, Lyon-Marseilles, and Bordeaux-Sète, linking Mediterranean and Atlantic.
- Franco-Russian trade treaty.
- Longchamp race track inaugurated.
- Napoleon III inaugurates the New Louvre and the Halles Centrales.
- Pasteur proves that lactic fermentation of milk is caused by living organisms.
- Rue Impériale, Lyon, is first French street to have permanent electric lighting.

Publications

Baudelaire, *Les Fleurs du mal*.
Champfleury, *Le Réalisme*.
Dumanoir and Barrière, *Les Toilettes tapageuses*.
Flaubert, *Madame Bovary*.
Gautier, *Jettatura*.
Monpont, *Les Femmes coquettes ou la ruine des maisons*.

1858

Events

- Attempt to assassinate Napoleon III by four Italians led by Orsini; Orsini executed.
- Decree establishing martial law.
- Faidherbe launches expedition in the Cayor (Sénégal).
- Delangle replaces Espinasse as Minister of the Interior; state of emergency ends.
- Franco-Chinese Treaty of Tientsin.
- Prince Napoleon appointed Minister for Algeria.
- Franco-Spanish expedition in Cochinchina.
- Inauguration of Paris-Cherbourg railway line.
- Franco-Japanese commercial treaty.
- Business paralysed by rumours of war.
- In Paris, demolition of Pont au Change; completion of Boulevard de Sébastopol; construction of Avenue du Trocadéro, Pont Solférino and spire of Notre Dame begins.
- Augustin Sommeiller invents compressed-air drill.
- Verguin invents fuchsine dye.

Publications

Delattre, *Tribulations des voyageurs et des expéditeurs en chemin de fer*.
Gautier, *De la mode*.
Gautier, *Le Roman de la momie*.
Michelet, *L'Amour*.
Ségur, *Les Petites filles modèles*.
Tessier, *La Mode*.

1859

Events

- Franco-Sardinian alliance signed in secret.
- French occupy Saigon.
- Secret Franco-Russian treaty of alliance.
- France declares war on Austria.
- Napoleon III leaves for Italy; Eugénie is regent.
- Battles of Magenta and Solferino.
- France signs Treaty of Zurich, bringing Austro-Sardinian war to an end.

- Britain and France prepare an expedition to China.
- Law annexing banlieu to city of Paris is signed.
- Plan for Parisian water supply and sewers approved; great collector sewer completed.
- Rue de Magenta laid out.
- Work begins on Suez canal.
- Lemoine invents steamroller.

Publications

Baudelaire, *Salon de 1859*.
Du Camp, *En Hollande: Lettres à un ami*.
Gagne, *Omégar ou le dernier homme*.
Monselet, *La Cuisinière poétique*.
Reculet, *Le Cuisinier praticien, ou la cuisine simple et pratique*.
Renan, *Essais de morale et de critique*.

1860

Events

- Anglo-French expedition reaches China and takes Peking.
- Nice-Savoy transferred to France after plebiscite.
- Napoleon III and Eugénie visit Algeria.
- Second Treaty of Tientsin.
- France opens branch of Comptoir d'Escompte in Shanghai.
- Extension of Paris city limits; population is now 1,525,942.
- Cession of Bois de Vincennes to city of Paris.
- Jardin zoologique d'acclimatation in Bois de Boulogne opens to public.
- Temporary relaxation of press restrictions.
- Founding of *Le Monde*, *La Mode illustrée*, *La Revue nationale* and *La Revue archéologique*.
- Napoleon III sponsors a biennial science prize of 20,000 francs.
- Bazar de l'Hôtel de Ville opens.
- Pasteur sterilises milk at 125°C.

Publications

Figuier, *La Photographie au salon de 1859*.
Goncourt, *Charles Demailly* [first published as *Les Hommes de lettres*]
Labiche, *Le Voyage de monsieur Perrichon*.
Lavergne, *Ruines historiques de France. Châteaux et abbayes*.
M. ***, *Le Voyageur, les chemins de fer et l'hôtel. Les Dames en voyage*.
Marchal, *Les Ruines romaines de Champlieu (Campi locus)*.

1861

Events

- France conquers Saigon province.
- France purchases a third of Monaco for 4 million francs.
- Bishop of Poitiers compares Napoleon III to Pilate.
- Franco-Italian boundary treaty signed.
- Remains of Napoleon I are entombed in les Invalides.
- Circular forbids priests from meddling in politics.
- Last French troops leave Syria.
- French take Bien Hoa citadel in Cochinchina.
- Commercial treaties with Turkey and Belgium.
- Network of secondary rail lines for France and a rail system for Algeria projected.
- Napoleon III promises financial reforms.
- Completion of the Canal du midi, connecting Atlantic and Mediterranean.
- Garnier wins competition for design of new Paris opera house; excavations begin.
- Pavillon de Flore demolished.
- Electric lights installed in Place du Carrousel.
- Calls for freedom of the press; Napoleon III says he will never agree to press freedom.

Publications

Baudelaire, *Les Fleurs du mal* (new edition).
Capendu, *Mademoiselle la Ruine*.
Gastineau, *Les Romans du voyage: La Vie en chemin de fer*.
Labiche, *La Poudre aux yeux*.

1862

Events

- French expeditionary force lands in Mexico; war is declared.
- Franco-Prussian treaty of commerce, navigation and copyright.
- Franco-Spanish boundary treaty.
- French defeated at Puebla, Mexico.
- Three eastern provinces of Cochinchina ceded to France.
- Three million francs made available for building secondary railway lines.
- Inauguration of the Théâtre Lyrique Impérial, Théâtre de la Gaîté, and Théâtre des Folies Dramatiques.

- Notre Dame re-consecrated after restoration.
- Duruy, *inspecteur générale* of education, introduces contemporary history into school curriculum.
- Introduction of Paris public libraries.

Publications

Bertherand, *Les Chemins de fer au point de vue sanitaire.*
Blanquet, *La Cuisinière des ménages, ou manuel pratique de cuisine et d'économie domestique pour la ville et la campagne.*
Claudin, *Paris.*
Flaubert, *Salammbô.*
Fromentin, *Dominique.*
Hugo, *Les Misérables.*
Leconte de Lisle, *Poèmes barbares.*
Michaux, *La Cuisine de la ferme.*

1863

Events

- French take Puebla, Mexico, after a two-month siege.
- Anglo-French squadron bombards points in Japan.
- Cambodia becomes a French protectorate.
- Maximilian is pressed by Napoleon III to accept the Mexican throne.
- France takes possession of the Loyalty Islands (New Caledonia).
- Franco-Italian commercial treaty.
- First 'Salon des refusés'.
- Decree freeing Paris bakers from government control.
- New statue of Napoleon I dressed as Roman emperor is placed on Vendôme column.
- Construction of Gare du Nord begins.
- Nadar founds Society for Encouragement of Heavier-than-Air Machines.
- Nadar's balloon, Le Géant, ascends with fourteen passengers.
- First self-propelled submarine, Le Plongeur, launched at Rochefort.

Publications

Gautier, *Le Capitaine Fracasse.*
Gautier, *Romans et contes.*
Merlet, *Portraits d'hier et d'aujourd'hui.*
Ségur, *L'Auberge de l'ange gardien.*

1864

Events

- Arrest of Greco and others for plotting to kill Napoleon III.
- Failure of Schleswig-Holstein conference.
- *Les Misérables* and *Madame Bovary* placed on Index.
- King of Spain visits France.
- MacMahon appointed governor of Algeria.
- Inauguration of steamship service from Le Havre to New York.
- First Deauville 'season'.
- Construction of new Hôtel Dieu on Ile de la Cité ordered.
- Free public evening courses at the Sorbonne open.

Publications

Decaisne, *Guide médical et hygiénique du voyageur.*
Feer, *Les Ruines de Ninive.*
Goncourt, *Germinie Lacerteux.*
Goncourt, *Renée Mauperin.*
Hugo, *William Shakespeare.*
Taine, *Histoire de la littérature anglaise.*
Verne, *Voyage au centre de la terre.*

1865

Events

- Napoleon III goes to Algeria; Eugénie regent in his absence.
- French evacuation of Rome begins.
- Announcement of Universal Exhibition in 1867 in Paris.
- Commercial treaties with Norway-Sweden, Hanseatic cities, Mecklenburg, Spain and Netherlands.
- Strike of drivers of the Paris Compagnie des Petites Voitures; company loses its monopoly.
- Strike of 2000 velvet-makers in Saint Etienne.
- Le Printemps department store established.
- Phylloxera observed in the south of France.
- First water from the Dhuis reaches Paris from new Ménilmontant reservoir.
- First daily newspaper on economic affairs, *Le Messager de Paris.*
- Demolition of Théâtre des Folies Dramatiques.
- Pasteur cures silkworm disease, saving French silk industry.
- Inauguration of Paris-Lyon line for pantelegraph facsimile transmission.

Publications

Bernard, *Introduction à l'étude de la médecine expérimentale.*
Delvau, *Histoire anecdotique des barrières de Paris.*
Fournel, *Paris nouveau et Paris futur.*
Larousse, ed., *Grand dictionnaire universel du XIXe siècle* [first volume published].
Verne, *De la terre à la lune.*

1866

Events

- Napoleon III announces withdrawal from Mexico; advises Maximilian to abdicate.
- Ollivier's call for further reform is defeated.
- Napoleon III ill at Vichy.
- Mass arrest of Blanquists at Café de la Renaissance.
- French garrison leaves Rome.
- Commercial treaties with Portugal and Austria.
- Commission to encourage worker education is named.
- Shop selling horsemeat opens in Paris.
- Paris population reaches 2,150,916.
- Opening of Théâtre des Délassements Comiques, Théâtre des Nouveautés, Théâtre des Menus Plaisirs, Théâtre des Fantaisies Parisiennes and Théâtre du Prince Impérial.
- Opening of Magasins Réunis.

Publications

Cordier, *Traité des insuccès en photographie.*
Delvau, *Les Heures parisiennes.*
Feydeau, *Du luxe, des femmes, des mœurs, de la littérature et de la vertu.*
Hugo, *Les Travailleurs de la mer.*
Mariette, *L'Art de la toilette.*
Meilhac and Lévy, *La Vie parisienne.*
Mérimée, *La Chambre bleue.*
Taine, *Notes sur Paris: Vie et opinions de monsieur Frédéric Thomas Graindorge.*

1867

Events

- Napoleon III publishes reform plans.
- French complete withdrawal from Mexico. Maximilian executed.

- Proposed laws on press and public meetings submitted to Corps Législatif.
- Failure of negotiations for France's purchase of Luxembourg.
- Three western provinces of Cochinchina annexed to France.
- Law extending powers of municipal councils in local affairs.
- Napoleon III meets Francis Joseph and other German rulers at Salzburg; makes speech alluding to 'des points noirs' on the horizon.
- French defeat Garibaldi at Mentana.
- Strike of garment workers.
- International monetary conference in Paris; gold standard agreement adopted.
- Inauguration of La Villette abattoir.
- Universal Exhibition in Paris.
- Work begins on project to bring water to Paris from the Vanne.
- Baudelaire dies.
- Primary education law voted.
- Duruy announces creation of secondary education for girls.
- Tellier begins experiments on 'dry freezing' meat.
- Mège-Mouries works to develop margarine, encouraged by Napoleon III.

Publications

Anon., *Guide officiel à l'exposition universelle de 1867: Vade mecum du visiteur*.
Anon., *Histoire chronologique du vêtement (homme) suivie de l'Art de se vêtir au XIXe siècle*.
Anon., *Itinéraires dans Paris, précédé de Promenades à l'exposition*.
Champfleury, *L'Hôtel des commissaires-priseurs*.
Goncourt, *Manette Salomon*.
Labiche, *Les Chemins de fer*.
Paris-Guide, par les principaux écrivains et artistes de la France.
Renaudin, *Paris-Exposition ou guide à Paris en 1867*.
Zola, *Thérèse Raquin*.

1868

Events

- Bank of France reserves reach one billion francs.
- Students and police clash in Paris over banning of Hugo's *Ruy Blas*.
- Demonstration in Montmartre at Baudin's rediscovered tomb; Gambetta unsuccessfully defends newspaper editors prosecuted for their support.
- Ten Paris newspapers fined for discussing legislative debates.
- Napoleon III establishes his own newspaper, *L'Époque*, with Duvernois as editor.

- Napoleon III proposes alliance of France, Italy and Austria-Hungary.
- Attack on free trade fails in Corps Législatif.
- Bakunin founds Alliance Internationale de la Démocratie Sociale.
- Siphon system under Seine connecting the great sewer collectors is completed.
- Théâtre de la Gaîté-Montparnasse established.
- Government grants 20-year concession to French Atlantic Telegraph Co. to lay cable to America.

Publications

Brisse, *Recettes à l'usage des ménages bourgeois et des petits ménages*.
Feydeau, *La Comtesse de Châlis ou les mœurs du jour*.
Zola, Preface to second edition of *Thérèse Raquin*.

1869

Events

- Persigny and Ollivier advise Napoleon III to turn to new men.
- Disturbances in Paris.
- 116 deputies sign demand for interpellation on responsible government.
- In October, threatened uprising in Paris fails to materialise.
- Strike of Loire silk workers (July), and Elbeuf textile workers (Sept.)
- Strike of employees of Paris *magasins de nouveautés*.
- Miners' strikes; miners and troops clash.
- Eugénie attends opening of Suez canal.
- Inquiry ordered into free trade.
- *La Revue contemporaine* fined for discussing constitution; general crackdown on the press.
- Duruy resigns as minister of education.
- Opening of Folies Bergère.
- Margarine first produced commercially.

Publications

Astrié, *Indispensable guide-manuel du voyageur en chemin de fer*.
Baudelaire, *Petits poèmes en prose*.
Du Camp, *Paris, ses organes, ses fonctions et sa vie dans la seconde moitié du XIXe siècle* [first of 6 vols.].

1870

Events

- Pierre Bonaparte kills Victor Noir; 100,000 attend Noir's funeral.
- Napoleon III rejects Prince Napoleon's idea of a true parliamentary regime.
- Plebiscite on the Liberal Empire: 7,527,379 for; 1,530,909 against. Riots in Paris.
- New constitution promulgated.
- Internationale again dissolved in France and leaders arrested.
- Failed uprising in Marseilles.
- Gold standard suspended.
- Blanquist uprising fails at La Villette.
- Napoleon III visits site of newly-discovered Arènes de Lutèce; agrees to allow Rue Monge to be built over it.
- Death of Jules de Goncourt.
- France declares war on Prussia.
- South German states declare war on France.
- All French males aged 25 to 35 called up.
- French navy blockades the Baltic.
- Series of French defeats, culminating in the loss of decisive battles around Sedan.
- Armistice signed 2 September; Napoleon III, his generals and the Army of Châlons enter German captivity.
- Paris learns of Sedan disaster on 4 September; mob invades Palais Bourbon.
- Second Empire ends on 4 September. Moderate republic is declared and provisional government formed.
- Eugénie and Prince Imperial flee to England. Siege of Paris begins.

Publications

Verlaine, *La Bonne chanson.*
Verne, *Vingt mille lieues sous les mers.*

BIBLIOGRAPHY

Allem, Maurice. *La Vie quotidienne sous le Second Empire*. Paris: Hachette, 1948.
Angot, Albert. *Nos ruines*. Paris: Ch. Douniol et cie, 1871.
Anon. *Histoire chronologique du vêtement (homme) suivie de l'Art de se vêtir au XIXe siècle*. Paris: Vanier, 1867.
Anon. *Les Étrangers à l'exposition*. Paris: Ch. Lahure, 1855.
Anon. *Les Petits Paris: Paris-en-omnibus*. Paris: Alphonse Taride, 1854.
Armstrong, Nancy. *Fiction in the Age of Photography: The Legacy of British Realism*. Harvard: Harvard University Press, 1999.
Arnoux, J. J. *Le Travail universel, revue complète des œuvres de l'art et de l'industrie exposées à Paris en 1855*. Paris: Bureaux de la patrie, 1856.
Aron, J. P. *Le Mangeur du dix-neuvième siècle*. Paris: Robert Laffont, 1973.
Astrié, Théophile. *Indispensable guide-manuel du voyageur en chemin de fer, indiquant les dispositions légales et réglementaires, les moyens et les formes propres à faire valoir les droits et aboutir les réclamations du voyageur*. Paris: Le Bailly, 1869.
Audebrand, Philibert. *Un café de journalistes sous Napoléon III*. Paris: Dentu, 1888.
Audot, L. E. *La Cuisinière de la campagne et de la ville*. 47th ed. Paris: Audot, 1868.
Baguley, David. *Napoleon III and his Regime. An Extravaganza*. Baton Rouge: Louisiana State University Press, 2000.
Balzac, Honoré de. *La Peau de Chagrin*. 1831; Paris: Garnier-Flammarion, 1971.
Barthes, Roland. 'Pour une psycho-sociologie de l'alimentation contemporaine'. In J. J. Hémardinguer, *Pour une histoire de l'alimentation*. Paris: Colin, 1970.
Baudelaire, Charles. *Correspondance*. Edited by Claude Pichois. 2 vols. Paris: Gallimard-Pléiade, 1973.
Baudelaire, Charles. *Œuvres complètes*. Edited by Marcel A. Ruff. Paris: Seuil, 1968.
Baudrillard, Jean. *Symbolic Exchange and Death*. Reprinted in Julie Rivkin and Michael Ryan, eds., *Literary Theory: an Anthology*. Oxford: Blackwell, 1998.
Barrière, Théodore and Dumanoir. *Les Toilettes tapageuses: Le Théâtre contemporain illustré*. Paris: Lévy, 1857.
Bayle, St. John. *Purple Tints of Paris: Characters and Manners in the New Empire*. 1854; New York: Riker, Thorne & Co., n.d.
Benjamin, Walter. 'A Small History of Photography'. In *One-Way Street and Other Writings*. Translated by E. Jephcott and K. Shorter. London: Verso, 1985.
Benjamin, Walter. *The Arcades Project*. Translated by Howard Eiland and Kevin McLaughlin. London: Belknap Press, 1999.
Bernard, Claudie. *Le Passé recomposé: Le Roman historique français du dix-neuvième siècle*. Paris: Hachette, 1996.
Bertherand, E. L. *Les Chemins de fer au point de vue sanitaire*. Paris: Arbois, 1862.

Blanquet, Rosalie. *La Cuisinière des ménages, ou manuel pratique de cuisine et d'économie domestique pour la ville et la campagne*. Paris: Théodore Lefèvre, 1863.

Blix, Göran. *From Paris to Pompeii: French Romanticism and the Cultural Politics of Archaeology*. Philadelphia: University of Pennsylvania Press, 2008.

Blood, Susan. 'Baudelaire Against Photography: An Allegory of Old Age'. *Modern Language Notes* 101 (1986): 817–37.

Brisse, Le Baron. *Recettes à l'usage des ménages bourgeois et des petits ménages, comprenant la manière de servir à nouveau tous les restes*. Paris: E. Donnaud, 1868.

Burton, Richard D. E. *The Flâneur and his City: Patterns of Daily Life in Paris, 1815–1851*. Durham: University of Durham, 1994.

Capendu, Ernest. *Mademoiselle la Ruine*. Paris: Alexandre Cadot, 1861.

Caraion, Marta. *Les Philosophes de la vapeur et des allumettes chimiques*. Paris: Droz, 2008.

Castille, Hippolyte. *Les Hommes et les mœurs en France sous le règne de Louis-Philippe*. Paris: Paul Henneton et cie, 1853.

Chambers, Ross. *Gérard de Nerval et la poétique du voyage*. Paris: Corti, 1969.

Champfleury. *L'Hôtel des commissaires-priseurs*. Paris: Dentu, 1867.

Champfleury. *Les Aventures de Mlle Mariette, contes de printemps*. Paris: V. Lecou, 1853.

Chapus, Eugène [M. le Vicomte de Marennes, pseud.]. *Manuel de l'homme et de la femme comme il faut*. Paris: Librairie nouvelle, 1855.

Chapus, Eugène. *Voyageur, prenez garde à vous!* Paris: Decaux et Dreyfous, 1855.

Christiansen, Rupert. *Tales of the New Babylon*. London: Minerva, 1994.

Citron, Pierre. *La Poésie de Paris dans la littérature française de Rousseau à Baudelaire*. 2 vols. Paris: Éditions de minuit, 1961.

Claudin, Gustave. *Paris*. Paris: Dentu, 1862.

Coates, Carroll F., ed. *Repression and Expression: Literary and Social Coding in Nineteenth-Century France*. New York: Peter Lang, 1996.

Collier, Peter and Robert Lethbridge, eds. *Artistic Relations: Literature and the Visual Arts in Nineteenth-Century France*. New Haven and London: Yale University Press, 1994.

Cooper, T. and M. Donaldson-Evans, eds. *Moving Forward, Holding Fast: The Dynamics of Nineteenth-Century French Culture*. Amsterdam/Atlanta GA: Rodopi, 1997.

Cordier, V. *Traité des insuccès en photographie: Causes et remèdes*. Paris: Lieber, 1866.

Cuisin, J. P. R. [M. Velocifère, pseud.]. *L'Amour au grand trot, ou la Gaudriole en diligence: manuel portatif et guide très-précieux pour les voyageurs*. Paris, 1820.

Decaisne, Émile. *Guide médical et hygiénique du voyageur*. Paris: Albessard, 1864.

Delattre, Eugène. *Canaux et chemins de fer*. Paris: Guillaumin & Cie., 1861.

Delattre, Eugène. *Tribulations des voyageurs et des expéditeurs en chemin de fer. Conseils pratiques*. 2nd ed. Paris: Taride, 1858.

Delvau, Alfred. *Histoire anecdotique des barrières de Paris*. Paris: Dentu, 1865.

Delvau, Alfred. *Les Heures parisiennes*. Paris: Librairie centrale, 1866.

Destaminil, M. *Le Cuisinier français perfectionné, contenant les meilleurs prescriptions de la cuisine ancienne et moderne*. Paris: Renault, 1861.

Du Camp, Maxime. *Égypte, Nubie, Palestine et Syrie: dessins photographiques*. Paris: Gide et Baudry, 1852.

Du Camp, Maxime. *En Hollande. Lettres à un ami*. Paris: Poulet-Malassis et De Broise, 1859.

Du Camp, Maxime. *Les Chants modernes*. Paris: A. Bourdilliat et cie, 1860.

Du Camp, Maxime. *Paris, ses organes, ses fonctions et sa vie dans la seconde moitié du XIXe siècle*. 6 vols. Paris: Hachette, 1869–1875.

Du Camp, Maxime. 1882–83. *Souvenirs littéraires*. Paris: Aubier, 1994.

Dumas, Alexandre, Théophile Gautier et al. *Paris et les Parisiens au XIXe siècle: Mœurs, arts et monuments.* Paris: Morizot, 1856.

Dumas, Alexandre. *Grand dictionnaire de cuisine.* Paris: Alphonse Lemerre, 1873.

Echard, William E., ed. *Historical Dictionary of the French Second Empire, 1852–1870.* Westport, CT: Greenwood Press, 1985.

Exposition des produits de l'industrie de toutes les nations: Catalogue officiel publié par ordre de la commission impériale. Paris: E. Panis, 1855.

Fairlie, Alison. *Imagination and Language: Collected Essays on Constant, Baudelaire, Nerval and Flaubert.* Cambridge: Cambridge University Press, 1981.

Feer, H. L. *Les Ruines de Ninive.* Paris: Société des écoles du dimanche, 1864.

Ferguson, Priscilla Parkhurst. *Accounting for Taste: The Triumph of French Cuisine* Chicago and London: University of Chicago Press, 2004.

Feydeau, Ernest. *Du luxe, des femmes, des mœurs, de la littérature et de la vertu.* Paris: Clichy, 1866.

Feydeau, Ernest. *La Comtesse de Châlis ou les mœurs du jour.* Paris: M. Lévy, 1868.

Figuier, Louis. *La Photographie au salon de 1859.* Paris: Hachette, 1860.

Flaubert, Gustave. *Œuvres complètes.* Edited by Bernard Masson. 2 vols. Paris: Seuil, 1964.

Flaubert, Gustave. *Madame Bovary: Plans et scénarios.* Edited by Yvan Leclerc. Paris: Zulma, 1995.

Flaubert, Gustave. *Bouvard et Pécuchet.* Edited by Claudine Gothot-Mersch. Paris: Gallimard, 1979.

Flaubert, Gustave. *Carnets de travail.* Edited by P. M. de Biasi. Paris: Balland, 1988.

Flaubert, Gustave. *Correspondance.* Edited by J. Bruneau and Y. Leclerc. 5 vols. Paris: Gallimard-Pléiade, 1973–2007.

Flaubert, Gustave. *Le Dictionnaire des idées reçues et Le Catalogue des idées chic.* Edited by Anne Herschberg-Pierrot. Paris: Livre de Poche, 1997.

Flaubert, Gustave. Unpublished notes to M. Sénard. February 1857. Transcribed in *Bulletin Flaubert* 3 (10 May 2001).

Fournel, Victor. *Paris nouveau et Paris futur.* Paris: Jacques Lecoffre, 1865.

Fournier, Édouard. *Paris démoli.* Paris: Dagneau, 1852.

Freeman, Michael. *Railways and the Victorian Imagination.* New Haven and London: Yale University Press, 1999.

Freund, Gisèle. *Photographie et société.* Paris: Seuil, 1974.

Frizot, Michel, ed. *A New History of Photography.* Köln: Könemann, 1998.

Fromentin, Eugène. 1862. *Dominique.* Paris: Flammarion, 1987.

Furst, Lilian. 'The Rôle of Food in Madame Bovary'. *Orbis Litterarum* 34 (1979): 53–65.

Gagne, Élise. *Omégar ou le dernier homme, proso-poésie dramatique de la fin du temps.* Paris: Didier, 1859.

Gastineau, Benjamin. *Les Romans du voyage: La Vie en chemin de fer.* Paris: Dentu, 1861.

Gautier, Théophile. 'Théophile Gautier à Charles Garnier'. *L'Univers illustré* (18 January 1868).

Gautier, Théophile. *De la mode.* Paris: Poulet-Malassis et de Broise, 1858.

Gautier, Théophile. 1852 and 1856. *Emaux et camées.* (Lille and Geneva: Giard and Droz, 1947.

Gautier, Théophile. 1863. *Le Capitaine Fracasse.* Paris: Garnier-Flammarion, 1967.

Gautier, Théophile. 1857. *Le Roman de la momie.* Edited by G. van den Bogaert. Paris: Garnier-Flammarion, 1966.

Gautier, Théophile. *Romans et contes.* Paris: Charpentier, 1880.

Gautier, Théophile. *Tableaux de siège, 1870–1871.* Paris: Charpentier, 1871.

Giafferri, Paul Louis de. *L'Histoire du costume féminin français: Les Modes du Second Empire 1852–1870*. Paris: Nilsson, 1922.
Goncourt, Edmond and Jules de. *Journal: Mémoires de la vie littéraire*. Edited by Robert Ricatte. 3 vols. Paris: Robert Laffont, 1989.
Goncourt, Edmond and Jules de. 1860. *Charles Demailly*. Paris: Charpentier, 1876.
Goncourt, Edmond and Jules de. 1864. *Germinie Lacerteux*. Paris: Union Générale d'Editions, 1979.
Goncourt, Edmond and Jules de. 1867. *Manette Salomon*. Paris: Union Générale d'Editions, 1979.
Goncourt, Edmond and Jules de. 1864. *Renée Mauperin*. Paris: Charpentier, 1876.
Gray, Francine Du Plessix. *Rage and Fire: A Life of Louise Colet*. London: Hamish Hamilton, 1994.
Green, Anne. 'Flaubert costumier: le rôle du vêtement.' In D. Fauvel and Y. Leclerc, eds., *Salammbô de Flaubert: Histoire, fiction*. Paris: Champion, 1999. 121–128.
Green, Anne. 'La Contribution inattendue de Flaubert à un manuel de chemin de fer.' *Bulletin des Amis de Flaubert et de Maupassant*, 8 (2000): 13–21.
Green, Anne. '*Sous Napoléon III* de Flaubert: ébauches abandonnées?' In Sonya Stephens, ed., *Esquisses/Ébauches: Projects and Pre-Texts in Nineteenth-Century French Culture*. New York: Peter Lang, 2007. 90–101.
Green, Anne. 'Time and History in Madame Bovary'. *French Studies* 49, no. 3 (July 1995): 283–291.
Guénée, A., C. Potier, and E. Mathieu. *Dzing! Boum! Boum! Revue de l'exposition*. Paris: Mifliez, 1855.
Guide officiel à l'exposition universelle de 1867: Vade mecum du visiteur. Paris: Dentu, 1867.
Hamon, Philippe. *Expositions: Littérature et architecture au XIXe siècle*. Paris: Corti, 1989.
Hans, L. and J. J. Blanc. *Guide à travers les ruines: Paris et ses environs*. Paris: Lemerre, 1871.
Herschberg-Pierrot, Anne. 'Flaubert journaliste: présentation.' *Littérature* 88 (December 1992): 115–126.
Honour, Hugh. *Romanticism*. London: Pelican Books, 1981.
Hooker, Sir William et al. *Notes of Some Remarkable Objects Exhibited in the French, Foreign and British Colonial Departments of the Paris Universal Exhibition*. Part I. London: Chapman and Hall, 1855.
Hugo, Victor. 1853. *Les Châtiments*. Edited by René Journet. Paris: Gallimard, 1977.
Hugo, Victor. 1862. *Les Misérables*. Edited by Yves Gohin. 2 vols. Paris: Gallimard, 1973 & 1995.
Hugo, Victor. 1866. *Les Travailleurs de la mer*. Edited by Y. Gohin. Paris: Gallimard, 1980.
Hugo, Victor. *The Toilers of the Sea*. Translated by W. May Thomas. London: Dent, 1961.
Hugo, Victor. 1864. *William Shakespeare*. Paris: Nelson, 1930.
Itinéraire des ruines de Paris: notices historiques sur les monuments incendiés. Paris: Librairie Madre, 1871.
Jammes, André and Emma Parry Janis. *The Art of French Calotype*. Princeton: Princeton University Press, 1983.
Jammes, André and Marie-Thérèse. *En Égypte au temps de Flaubert, 1839–1860: Les Premiers photographes*. Kodak-Pathé exhibition catalogue, 1981.
Journal des débats. 26 May 1857.
Kelly, Jill. 'Photographic Reality and French Literary Reaction: Nineteenth-Century Synchronism and Symbiosis'. *French Review* 65, no. 2 (December 1991): 195–205.

L'Art en France sous le Second Empire. Paris: Editions de la Réunion des musées nationaux, 1979.
Labiche, Eugène. *Théâtre complet*. 10 vols. Paris: Calmann-Lévy, 1898.
Lacan, Ernest. *Esquisses photographiques à propos de l'exposition universelle et de la guerre d'Orient*. Paris: Grassart et Gaudin, 1856.
Larousse, Pierre. *Grand dictionnaire universel du XIXe siècle*. 17 vols. Paris: Administration du grand dictionnaire, 1865–90.
Lavergne, Alexandre de. *Ruines historiques de France: Châteaux et abbayes*. Paris: Amyot, 1860.
Le Miroir parisien. October 1862; January 1863; February 1863; June 1863.
Le Moniteur de la mode. 15 February 1853; 25 March 1853; May 1853.
Leclerc, Yvan. 'Portraits de Flaubert et de Maupassant en photophobes.' *Romantisme* 105 (August 1999): 97–106.
Leconte de Lisle, Charles. 1862. *Poèmes barbares*. Edited by C. Gothot-Mersch. Paris: Gallimard, 1985.
Les Douze expositions de l'industrie en France de 1798 à 1855. Paris: Martinon, 1855.
Lespès, Léo [Timothée Trimm, pseud.]. *Les Ruines de Paris: Chronique du Paris brûlé. Description des monuments, palais, maisons incendiées, scènes de dévastation, état actuel des ruines, etc*. Paris: Librairie et imprimerie universelles, 1871.
M. ***, Avocat. *Le Voyageur, les chemins de fer et l'hôtel: Les Dames en voyage*. Paris: Dezobry, S. Magdeleine et cie, 1860.
Mainardi, Patricia. *Art and Politics of the Second Empire: The Universal Expositions of 1855 and 1867*. New Haven and London: Yale University Press, 1987.
Mallarmé, Stéphane. *Œuvres complètes*. Edited by Carl Barbier and Gordon Millan. Paris: Flammarion, 1983.
Maneglier, Hervé. *Paris impérial: La Vie quotidienne sous le Second Empire*. Paris: A. Colin, 1990.
Marchal, Charles. *Les Ruines romaines de Champlieu (Campi locus)*. Paris: Dentu, 1860.
Marien, Mary Warner. *Photography and its Critics: A Cultural History, 1839–1900*. Cambridge: Cambridge University Press, 1997.
Mariette, Pauline. *L'Art de la toilette: Méthode nouvelle pour tailler, exécuter ou diriger avec économie et élégance tous les vêtements de dames et d'enfants*. Paris: Librairie centrale, 1866.
Marx, Karl and Friedrich Engels. *The Communist Manifesto*. Translated by S. Moore. London: Penguin Books, 1967.
Mazure, P. Adolphe. *Illustrations, ruines et souvenirs des capitales anciennes et modernes*. Paris: Lehuby, 1852.
McCauley, Elizabeth Anne. *A. A. E. Disdéri and the Carte de Visite Portrait Photograph*. New Haven and London: Yale University Press, 1985.
McCauley, Elizabeth Anne. *Industrial Madness: Commercial Photography in Paris, 1848–1871*. Newhaven and London: Yale University Press, 1994.
Meilhac, Henri and Ludovic Halévy. *La Vie parisienne*. Paris: M. Lévy, 1866.
Mérimée, Prosper. *Romans et nouvelles*. Edited by M. Parturier. 2 vols. Paris: Garnier, 1967.
Merlet, Gustave. 'Le Roman physiologique: *Madame Bovary*.' *Portraits d'hier et d'aujourd'hui*. Paris: Didier, 1863.
Michaux, Marceline. *La Cuisine de la ferme*. Paris: Librairie agricole de la maison rustique, 1862.
Michelet, Jules. 1858. *L'Amour*. Paris: Hachette, 1859.
Monpont. *Les Femmes coquettes ou la ruine des maisons*. Paris: Ledoyen, 1857.
Monselet, Charles. 1859. *La Cuisinière poétique*. Paris: Michel Lévy, 1877.

Mortier, Roland. *La Poétique des ruines: Ses origines, ses variations de la Renaissance à Victor Hugo.* Geneva: Droz, 1974.
Nadar. *Le Droit au vol.* Paris: Hetzel, 1865.
Nadar. 1900. *Quand j'étais photographe.* Paris: Babel, 1998.
Nerval, Gérard de. *Œuvres complètes.* Edited by J. Guillaume & C. Pichois. 3 vols. Paris: Gallimard Pléiade, 1993.
Nochlin, Linda. *Realism.* London: Penguin Books, 1971.
Oster, D. and J. Goulemot. *La Vie parisienne. Anthologie des mœurs du XIXe siècle.* Paris: Sand/Corti, 1989.
Paris-Guide, par les principaux écrivains et artistes de la France. 2 vols. Paris: Librairie internationale, 1867.
Parville, M. de. *Itinéraires dans Paris, prédédé de Promenades à l'exposition.* Paris: Garnier, 1867.
Perrot, Philippe. *Les Dessus et les dessous de la bourgeoisie: Une histoire du vêtement au XIXe siècle.* Paris: Fayard, 1981.
Poésie des chemins de fer, par un chauffeur. Paris & Lyon, 1855.
Prendergast, Christopher. *Paris and the Nineteenth Century.* Oxford: Blackwell, 1995.
Rabb, Jane M., ed. *Literature and Photography: Interactions, 1840–1990.* Albuquerque: University of New Mexico Press, 1995.
Raitt, A. W. 'L'Éducation sentimentale et la pyramide'. In *Histoire et langage dans 'L'Éducation sentimentale' de Flaubert.* Paris: CDE et SEDES, 1981. 129–142.
Reculet, Charles. *Le Cuisinier praticien, ou la cuisine simple et pratique.* Paris: Dentu, 1859.
Renan, Ernest. *Essais de morale et de critique.* Paris: Lévy, 1859.
Renaudin, Edmond. *Paris-Exposition ou guide à Paris en 1867.* Paris: Ch. Delagrave et cie, 1867.
Richard, Jean-Pierre. *Stendhal et Flaubert: Littérature et sensation.* Paris: Seuil, 1954.
Roqueplan, Nestor. *Regain: La Vie parisienne.* Paris: V. Lecou, 1853.
Rouillé, André. *La Photographie en France: Textes et controverses; Une anthologie 1816–1871.* Paris: Mancula, 1989.
Sainte-Beuve, Charles Augustin. '*Salammbô* par Monsieur Gustave Flaubert.' *Le Constitutionnel.* 15 December 1862.
Schivelbusch, Wolfgang. *The Railway Journey: Trains and Travel in the 19th Century.* Translated by Anselm Hollo. Oxford: Basil Blackwell, 1979.
Ségur, Mme la Comtesse de. *L'Auberge de l'ange gardien.* Paris: Hachette, 1863.
Ségur, Mme la Comtesse de. 1858. *Les Petites filles modèles.* Paris: Hachette, 1909.
Seznec, Jean. *Flaubert à l'exposition de 1851.* Oxford: Clarendon Press, 1951.
Simon, Marie. *Fashion in Art: The Second Empire and Impressionism.* London: Zwemmer, 1995.
Taine, Hippolyte. 1864. *Histoire de la littérature anglaise.* Paris: Hachette, n. d.
Taine, Hippolyte. *Notes sur Paris: Vie et opinions de monsieur Frédéric Thomas Graindorge.* Paris: Hachette, 1867.
Tanner, Tony. *Adultery in the Novel: Contract and Transgression.* Baltimore and London: Johns Hopkins University Press, 1979.
Tessier, Henri. *La Mode.* Paris: M. Lévy, 1858.
Tocqueville, Alexis de. 1856. *L'Ancien régime et la révolution: Œuvres complètes.* Paris: Gallimard, 1952.
Truesdell, Matthew. *Spectacular Politics: Louis-Napoleon Bonaparte and the Fête Impériale, 1849–1870.* New York and Oxford: Oxford University Press, 1997.
Vanier, Henriette. *La Mode et ses métiers: Frivolités et luttes des classses, 1830–1870.* Paris: A. Colin, 1960.

Varin, Saint Yves and Bureau. *L'Amour au daguerréotype: Le Théâtre contemporain illustré.* Paris: Lévy, 1854.
Verlaine, Paul. *La Bonne chanson.* Paris: Alphonse Lemerre, 1870.
Verne, Jules. 1865. *De la terre à la lune.* Paris: Librairie générale française, 2001.
Verne, Jules. 1870. *Vingt mille lieues sous les mers.* Paris: Hetzel et cie, n. d.
Watson, Janell. *Literature and Material Culture from Balzac to Proust: The Collection and Consumption of Curiosities.* Cambridge: Cambridge University Press, 1999.
West-Sooby, John, ed. *Consuming Culture: The Arts of the French Table.* Newark: University of Delaware Press, 2004.
Zeldin, Theodore. *France, 1848–1945.* 2 vols. Oxford: Oxford University Press, 1977.
Zola, Émile. *Correspondance.* Edited by B.H. Bakker. 10 vols. Montreal-Paris: Presses de l'Université de Montréal – CNRS, 1978–95.
Zola, Émile. 1890; *La Bête humaine.* Paris: Fasquelle, 1979.
Zola, Émile. 1867; *Thérèse Raquin.* Paris: Garnier-Flammarion, 1970.

INDEX

About, Edmond 157
accidents 45–7, 49, 147
Africa 12
Alexander II of Russia 80
Alexander III of Russia 80
Algeria 2
America 12
Angot, Albert 153
Arnoux, J.-J. 24
Asia 12
Astrié, Théophile 44, 46n48
Auber, Daniel 21
Audebrand, Philibert 66
Aunet, Léonie d' 124
Austria 2, 9, 10
Auvergne 23

Babylon 152, 157
Backhuysen, Ludolf 21
balloon 60
Balzac, Honoré de 108, 124, 152
   Peau de Chagrin, La 25, 66n8
barricades 154, 159–61, 165
Barrière, Théodore: *see* Dumanoir
Baudelaire, Charles 2, 56, 83, 86, 87, 95, 96–7, 123, 124, 125, 138, 141n84, 151, 161, 170
Baudrillard, Jean 135–6
Beethoven, Ludwig van 21
Béranger, Pierre-Jean de 128
Berry 23
Bertherand, E. L. 45n42
Bethéder and Schwabbe 101
Bismarck, Otto von 80
Bisson, Louis-Auguste and Auguste-Rosalie 115
Blanc, J.-J. 166

Blanquart-Evrard, Louis-Désiré 99–100
Boileau, Nicolas 128
Bonaparte, Louis-Napoleon:
   see Napoleon III
Borie, Victor 77–8
Bossuet, Jacques-Bénigne 128
Bouilhet, Louis 115, 151, 154
Bourdieu, Pierre 20
Brisse, Baron 66, 68n12, 69, 74, 82
Brittany 23
Burgundy 23

Capendu, Ernest
   Mademoiselle la Ruine 78–9
Caraguel, Clément 87, 88
Castille, Hippolyte 93
catalogues 6, 16, 18, 20–2, 24, 25, 26, 29, 120
censorship 2, 4
Champ de Mars 7, 10, 12, 24, 52
Champfleury 17, 102, 103, 104
   Aventures de Mademoiselle Mariette, Les 82n61, 98n27, 137
   Hôtel des commissaires-priseurs, L' 17
   Légende du daguerréotype, La 98
Chapus, Eugène 42
   Voyageur, prenez garde à vous ! 41
   Manuel de l'homme et de la femme comme il faut 122–3, 125, 126
Charles V, King 151
China 128, 166
Claudin, Gustave 41, 157, 163
coach travel 36, 42–3, 47, 51–2, 54, 61
Colet, Louise 57, 62, 86, 107, 124, 128
Coligny, Gaspard de 151
Coliseum 8, 10
Communist Manifesto 13

Cormenin, Louis de 95–6
Corneille, Pierre 62
Correggio, Antonio da 20
corsets 121, 125, 130, 130n49, 134, 137
costume 12, 23, 117–45, 147
coup d'état 1, 2, 18, 162, 170
Crimea 2, 9, 10, 35
crinoline 117, 119, 127, 130, 131–3, 134, 141, 144
Cuvillier-Fleury, Alfred-Auguste 106

Daguerre, Louis 92
Daubigny, Charles-François 21
Decaisne, Émile 35, 43, 47, 57
Decamps, Alexandre-Gabriel 21
Delacroix, Eugène 21, 97
Delattre, Eugène 41, 43, 45–6, 47, 54
Delvau, Alfred 70, 130n49
Destaminil 74, 88
Disdéri, André-Adolphe 91, 111
Dow, Gerard 21
dress: *see* costume
Du Bellay, Joachim 147
Du Camp, Maxime 2, 36, 37–8, 45, 48, 59, 65, 80–1, 101, 127, 163, 164, 170
Dumanoir and Barrière, Théodore
   Les Toilettes tapageuses 126–7, 130–1, 132n57, 135
Dumas, Alexandre 70, 102
Dzing ! Boum ! Boum ! 22

Egypt 101, 149, 157
Engels, Friedrich 13
England 9, 10, 68, 70, 73, 74–5, 104, 125, 154, 162
Eugénie (de Montijo), Empress 5, 117, 118–9, 120
Europe 12, 15, 132
exhibitions: *see* universal exhibitions
exposition universelle: *see* universal exhibitions

fabrics 23, 117, 118, 123, 126, 129–30, 137–9, 169
Feer, H. L. 149–50
Feydeau, Ernest 17, 111
   Comtesse de Châlis ou les mœurs du jour, La 17, 129n47, 131–2
   Daniel 103

Figuier, Louis 100
Flaubert, Gustave 4, 9, 24, 25, 27, 46, 47–8, 57, 62, 72, 86, 94, 101–2, 103–4, 105, 106–8, 124, 125, 128–9, 141, 166, 167, 169, 170
   Bouvard et Pécuchet 162
   Carnets de travail 108n53, 140
   Château des cœurs, Le 83, 121n15
   Dictionnaire des idées reçues 14, 35–6n1, 54, 99, 140, 147
   Éducation sentimentale, L' 16, 17, 18, 24–5, 26, 48–9, 51–2, 55, 57, 60, 69, 72, 74, 89–90, 107, 108–15, 130n48, 142, 159–61, 162
   Madame Bovary 25, 27–33, 42, 51, 60n89, 62, 72, 80, 81–2, 89, 90n87, 102–3, 105–6, 107, 121, 127, 129–30, 131, 136, 137, 139, 150, 162
   Salammbô 18–19, 20, 22, 73–4, 75, 76, 90n87, 105n45, 131n52, 148–9, 150
   Sous Napoléon III 170
   Tentation de saint Antoine, La 153n21
   Voyage en Orient 13n35
Fontainebleau 18, 25, 51, 55, 110, 111, 112, 159
food 65–90, 121, 125n29, 147, 169, 171
Fournel, Victor 14
Fromentin, Eugène
   Dominique 2n4, 105, 126n37

Gagne, Élise 158n37
Gascony 22
Gastineau, Benjamin 36, 37, 38, 39, 41, 45, 58–9, 62
Gautier, Théophile 2, 50, 51n62, 87–8, 100, 101, 102, 124, 129n47, 138, 161n47, 166n69, 167
   Arria Marcella 56, 58, 158–9
   Capitaine Fracasse, Le 75, 76–7, 84–5, 89, 156–7
   Émaux et camées 2, 50, 125, 141–2, 145n93
   Jettatura 104
   'Mosaïque de ruines' 151–2, 157, 163
   Roman de la momie 19, 85n70, 126, 149, 150
Géricault, Théodore 21, 77
Germany 35, 70

gloves 133, 140, 141
Goncourt, Edmond and Jules de 14, 15, 20, 97, 98, 152, 165, 170
  Charles Demailly 107n52
  Germinie Lacerteux 15, 136–7, 140, 152–3
  Manette Salomon 23–4, 25, 27, 51, 53, 74n40
Gounod, Charles 21
Gozlan, Léon 136
Great Exhibition of 1851 6, 27
Greece 102, 161
Guénée, A.: *see Dzing ! Boum ! Boum !*
guidebooks 3, 4, 6, 10, 12, 39–48, 49, 51, 52, 54, 66, 68, 118, 119, 120–3, 129, 142, 159n44, 163, 165–7

habit noir 121, 122–3, 124, 133, 141, 142n85
Hadyn, Franz Joseph 21
Halévy, Ludovic: *see* Meilhac, Henri
Hamon, Philippe 124
Hans, L. 166
Hassan-ibn-Sabbah 2
Haussmann, Baron Georges 148, 150, 157, 169
Herold, Ferdinand 21
Hetzel, Pierre-Jules 102
Holbein, Hans 20
Holland 59, 70
Hortense (de Beauharnais), Queen 120
Houssaye, Arsène 128
Hugo, Charles 94, 102
Hugo, Victor 20, 67, 83–4, 94, 102, 154, 163, 167
  Châtiments, Les 84
  Misérables, Les 160–1
  Napoléon le petit 32
  Travailleurs de la mer, Les 19–20, 57–8, 153n21, 154–6, 159n40, 162
Humboldt, Alexander von 92

Indochina 2
Ingres, Jean Auguste Dominique 21, 97
Italy 2, 35, 70, 147

Jud, Charles 50
July monarchy 35

Kaempfer 10

Labiche, Eugène 49
  Chemins de fer, Les 49
  Poudre aux yeux, La 82n62, 90n87, 111n63
  Voyage de M. Perrichon, Le 49
Laborde, Léon de 96
La Bruyère, Jean de 128
Lacan, Ernest 93, 95, 96
lace 125, 127, 132, 133, 138, 139–40, 141
Lacretelle, Henri de 95
La Harpe, Jean-François de 128
Lamartine, Alphonse de 97
language 26–7, 38, 52, 53, 61, 66, 85, 86, 87–9, 92, 120, 122n20, 124–5, 126, 127, 158, 162–3, 171
Leconte de Lisle, Charles-Marie 157–8
Legislative Assembly 1
Le Gray, Gustave 96, 101, 102, 104, 105, 110, 111, 115
Leonardo da Vinci 20
Lesage, Alain-René
  Gil Blas 128
London 6, 7, 27, 152
Louis XIV, King 128
Louis, Saint 151
Luchet, Auguste 65

Mainardi, Patricia 8n11
Maintenon, Madame de 120
Mallarmé, Stéphane 125
manuals: *see* guidebooks
Marcelin 97
Marennes, Vicomte de: *see* Chapus, Eugène
Marie-Antoinette, Queen 120
Marien, Mary Warner 92
Mariette, Pauline 119
Marmontel, Jean-François 128
Marseilles 23, 54
Marx, Karl 13
Mary, Queen of Scots 120
Mathieu, E.: *see Dzing ! Boum ! Boum !*
Mayer, Léopold 101
Mayer, Louis 101
Meilhac, Henri and Halévy, Ludovic
  La Vie parisienne 132n57

Meissonier, Jean-Louis-Ernest 21
Mérimée, Prosper 50, 102, 164
Merlet, Gustave 102, 103, 104
Metsu, Gabriel 21
Metternich, Pauline 117n2
Mexico 2, 10
Meyerbeer, Giacomo 21
Michelangelo 19
Michelet, Jules 67, 75, 77, 80
    L'Amour 135
Molière, 128
Monnier, Henry 102
Monselet, Charles 71–2, 87, 88, 153
Monpont 129
Mozart, Wolfgang Amadeus 21
Murillo, Bartolomé Esteban 20
museum 16, 21–2, 23
Musset, Paul de 121

Nadar, Félix 60–1, 102, 113, 115
Naples 56
Napoléon III, Emperor 1, 2, 3, 5, 8, 9, 18, 20, 32, 33, 37, 57, 84, 91, 111, 117, 120, 148, 150, 154, 164, 166, 167, 169
Napoléon, Joseph Charles Paul Bonaparte, Prince 5, 6, 9

national identity 5–6, 8–13, 31
Near East 3
Nerval, Gérard de 2, 101, 141, 167, 170
    Nuits d'octobre, Les 54–5, 56–7, 72, 97
    Sylvie 56n78, 139–40, 159
New Caledonia 2
Nibelle, Paul 110
Nice 2
Nineveh 149, 157, 165
Normandy 22, 30, 106
North Africa 3, 119

Oceania 12
Offenbach, Jacques 61
omnibus 43–4, 51, 53–4, 62n97, 79
Orient 13n35, 14, 38, 89, 95

Palace of Industry 6, 7, 8, 10, 11, 18, 19, 27, 28–9
photography 3, 92–115, 147, 169, 170

Pierson, Pierre-Louis 101
Piot, Eugène 100
Pitre-Chevalier, Pierre-Michel-François 128
plebiscite 1
Pompadour, Madame de 120, 128
Pompeii 56, 58, 158
Pontmartin, Armand de 106
Potier, C.: see *Dzing ! Boum ! Boum !*
Potter, Paul 21
Prudhon, Pierre-Paul 21
Prussia 3, 10, 80, 164
public transport 3; *see also* coach travel, omnibus, railways

Rabelais, François 66
Racine, Jean 62, 151
railways 3, 30, 35–64, 65, 66, 91, 95, 118, 158, 169, 171
railway station 35, 40–1, 43, 45, 49, 51, 52, 54, 59, 60
Raphael 20
Raynal, Guillaume 128
Reculet, Charles 70–1
Renan, Ernest 13
Revolution of 1789 1, 7–8, 67
Revolution of 1848 1, 60, 115, 120
Ribera, José de 20
Rome 8, 31, 148, 150, 159n44
Roqueplan, Nestor 67, 138–9
Rossini, Gioachino Antonio 21
Rouen 25, 29, 32
Rubens, Peter Paul 20
ruins 147–67, 171
Russia 2

Sainte-Beuve, Charles Augustin 20, 22, 128
salerooms 16–18
Sand, George 9, 14
Savoy 2
Schivelbusch, Wolfgang 54
Schwabbe *see* Bethéder
Sedan 3, 164
Ségalas, Anaïs 151
Ségur, Sophie, comtesse de 68
    Auberge de l'ange gardien, L' 68, 75–6
    Petites filles modèles, Les 133–5

Sénard, Jules 86n72
Shakespeare, William 125
Soulié, Frédéric 125
Souvestre, Émile 128
Spain 35, 70, 100, 101
Stendhal 108
Sue, Eugène 128
Switzerland 9, 35
Syria 2

Taine, Hippolyte 15, 75n41, 107, 108, 132n57, 150n8
Teniers, David 21
Tessier, Henri
 La Mode 130, 131
time 3, 51, 54, 55–56, 58, 159, 167
Titian 20
Troyon, Constant 21
Turkey 102

universal exhibitions 5–33, 35, 66, 94, 100, 147, 170
Unwin, Timothy 86n71

Velasquez, Diego 20
Verlaine, Paul 62–3

Verne, Jules 20, 25, 36, 86n71, 102
 Vingt-mille lieues sous les mers 19, 20–2, 69n18, 86n71, 163–4
 Voyage au centre de la terre 77
Vernet, Claude-Joseph 21
Véron, Pierre 151
Veronese, Paolo 20
Viennet, Jean 61
Viollet-le-Duc, Eugène-Emmanuel 165
Virgil 38

Wagner, Richard 21
Waterloo 9
Watson, Janell 20, 25n68
Weber, Carl Maria von 21
West Africa 2
Wey, Francis 96, 100n29, 109n57
William I of Prussia 80

Zola, Émile 3, 48, 107n52, 170, 171
 Au bonheur des dames 171
 Bête humaine, La 48, 171
 Curée, La 171
 Thérèse Raquin 19, 142–5
 Ventre de Paris, Le 171

www.ingramcontent.com/pod-product-compliance
Lightning Source LLC
Chambersburg PA
CBHW021828300426
44114CB00009BA/372